CW01501898

ON ADOLESCENCE

Adolescence and adolescent states of mind have seldom captured so much attention publicly, nor have they stirred so much anxiety and disturbance privately. This long-acknowledged, problematic, transitional world between childhood and adulthood is especially fraught these days, with the assaults and pressures of contemporary culture and modern technology.

The heart of the book lies in the exploration of the inner lives of these young people, whether or not they find their way to clinical services. It sets out to illuminate the sorts of things that go wrong, and how we can help to address them—the crises of identity, gender, loss, self-harm, bullying, depression, anger, suicidal impulses, anxiety, and so much more. *On Adolescence: Inside Stories* is intended for all those concerned with adolescence, and adolescent states of mind, at whatever age or stage.

Margot Waddell is a Fellow of the Institute of Psychoanalysis, where she is currently the Chair of Publications. She has a background in Classics and literature and took a PhD at Cambridge on George Eliot's novels. She is a Child Analyst and worked for many years as a Consultant Child and Adolescent Psychotherapist at the Tavistock Clinic, London. She co-edits the Tavistock Clinic Series. Her book *Inside Lives: Psychoanalysis and the Growth of the Personality* was published by Karnac in 2002.

Tavistock Clinic Series

Margot Waddell, Jocelyn Catty, & Kate Stratton (Series Editors)

Recent titles in the Tavistock Clinic Series

ON ADOLESCENCE
Inside Stories

Margot Waddell

Foreword by
Edna O'Shaughnessy

Routledge
Taylor & Francis Group
LONDON AND NEW YORK

Tavistock Clinic Series

Founded in 1920, The Tavistock Clinic is recognised and respected as one of the world's leading psychoanalytically based psychotherapy centres. It is a mental health institute with two departments – Children, Young Adults and Families, and Adult – and is also one of Britain's leading training institutions and a pioneer in infant observation research.

The Tavistock Clinic Series, written in a clear and accessible style, makes available the clinical and theoretical work that has been most influential at the Tavistock.

Future volumes will cover sexualities; social work, psychoanalysis and society; psychoanalytic work with children on an oncology unit; and new psychoanalytic readings of gender and sexuality.

*For my children, stepchildren, and grandchildren,
through whom and with whom I continue the life-long process
of growing up*

"If we had a keen vision and feeling of all ordinary human life,
it would be like hearing the grass grow and the squirrel's heart
beat, and we should die of that roar which lies on the other side
of silence."

George Eliot, *Middlemarch*, Part II, Ch. 20, p. 226

First published 2018
by Routledge
2 Park Square, Milton Park, Abingdon, Oxon OX14 4RN
52 Vanderbilt Avenue, New York, NY 10017

Routledge is an imprint of the Taylor & Francis Group, an informa business

British Library Cataloguing in Publication Data
A catalogue record for this book is available from the British Library

ISBN 13: 978-1-78220-526-5 (hbk)

Edited, designed, and typeset in Optima, Palatino, and Gill Sans
by Communication Crafts, East Grinstead

Printed and bound by CPI Group (UK) Ltd, Croydon, CR0 4YY

CONTENTS

SERIES EDITORS' PREFACE

Margot Waddell, Jocelyn Catty, & Kate Stratton

Since it was founded in 1920, the Tavistock Clinic—now the Tavistock and Portman NHS Foundation Trust—has developed a wide range of developmental approaches to mental health which have been strongly influenced by the ideas of psychoanalysis. It has also adopted systemic family therapy as a theoretical model and a clinical approach to family problems. The Tavistock is now one of the largest mental health training institutions in Britain. It teaches up to 600 students a year on postgraduate, doctoral, and qualifying courses in social work, systemic psychotherapy, psychology, psychiatry, nursing, and child, adolescent, and adult psychotherapy, along with 2,000 multidisciplinary clinicians, social workers, and teachers attending Continuing Professional Development courses and conferences on psychoanalytic observation, psychoanalytic thinking, and management and leadership in a range of clinical and community settings.

The Tavistock's philosophy aims at promoting therapeutic methods in mental health. Its work is based on the clinical expertise that is also the basis of its consultancy and research activities. The aim of this Series is to make available to the reading public the clinical, theoretical, and research work that is most influential at the Tavistock. The Series sets out new approaches in the understanding and treatment of psychological disturbance in children, adolescents, and adults, both as individuals and in families.

Margot Waddell's *Inside Lives: Psychoanalysis and the Growth of the Personality*, first published in 1998, has inspired a generation of clinicians, teachers, and students of the human condition. Now, in *On Adolescence: Inside Stories*, she turns her mind to the age group to which she has devoted so much of her professional life.

Waddell explains that she will be approaching her subject "not so much cognitively, nor behaviourally, nor in terms of theories of child development or social adaptation, but emotionally, psychically, in terms of the inside story". Her commitment to telling the "inside story" pervades this book, whether she is considering the history of the concept of adolescence, the numerous challenges faced by adolescents in today's society, or the vicissitudes of adolescent emotional life more generally.

At the heart of *On Adolescence* is a profound understanding of what Waddell describes as "the traditional wisdom of the Tavistock Adolescent Department"—namely, the liminal position of these young people in "the frame space between two states: of being no longer a child, but not yet an adult either; a state in which previous identities are dissolved before new ones are formed". As in *Inside Lives*, Waddell looks to literature for inspiration and understanding. Here, too, she holds in exquisite balance her twin focuses on the adolescent internal world and the psychoanalytic clinical endeavour. In working with this turbulent and, frequently, alarming group, Waddell's emphasis on the "underlying drive towards development in every person" is both helpful and hopeful. Without claiming that such distinctions can be made easily, she draws attention to how one troubled adolescent may gradually work through his or her disturbance without therapeutic help, while another may become increasingly entrenched within it.

In thinking about the adolescent in his or her social and educational context, Waddell acknowledges the increasing pressure exerted by the current education system and its impact, sometimes dire. This is a world where "mental performance is frequently mistaken for mental health" and where "the B word"—for a grade, rather than as an expletive—can inspire horror. In this context, the realization of one failing student that he needs to "grow up on the inside with his 'real' self" is particularly significant. How appropriate that this young man dreamt, with alarm, that he had lost his copy of Bion's *Learning from Experience*.

Looking back on her fifty years of clinical work with adolescents, Waddell makes it clear that, despite all, she has been able to hold on to hope. Yet she never fails to acknowledge the difficulties involved in this exacting and disturbing endeavour, nor the importance of letting go of ideas of "happy ever after". Working on the border, "one learns the importance of eschewing notions that we might ever be 'in the clear'".

On Adolescence is the fiftieth book in the Tavistock Clinic Series and comes in the cross-over phase between Karnac and Routledge. Alongside her central role in the Tavistock Adolescent Department, Margot has tirelessly edited the Series since its inception, first with Duckworth, then for sixteen years with Karnac, and now with Routledge. In this ongoing task—in which, latterly, we (KS and JC) have joined her—she has brought the work of the Tavistock tradition to an international audience, inspiring generations of writers and readers. We are confident that this latest volume will carry that understanding still further.

ACKNOWLEDGEMENTS

It is hard to pay tribute or to extend sufficient gratitude to all those who have contributed to this book, sometimes unbeknownst even to themselves. I have in mind, first and foremost, the patients, but also colleagues, supervisors, and supervisees from whom, and with whom, I have learned so much. Because some of the work described here stretches back over many years, it has not always been possible to acknowledge nor adequately to mark all those involved. The following pages are testimony to how deeply I valued my years spent training and practising as a Child and Adolescent Psychotherapist in the Adolescent Department and also, before that, in the Classics and English Faculties at Cambridge, where I learned to read and to think with, among others, John Raven, Anne Barton née Righter, and John and Gillian Beer.

I have John Bowlby and Martha Harris to thank for my being at the Tavistock in the first place and Anton Obholzer for my home in the Adolescent Department. In addition to these three, many of those from whom I learned and with whom I worked over the years have had an inestimable influence: Isca Wittenberg, Dugmore Hunter, Jorge Thomas, Arthur-Hyatt Williams, Donald Meltzer, Beta Copley, Sally Box, Anna Dartington née Halton, Gianna Williams, Robin Anderson, and so many others.

Practically, I don't know how this book could have been written without the immense generosity of the financial support from the Tavistock Clinic Foundation Child Psychotherapy Research Fund through the Nicola and Denzil Cleminson Memorial Bequest. With the benefit of this fund, I have been able to draw on the invaluable talents—those of typing, referencing, researching, thinking, and cheering-up—of Amber Segal, without whom this book would not have seen the light of day. I am grateful, too, to Carol MacBroom and Florence Graham for practical assistance and good will, as well as to long-suffering family and wonderful friends for patience and ongoing support. For textual advice and careful reading, I must thank Margaret Rustin, in particular, and also Toni Griffiths, Jill Vites, Jocelyn Catty, Kate Stratton, Lisa Miller, Edna O'Shaughnessy, and Barbara McLean; for introducing me to Young Adult fiction and guiding me through this literature, my thanks to Joanna de Guia.

I am grateful to Karnac Books, in particular Oliver Rathbone and Rod Tweedy, for general trust, expertise, and encouragement as well as for permission to quote extensively from work that has previously appeared in my earlier book *Inside Lives* and as chapters or extracts from other books in the Tavistock Clinic Series. An earlier version of Chapter 7, on bullying, was first published by *Free Associations* (2002), and of chapter 10, on narcissism, by the *Journal of Child Psychotherapy* (2006)—my thanks for permissions to both Karnac and Routledge. I am also grateful to Bloodaxe for the use of Ann Stevenson and Carole Satyamurti's wonderful poems and to Faber & Faber for T. S. Eliot and Sylvia Plath. Warm thanks to Nicola Bion Vick and © The Estate of W. R. Bion. Eric and Klara King of Communication Crafts cannot be thanked enough for making this book happen so swiftly and smoothly, for their dedication to textual accuracy, and for their commitment to our overall project.

PREFACE

The reflections that make up this volume are rooted in the clinical home in which I grew up: where I trained, worked, taught, supervised, and wrote and from which I have now retired: the Adolescent Department of the Tavistock Clinic, London. This book is, in part, a record of aspects of the work that I learned from, that I found so anxiety-provoking, so revelatory, even inspiring. It is also, in part, an attempt to register the significance of such a "work group" of psychoanalytically and community-minded professionals, staff, and trainees—those who work and worked in the Department, devotedly and creatively, over the forty-five or so years during which I had the privilege to "live" there and was encouraged to find my own way and my own voice.

To write about adolescence is to trace the process of becoming, one that begins with puberty and ends, these days, sometime during the twenties. For, as we shall see, "the agitation of inexperience" threads its way through these years, ever presenting and transforming itself in myriad ways, ones that are both characteristic and generalizable, yet also unique in each case. For beneath the generalizations must lie a specificity to any one individual's confusion, pain, excitement, fear, passion, so often rooted in infantile states, ones that are puzzlingly opaque, by turn infuriating and engaging, and, clinically, extremely challenging.

The theoretical framework for thinking in this book is the one that I grew up with, one that will, I hope, become clear as we go along. As Freud (1905d) suggested, given the complexity of the tasks—psychological, behavioural, intellectual, sexual—of the adolescent agenda, it is a wonder that anyone gets through these years at all. Indeed, some take a lot longer than others and stumble a little, even fall, along the way. But, on the whole, most do make it. These chapters will be tracing some of the vicissitudes of the inside stories of this troubled age group and their families, although I prefer to move away from the chronologically defined notion of *age* group, as such, and to concentrate, rather, on states of mind. For the states of mind that I shall be describing are characteristic of these years, yet can also be found, perhaps fleetingly, in an 8-year-old, or even a 38-year-old and beyond.

The particularities of the joys and horrors of the ways in which young people "grow up", and the individual and group manifestations of this, are chronologically and culturally very specific, and such specificities will have a prominent place in these "reflections". I refer, especially, to the technological revolution that has occurred in the last twenty years, ushering in changes that would have been unthinkable at the time of the establishment of the Adolescent Department. Yet, in tracing the dynamics of the development of this age group in the consulting room, in culture, and in literature across the ages, one can clearly see that, whatever the contemporary sociological manifestations, human nature has its own slower ways of evolving. The transitional years under discussion especially need to be embedded in the increasingly and rapidly changing demands and pitfalls of what the teenage years throw up. Yet they also need to be viewed across the ages, a view most easily accessible in literature, offering, as it does, the timeless aspect of development. The external circumstances change, but less so the internal dynamics of the formation, or destruction, of a true, or truer, sense of the self and of the ongoing and ever differing *mores* of each generation.

The heart of this book lies in the exploration of the inner lives of these young people, whether or not they find their way to clinical services—an exploration of what is going on inwardly during these years of protracted transitional angst, what sorts of things go wrong and how we can help to address them, how we can support these young people's emergence from a kind of mayhem of enactment or retreat, towards a feeling of having a self of their own. The book is intended for all those concerned with adolescence and adolescent states of mind, at whatever age or stage.

FOREWORD

Edna O'Shaughnessy

The author of this volume, Margot Waddell, brings the world of adolescence vividly into view. She has written her book with a double approach, drawing both on her long experience of psychoanalytic psychotherapy with adolescents at the Tavistock Clinic, and on her own deep engagement with literature. The ideas here have their basis in her encounters with young people in the consulting room as well as in her understanding of fictional adolescents, their relationships and their imagined psychic lives. Sensitively and subtly, Waddell interweaves psychoanalysis and literature in a way that enriches both fields and makes an original and in itself beautiful contribution to the understanding of a fundamental period of change and transition.

Waddell shows how sexual maturation and the impending loss of the shelter of the family make adolescence a time that disorganizes the internal world of the middle years of childhood and unsettles also the adolescent's external relations to parents, siblings, peers, and other elders. Moreover, even as adolescence is a call for the new and for independence, contradictorily it reawakens the earliest needs and sexual strivings. In successive chapters, this book illuminates the growth and the losses involved in adolescent development. The focus is on the psychic disruptions of this period and the internal and external forces that can promote or impede the young person's attempts to work out—or work through—a sense of self-hood in the adult world.

The reader will find that both the clinical and the literary illustrations bring the uncertainties, problems, and extremities of adolescent states of mind into sharp focus. All too often they highlight the hardly bearable—and sometimes unbearable—feelings that can exert such a force on the young person. And yet in her final chapter Waddell writes that, "despite the many indications to the contrary, some hope can, nonetheless, be found in the 'inside stories' of adolescents". This idea is deeply ingrained in her book: at once challenging and inspiring, it is a volume that will expand our thinking about the complexities of adolescent psychic life, offering an understanding to sustain and enrich us both in the consulting room and far beyond it.

PART I

CONTEXT AND BACKGROUND

CHAPTER ONE

Historical context

In the late summer of 1909 Freud, accompanied by his then friend Carl Jung and by Sandor Ferenczi, made his first and only visit to the United States. At Clark University, Worcester, Massachusetts, Freud was to be awarded an honorary degree and to give five lectures (in German) on the history and nature of psychoanalysis. He later described the visit in memorable terms:

> In Europe I felt as though I were despised; but over there I found myself perceived by the foremost men as an equal. As I stepped on to the platform at Worcester to deliver my *Five Lectures on Psychoanalysis* [1910a] it seemed like the realization of some incredible day-dream: psycho-analysis was no longer a product of delusion, it had become a valuable part of reality. [1925d, p. 52]

Freud delivered the lectures extempore and spoke without notes. The lectures were written down and published on his return to Vienna, and he dedicated this first account of psychoanalysis to G. Stanley Hall. He declared at the time that the invitation to lecture "was the first recognition of the young science". The lectures included reflections on hysteria, the role of sexuality, the Oedipus complex, repression, the existence of the unconscious in everyday life, and the importance of psychoanalysis in the treatment of neurosis. They proved to be his most popular publication.

The significance of this visit was twofold: not only was it clearly of immense importance to Freud personally, but the invitation was extended to and the event hosted by a figure who was to have considerable, though belated, influence on the understanding of the world of adolescence. This figure was G. Stanley Hall, the then President of Clark University. Freud (1925d) described him as "justly esteemed as a psychologist and educationalist", and as having "introduced psychoanalysis into his courses several years earlier" (p. 51).

During the last years of the nineteenth century, Hall had carried out a prodigious range of research into the pubertal and post-pubertal stages of development. The fruit of his work was published in 1904 in two huge volumes simply entitled *Adolescence*. The reach of the work was very considerable, especially in terms of an understanding of the multifold factors—biological, psychological, but also social, educational, anthropological, criminal, and political—that bore on an understanding of this newly designated age group. Jon Savage (2007, p. xv) calls *Adolescence* "a prophetic manifesto", because the impact of Hall's exhaustive work only became properly current about fifty years after the publication of the book.

Hall broke new ground in viewing adolescence, "as a separate stage of life subject to enormous stresses and strains—and therefore to be treated with special care and attention" (quoted in Savage, p. 66). Moreover, his term was rooted, for the first time, in a very specific age definition. He regarded what he called "adolescence" as a "definitive term for the elongated hiatus between childhood and adulthood", describing it as "more than puberty, extending over a period of years from twelve or fourteen to twenty-one or twenty-five in girls and boys respectively, but the culmination is at fifteen or sixteen" (p. 66). Presciently, he had written in 1894 that

> The study of soul evolution is just beginning, but it is becoming already the master-key for everyone who is trying to solve the problems of the human will, the emotions and feelings. The intellect was the beginning and the end of the old philosophy. The heart is the beginning of the new. [quoted in Savage, p. 67]

During his extensive travels in Europe, Hall had come across Freud's work, and he was among the first to cite Freud approvingly, viewing psychology as the discipline that could best understand this time of "mental and moral inebriation" (quoted in Savage, p. 71), noting that, "The dawn of adolescence is marked by a special consciousness of sex", and stating, in his Preface to *Adolescence*, that "Nature arms youth for conflict with all the resources at her command" (Hall, 1904, vol. 1, p. xiii).

It is not difficult to appreciate the importance of such an approach in the evolution of current thinking about adolescence, and my overview of the history of analytic work with adolescence must emphasize the significance of the role that Hall accorded to psychoanalysis in understanding this period of human development. It must also emphasize that around the same time, Freud, in *The Three Essays on the Theory of Sexuality* (1905d), nominates adolescence as one of the crucial developmental phases in the human life cycle: it was the time when changes set in that give infantile sexual life its final, normal shape. The tripartite achievement of this final shape was, according to Freud, the crystallization of sexual identity, the finding of a sexual object, and the bringing together of the two main stems of sexuality—the sensual and the tender. There was nothing of the later sense of adolescence as performing a major developmental task: that of providing a crucial period for the restructuring and final organization of the personality. The emphasis at this early stage was very much on adolescent sexuality, to be picked up again by Ernest Jones in a paper given in 1922, "Some Problems of Adolescence". This paper was delivered before a joint meeting of the General, Medical, and Educational Sections of the British Psychoanalytical Society and was published in the *British Journal of Psychology*. I stress this because the paper marked so significant a step forward in the understanding of the infantile components of the adolescent psychic make-up. Something was astir, even then, in the psychoanalytic community, although it took a further fifty years before the import of this thinking properly came into its own.

Jones's position was that:

> At puberty a regression takes place in the direction of infancy . . . and the person lives over again, though on another plane, the development he passed through in the first five years of life. As this correlation between adolescence and infancy is the most distinctive generalisation to which I wish to call your attention in this paper, I should like to dwell on it at some little length; it is one to which I would attach considerable importance as affording the key to many of the problems of adolescence. Put in another way, it signifies that the individual *recapitulates and expands* in the second decennium of life the development he passed through during the first five years of life . . . [1922, pp. 39–40]

Jones continues a little later in the paper:

> As was remarked above, these stages are passed through on different planes at the two periods of infancy and adolescence, but in very similar ways in the same individual. . . . Now it is surely noteworthy that the two periods of life at which the acquirement of inhibition is most active are those of infancy and adolescence. The lessons learnt in both may differ in their individual form, but they are of a similar order. . . . The most typical example from infancy would be the acquirement of control over the acts of excretion, where every feature of the description just given is illustrated. In adolescence a great part of both the natural changes and the training deliberately inculcated may be summed up under the term "acquirement of self-control". . . . A process that is closely connected with inhibition, being indeed in all probability one of its manifestations, is that of "repression", and again infancy and adolescence are the two ages at which this takes place on the most extensive scale. . . . In adolescence, a second great wave of repression sets in, reaching a height never attained at any other period of life. Ideas which were tolerable enough to consciousness up to puberty—for instance, the desire for the pleasure of parental caresses—now become repressed for ever, and ideas which later on will once more be freely admitted to consciousness—e.g., sensual ones—are often quite banned. [pp. 41–42]

The timing of this paper was affected by the cost to the younger generation of, as Philippe Ariès (1960) put it, the calamitous war of youth slaughter. It was with this slaughter, during the First World War, "in which troops at the front were solidly opposed to the older generations at the rear", that, Ariès suggests, "the awareness of youth really began" (p. 28). (W. R. Bion's early experience of war as a tank commander at the Front, aged 18, throws a fascinating and terrible light on the madness of the whole enterprise, as described in *The Long Week-End*, 1982.)

The post-war awareness of the fragmentation of the lives of so many families, and the immense cost to youth in particular, saw, in Europe, the emergence of three redoubtable women who, though working in very different ways each from the other, effectively pioneered work with young and not so young children: Anna Freud and Hermine von Hug-Hellmuth in Vienna, and Melanie Klein in Berlin and then in London. Anna Freud and Klein extended Freud's psychoanalytic work with disturbed adults into the realm of children—and, in Klein's case, very early childhood—and techniques emerged to access the inner world of the children's underlying experiences, drawing on Freud's theories of the unconscious, to understand the plight of the mental states of young children and adolescents. Klein's research and practice, much influenced by the thinking of her analyst, Karl Abraham, led to theories, based on the observation of infants as well as young children, that were to change the face of psychoanalytic theory and practice thereafter. The view of Abraham was that: "the future of psychoanalysis lies in the play technique" (quoted in Klein, 1932, p. 11).

Although clinical work had been being done in the period between the two world wars, it is striking that little was known about the nature and practice of child psychoanalysis outside the profession itself until the end of the Second World War. A colleague drew my attention, to my interest and amusement, to an entry in the 1948 edition of Elizabeth Craig's compendium of "Lively and Up-to-Date Information on Every Household Subject", unselfconsciously entitled *Enquire Within*. The book contains 2,000 hints on anything anyone might wish to know about how to run a household. It is an encyclopaedia of homely lore that takes "the guesswork out of housekeeping". I turned from "How to brighten burnt cake tins" and "How to wash taffeta" to the section on the family. At the end of a most enlightened entry on the "Psychology of Children", I found a section on "Nervous Children" which concludes as follows:

> If in spite of all your care and patience, a child continues to show signs of nervousness, never neglect them. The happiness of his whole life may depend on your seeking expert advice now. Psychoanalysis, which uncovers the core of the fears, examines it in the light of day and so minimises it and removes it, is a form of treatment that is becoming more and more widely used and successful. Your doctor may be able to help you set about obtaining this treatment or you can get into touch with the Institute of Child Psychology, 26 Warwick Avenue, London W9. [p. 132]

What struck me on reading Elizabeth Craig was how *little* knowledge about child analysis has, in fact, even now penetrated into popular culture since 1948, and how extraordinary it would be to find such a reference in any contemporary book of good housekeeping. The dating of the book is significant—1948. Not surprisingly, the awareness of the plight of children was particularly acute during and after the two world wars. Trauma, bereavement, and massive displacement of children characterized both periods, though more overwhelmingly after the Second World War, in the context of intensive bombing raids. A poignant fact is recounted that when Anna Freud escaped from Vienna with her father and other members of the family in 1939, her luggage included ten little stretcher beds—in anticipation of the War Nursery that she later helped to create. This detail is indicative of how the early child practitioners were acutely aware of the relationship between internal impulse life and the often extremely primitive nature of anxieties, and the vast array of defences against them, that are regularly encountered in the consulting room. Of necessity, these inner states were to be viewed in the context of scarcely imaginable conditions of external trauma and experiences of fracture and loss. The question was one of how these experiences, then as now, might be engaged with and mitigated, how to find a way of thinking about the interaction of internal states and external circumstances. It was, as we saw, after the First World War that work directly with children first began, and the end of the Second World War marked the founding of three training schools for the psychoanalytic treatment of children, funded both privately and by the NHS.

The significance of these developments for the understanding of adolescence cannot be overestimated. The important historical facts were that, building on the understanding of these early pioneers, there developed an interest in the provision of affordable training for those whose concern focused on the seriousness and relevance of the nature of psychic growth from the beginning. In 1948, John Bowlby—psychiatrist, psychoanalyst, and, by then, deputy director of the Tavistock Clinic and also head of the Department for Children and Parents—saw the importance of establishing within the newly formed NHS an analytic training for clinical work with children and their families. The training would be for non-medical personnel practising psychotherapy in publically funded clinics. In London, one such psychotherapy clinic was to be located at the Tavistock, which, by then, had been in existence for nearly thirty years.

As its "biographer", Henry Dicks (1970) gave an interesting and comprehensive account of *Fifty Years of the Tavistock Clinic* from its establishment in 1920. He describes the origin of the clinic as providing psychodynamic thought to the treatment of shell-shocked soldiers. Dicks also stresses the clinic's commitment, from the first, to understanding the patient as a product both of his environment and of his own history. The multidisciplinary team, comprising the psychiatrist, the psychologist, and the social worker, was regarded as central to the study of all aspects of the personality: "the child as father of the man and the parents as conditioning the new generation of children." The clinic was positioned "somewhere between official psychiatry and medicine on the one hand, and 'orthodox' psychoanalysis on the other" (pp. 1–2).

When the clinic became part of the NHS on 5 July 1948, it was located in Beaumont Street, in North London, and was divided into the Adult Department and the Department for Children and Parents. It was not until the end of the 1950s that a nascent unit for the treating of adolescents, nearby in Hallam Street, was also established. This was staffed by Dugmore Hunter, Elizabeth Hunter, Derek Miller, and also Isca Wittenberg who went on to set up the Young People's Consultation Service—a self-referral unit of brief psychotherapeutic consultations for up to 30-year-olds which continues to this day. In 1965, under the leadership of Derek Miller, the foundation stone for a new clinic was laid. The building was opened in 1967, and space was available to create a department especially for work with adolescents in this newly built Tavistock Clinic, in Swiss Cottage. Miller had been working with adolescents at the Menninger Clinic in the United States, and Dugmore Hunter was dedicated to realizing a professional initiative that would offer a service to the mounting problem of "disturbed and anarchic youth" (Dicks, 1970, p. 262), but also to their families and to the social settings that were involved with their care. (For a more recent account of this period, see Vaspe, 2017.)

Under Bowlby, it was Esther Bick, a close colleague and collaborator of Melanie Klein, who was chosen to be the first organizing tutor of the child and adolescent psychotherapy training, and she remained so for eleven years. The training brought together strong links with the community (the welfare state and the public sphere generally) and with a rootedness, through Mrs Bick's work, in observation. Observation was a discipline regarded by Freud, Klein, and certainly later by one of Klein's analysands, Wilfred Bion, as essential to a psychoanalytic frame of mind. Such links were central to a training in Adolescent psychotherapy. The goals and functions of the child and adolescent psychotherapist or psychoanalyst became clearer: to understand and render meaningful troubled aspects of the personality by bringing insight to bear on the nature of the internal world and its mixed population of figures, benign and persecutory. Where adolescence was concerned, and as Hall had emphasized forty-five years earlier, the worlds of this population must always be seen as significantly entangled both with the changes in the youngsters' bodies and brains and also with the external familial, social, cultural, and educational realities in which the teenage years are lived out.

In literary terms, it is interesting that adolescence, as we know it, and as Hall had described it—that is, as a protracted state of confusion and complexity—did not emerge until the end of the Second World War and, even then, not fully until the 1950s. J. D. Salinger had begun his great novel of adolescence, *The Catcher in the Rye*, during active service as a soldier in Europe. It was after he had written and published several short stories about the war that he resumed his work on the novel in 1949 and published it in 1951. My late friend and colleague, Anna Dartington (personal communication), compares the opening lines of Salinger's novel and of Camus's *The Outsider*.

Camus's novel, published in 1942, begins:

> Mother died today. Or, maybe yesterday; I can't be sure. The telegram from the Home says: *"Your mother passed away. Funeral tomorrow. Deep sympathy."* Which leaves the matter doubtful; it could have been yesterday.

Salinger's novel begins:

> If you really want to hear about it, the first thing you'll probably want to know is where I was born, and what my lousy childhood was like, and how my parents were occupied and all before they had me, and all that David Copperfield kind of crap, but I don't feel like going into it.

Dartington goes on:

> In each case, the reader is jolted straight into an unsettlement. The tone is stark, uncompromising, even menacing. The narrator doesn't seem very interested in the reader. In fact the reader could be forgiven for assuming that the narrator might coolly walk out of the novel at any moment.

Of course, she suggests, the Salinger voice is younger and less enigmatic, but the same message is conveyed: "Life is hard, nothing is sacred, honesty is more important than social convention. If you can take that, come into the novel, if you can't, stay out, it's your choice".

Dartington interestingly adds:

> The passing reference to *David Copperfield* is a comment on the radical change in literary style, not only since Dickens but also from early modernist writers such as James Joyce and D.H. Lawrence who wrote semi-autobiographical novels about their own adolescence, but in a different way. In their books, authority over one's destiny was something that was gained only gradually, usually by stealth or cunning. Salinger's character, Holden Caulfield, just takes that authority as his right and it was *The Catcher in the Rye* that seemed to proclaim the age of the teenager who demands to have an independent voice.

When the starting point for the understanding of adolescence became located in a combination of the theories of Ernest Jones with one of Klein's most important contributions to the understanding of the psyche, a much fuller set of possibilities for exploring the inside life of the adolescent was opened up. This contribution of Klein was an idea of psychic development described not so much in terms of stages—ones dominated, as Freud had suggested, by the anatomically related primacy of oral, anal, and phallic phases—but, rather, in terms of attitudes of mind or, as she called them, "positions". By this, Klein meant something like the perspective from which a person might view himself and his relationship with the world.[1] Such are the paranoid-schizoid position (Klein, 1946) and the depressive position (Klein 1935, 1940, 1945). A crude differentiation defines the relationship between, in the first, a primarily narcissistic attitude to the world, one in which self-preservation and ego-centricity take precedence over love and concern for the other, and, in the second, one wherein guilt and remorse predominate, lest hostile impulses and consequent guilt have damaged that which is so wanted, loved, and depended upon. In other words, much depends on the extent to which it has been possible, from the earliest days, to negotiate a shift away from being primarily enclosed within a frame of mind that is based in self-interest, fear for the survival of the self, and the tendency to see things from extreme points of view, usually solely from the standpoint of that self. The shift is towards one that could be described as involving a capacity to see things from the other's point of view, to bear being wrong, to tolerate ambivalence, and to survive guilt and remorse. Thus, a person may not be so overwhelmed by anxieties about his own psychic reality that he cannot properly engage with the outside world.

Rather than seeing the relationship between the two attitudes as a linear progression during the first year of life, as Klein had hypothesized, Bion tended to see it as a matter of a more immediate kind of to-and-fro, of an oscillation between moment-by-moment states of mind, as well as between ones that, in a more extended way, are linked to the broad constellations being described. This notion of ever-shifting mental states offers an account of growth and development in which there is a total interdependence between successive transitions from one developmental phase to the next (from infancy to childhood, from childhood to adolescence, from adolescence to adulthood) and the nature and quality of those states of mind that predominate at any one time, irrespective of the subject's actual years. For the adult may be found in the baby; the infant in the adolescent; the young child in the old man; the middle-aged man in the 7-year-old boy. These respective presences will make themselves felt in response to whichever mental attitude to the self and to the self-in-the-world has precedence at the time. Moreover, such states flicker and change with the nuances of internal and external forces and relationships, forever shifting between egoistic and altruistic attitudes. Such a to-and-fro characterizes adolescent mental functioning in particular—a matter of constant bafflement both to the self and to others.

This notion of the to-and-fro between different states of mind is beautifully caught in one of George Eliot's (1872) metaphors. She describes the distinction as being an alternation between gazing at the self in a mirror and looking out through a window at others' lives. Then, perhaps under the impact of renewed anxiety or loss, there could be a shift back again to the mirror (see, for example, chapter 10; see also Abrams, 1954).

Bion's belief (1963) was that mental development occurs not so much through ironing out difficulties, but consists, rather, in "an increase of capacity to bear reality and a decrease in the obstructive force of illusions" (p. 51). He was always very clear about just how painful it was to remain in touch with "reality". At the end of *The Long Week-End*, he commented with deep irony that man should do "anything to hold at bay the dark and sombre world of thought" (1982, p. 286). At no period is this more applicable than during the often tumultuous and confusing years of adolescence. Therapeutic work can be characterized as a process of reintegration of aspects of the personality that have been disowned, or disavowed, because of being felt, for whatever reason, to be too threatening to psychic equilibrium. The process of integration involves taking back projections and bearing the discomfort that occurs when a person is brought into relation with the less manageable aspects of the personality. This struggle starts very early in life. A 7-year-old boy, Ben, who greatly appreciated his "special time" with his "lady", shouted at her in one session, "I hate you Mrs T. I'm going to report you to the British Government and get you locked up for making me think for the rest of my life!" (Beverley Tydeman, personal communication).

Ben was finding it terribly hard to put together his desired version of himself with whatever new version his therapist was suggesting. The process entails an investigation of the unconscious area of psychic life, which is, as Bion believed, often so hard to accept. Such a process is by no means limited to children and adolescents, but concerns the overall meaning of "growing up". Parents of adolescents, as we shall see, are often faced with the "un-grown-up" aspect of themselves, as their adolescent children touch off areas that remain hard to think about or to accept.

The view of the novelist Ivy Compton-Burnett was that, "people have no time to grow up. A lifetime is not long enough" (quoted in Mantel, 2017). But it is, perhaps, at no time more arduous and potentially enriching than the "growing-up" process of the adolescent years. The present book acknowledges adolescence as perhaps the most rich, challenging, and unsettled period of the life cycle. How are adolescents, themselves, to address or understand what is happening to them? The following pages describe the temperature and the geography of the very varying experiences of the teenage years and something of the preludes and sequels of those years. They describe, too, the ever-changing nature of states of mind and body that can be so confusing and so engrossing, both for the adolescents themselves and for those concerned with their welfare.

Lewis Carroll was also especially aware of such difficulties, as Gillian Beer explains:

> Why do children so dislike that adult exclamation: "How you've grown!" Because of loss, because of swelling, because they are no longer who they were. Children endure growth. They also endure growing up. The two processes do not coincide comfortably in time. Alice is perhaps closer to the Caterpillar in Wonderland than she likes to acknowledge. She pleads that "being so many different sizes in a day is very confusing." [Beer, 2016, p. 231]
>
> Alice seeks to gain advantage over the Caterpillar by her schoolgirl knowledge of his necessary transformations within the life cycle (which he ignores and may be ignorant of), but the transformations, both physical and mental, that all humans undergo as they grow through the life cycle match his in strangeness.
>
>> "I never ask advice about growing," Alice said indignantly.
>> "Too proud?" the other [Humpty-Dumpty] enquired.
>> Alice felt even more indignant at this suggestion. "I mean," she said, "that one ca'n't help growing older."
>
> Humpty-Dumpty treats growing as a skill to be managed and Alice as a novice too proud to admit her need of advice. Indeed, Doctor Death creeps into the majestic malice of his retort to her remark, "one ca'n't help growing older":
>
>> "*One* ca'n't, perhaps," said Humpty-Dumpty; "but *two* can."
>
> [Beer, 2016, pp. 212–214]

Note

1. For purposes of clarity, I am reluctantly using masculine pronouns throughout. Since so many of the early processes under discussion describe interchanges with the mother, the build-up of feminine pronouns simply becomes too confusing, and the she/he formulation too clumsy. These days, by contrast with the 1920s, 1930s, and 1950s, many of the functions being ascribed here to mothers can be and are performed by fathers and other caretakers who have a close, sustained relationship to the infant.

CHAPTER TWO

Internal worlds

> God guard me from those thoughts
> Men think in the mind alone
> He that sings a lasting song
> Thinks in a marrow-bone.

These lines are from W. B. Yeats's poem "A Prayer for Old Age" (in Yeats, 1933). I think that they lie at the heart of the project of thinking about the development of the human mind across the ages. I shall be talking about adolescence not so much cognitively, nor behaviourally, nor in terms of theories of child development or social adaptation, but emotionally, psychically, in terms of the *inside* story. For the psychoanalytic picture is one that puts the emphasis on the complex relationship between internal states and external tasks; on *capacities* rather than *abilities*; with the stress always on what an experience *means* to a person and not on casual and contractual relationships. So, I am thinking less in terms of chronology as such than of *different states of mind*—ones that can predominate, if temporarily, at whatever the age and stage, for psychoanalysis is about the expansion of meaning if nothing else. In Keats's journal-letter to George and Thomas Keats (21 December 1817, in Gittings, 1970), he offers a wonderful description of the process—he calls it "Soul-making". It is a process that has become intrinsic, implicitly, to the contemporary psychoanalytic picture of human development: that development is rooted in the capacity to undergo experience, neither evading it nor being defeated by it, and that psychic growth only occurs insofar as a person's experience makes sense by having been worked on truthfully internally. More than a century later, Freud (1924c) drawing on Goethe, remarks on "a profitable return from grey theory to the perpetual green of experience" (p. 169). Perhaps following Freud, Marion Milner (1950) speaks of "a meeting of the conscious inner eye and the blind experience of colour" that keeps the reading experience perpetually green (p. 28).

A similar thought is to be found in T. S. Eliot's "The Dry Salvages":

> . . . The sudden illumination—
> We had the experience but missed the meaning,
> And approach to the meaning restores the experience
> In a different form, beyond any meaning
> We can assign to happiness.
>
> [1963, pp. 92–96]

As I have suggested, with the exception of the work of G. Stanley Hall, the link between psychoanalysis and an understanding of the nature and function of adolescence is a relatively recent one. There has slowly evolved a fundamental shift in the psychoanalytic model of the mind from Freud's archaeological emphasis on retracing a patient's symptoms back into his early past and unearthing there repressed traumatic experiences, long consigned to the "bin" of the unconscious—a shift from that picture of things to a more forward-looking interest in the factors that fostered a person's development, the realization of his potential, his capacity "to become the person one might have been", as George Eliot is said to have put it much earlier. This latter approach was, as we shall see, rooted in the work of Melanie Klein and of those influenced by her thinking.

It is on Klein's thinking and on that of two, perhaps three, of her analysands that most of what I have to say is based. The analysands were Wilfred Bion, Donald Meltzer, and, less famously, but very importantly, Esther Bick. It was these analysts who particularly contributed to a specific "climate of thought" that began to make itself felt in this country in the 1960s and 1970s. Not only were the roots of extreme pathological states explored in the context of earliest development—states hitherto thought scarcely to be amenable to any kind of psychodynamic thinking (adult psychosis, for example, schizophrenic disorders, autistic spectrum disorders)—but what was also explored was the more ordinary developmental picture, with an eye to the future rather than explorations on the model of an archaeological dig. Central to this picture was an interest in the nature and integrative function of psychic containment in earliest mental life. The focus was, that is, on the kinds of experience that fostered ordinary developmental capacities and what even very young children resorted to in order to hold themselves together in the absence of such containment.

Development, at whatever age or stage of the life cycle, depends on the state of mind that prevails at the time, and, in turn, *that* state of mind depends on the way in which psychic pain has been managed and, to use a now familiar term, contained from the first. (By psychic pain, I mean the recognizable states of fear and anxiety that are part of all ordinary human experience.) Moreover, how a person manages the stage that he is currently in, whether during childhood, adolescence, or adult life, very much depends on the success or otherwise of the preceding state or stage.

Since the concept of "containment" is so central to what I shall be saying throughout this book, I shall briefly define what I mean, for it is a term of enormous conceptual potency. It was introduced by Wilfred Bion (1962a), originally to describe the circumstances in an individual's very early life that fostered and helped to integrate the emotional elements of a particular kind of thinking process. Bion's sense was that anxiety, at this point often stirred by frustration and fear, militated against the kind of emotional thinking that he was concerned with, and that if anxiety could be somehow mentally held and thought about, people would be better able to bear their experience and to learn from it. Initially, that mental "holding" is the task of the main carer, usually the mother. It was Bion's belief that the baby, even at the outset of life, has contact with reality sufficient to enable him to act in a way that engenders in the mother feelings that are either not wanted (and need to be evacuated) or which the baby wants the mother to have as a form of communication of the emotional experiences being undergone.

One can observe how, in infancy, it becomes clear that emotions at their most primitive level are rooted in bodily states and sensations—sensations that slowly become "educated" and thereby achieve meaning. One can observe, too, how they become organized and subject to discrimination, to judgement, and to learning. This occurs by way of the mother's or early caretaker's emotional responses—on the capacity, in Martha Harris's words, to be "continent and cognisant" (1982/2011, pp. 69–70) of her own infantile emotions and to respond to the projections and communications of her own infant in its own particular context. Bion's word for this beautifully encompasses the conscious and unconscious processes involved: it is "rêverie" (1962a, p. 36). Much hangs on the capacity to perform not just physical functions for the baby—warmth, nourishment, holding, and so forth, but mental functions. The issue is not simply one of gratification and frustration, but of understanding and failing to understand. It is to do with being open emotionally and psychologically to the baby's experience, with being able to register and, at least some of the time, to metabolize that experience *for* the baby. In so doing, the carer becomes the modulator of mental pain, thus allowing the baby to proceed with his development. One of the things that is happening in the course of this process is that the infant is enabled to undergo his *own* experience in tolerable form, neither intruded into by the parents' preconceptions nor by emotional states—depression, for example—nor by their identifications and anxieties. Gradually, the infant can begin to develop a sense of being him*self*.

If, by contrast, anxiety is felt to be too intense, or too often misunderstood or misread, ways have to be found variously, in Bion's terms, to avoid it, to master it, or to deny it. These ways will be different at different ages. Later on, for example, one uncontained child will constantly and manically rush around; another will retreat, silent; another will show off; another, as we shall see, may become depressed, listless, and bored; another a gang leader, or a gang follower.

A brief, and perhaps familiar, example will throw some light, from the slightly later perspective of the world of the 7-year-old, on what would seem to have been going on in each of these little children's minds, from a very much earlier date. It will also bring together the relationship between the containment of anxiety, or lack of such containment, and the nature of internal realities. I shall be drawing on and extending an anecdotal account by my colleague Gianna Williams of an exhibition of pictures in the hall of an Italian primary school. I shall describe it in order to indicate how very differently a group of 7-year-olds experienced a small flood that swept through their village when a dam further up the mountain burst and water came rushing down the hillside. In one sense, every child had a similar experience of the depth of the water and of the degree of actual danger or absence of danger involved. But the pictures painted told otherwise. They were fundamentally different each from the other.

Very briefly, one child had depicted a church tower with a small huddle of people at the top and water almost reaching the parapet.

The sky was dark and scary with clouds scudding by and no moon in sight. There were sharks and whales thrashing around, and a look of terror on everybody's face. The picture beside that one was quite different—it could almost have been a holiday. There were puddles on the ground, buckets and spades, a few rubber balls and plastic ducks. The sky was bright with a smiley sun up in one corner. There were red wellies around and signs of water, but, on the whole, simply rather small and shallow puddles. The third picture was of a parental-looking figure with a sack marked "provisions" on his back, leading a group of children two-by-two in crocodile formation up the steps of the local church and above the waterline. The line was drawn more or less exactly as it had been in reality.

A fourth picture was very precise, ruled with lines and measurements of the distances between the village square, for example, and the church, or the butcher and the pizzeria, with prolific labels: "this is my house"; "this is where my gran lives"; "this is my school"; and so on.

A fifth picture was simply a black wash of paint with no figurative representation at all.

The disparity between these symbolic expressions of the internal feelings of the children and the external facts was made starkly clear in these little works of art. The first child clearly brought to the experience of the flood an enormously over-anxious perception of things. Setbacks were catastrophes. The external world dangers were greatly exaggerated. Perhaps this child had very anxious parents who *did* view setbacks as catastrophes and were not able really to help their child with his or her unrealistic fears and fantasies. By contrast, the second picture was equally unrealistic. The flood, real enough in itself, had been wholly underrated and its consequences had been turned into some kind of manic holiday atmosphere with a few puddles and plenty of ducks and wellies. The third picture approximated much more closely to the actual event. This child carried with him or her an internal experience of a parent who could always be relied upon to have foresight; who would provide; who had a realistic expectation of life events; who was able to protect and wisely to lead the children to safety. The fourth child seemed to suffer from something quite obsessional, in that no ordinary imaginary expression of things was possible, simply quantification, labelling, and exactness—a rigid, factual defence against anxiety rather than a capacity to express it symbolically, which would indicate some degree of psychic digestion. The fifth child was just too utterly overwhelmed by the experience to find any symbolic means at all of representing it on paper.

Each of these children was demonstrating the nature and culture of what I am calling their "inner world", a world that had been forming since the moment they were born—indeed, before they were born. What I am trying to illuminate is the fact that internal reality is by no means the same as external reality and that external reality is experienced through the lens of internal experiences of the world. As Edna O'Shaughnessy so clearly puts it: "[the] inner world is the source of the subjective meaning of the external event" (1994/2015, p. 170).

We can see in this example the consequences of the very varying early experiences of the containment of anxiety among the young painters described. On the whole, we observe a range of defensive strategies clearly adopted very early on to manage scary or persecutory experiences in the absence of any properly secure internal structure for so doing. One child has a rather paranoid take on reality, another a somewhat manic one, a third a realistic one, a fourth an obsessional one, and so on. It is important to keep this in mind when thinking not just about infants and young children, but about adolescents in particular. Later on in her life, Klein (1959) wrote conclusively that "nothing that ever existed in the unconscious completely loses its influence on the personality" (p. 262). The psychoanalyst Donald Meltzer put it another way:

> The impact of interferences such as prematurity, incubation, early separations, failures of breast-feeding, physical illness in mother or baby reveal themselves in character development as unmistakeably as the "shakes" in a piece of timber mark early periods of drought. [Meltzer & Harris Williams, 1988, pp. 25–26]

Let us take a simple example from the beginning of the life cycle. As a mind is observed encountering another mind, it is possible to identify both the seeds of those factors that may nurture, and also of those that may obstruct potential mental and emotional development. The following is an extract from an observer's notes on baby Fred when he was 4½ months old. Hopefully, it will convey something of the joys and tensions of Fred's early relationship with his mother: we see development in action, development that will be laying the foundations for later capacities to undergo and understand his own experiences.

> When I came in today, Fred was sitting in his bouncy chair in front of the washing machine—watching the drum going around. His mum is leaning back against the worktop watching him. Laughing, she said

that he was going mad with it. He was, indeed, very excited. As the machine rumbled and spun he waved his arms and legs, but the excitement peaked as his mum, in imitation, made a low, rumbling sound deep in her chest. While she did this, Fred's face was alert, watching, listening intently to the sound. His mouth was open as if he was literally "taking her in". Every time she finished her performance, his arms and legs were released in a frenzy of activity, his legs stiffening and suddenly drawn back against his chest, his arms waving up and down, his hands alternately clenched and shooting open, all fingers rigidly extended. He made a variety of explosive noises: squeals, lip-bubbling, dribbling and spraying saliva, and rich chortles which seemed almost like laughing. As if exhausted by these outbursts, he would lapse back into relative stillness while his face tensed in expectation, his eyes riveted to his mum's face, waiting for her to take up the dialogue. When, for example, she turned to talk to me to tell me that Fred had discovered the mouth bubbling only this week, he remained tense but his expression changed as if a light had gone out. This happened two or three times. During these interruptions, Fred seemed to wait patiently, suspended, his face losing its animation but ready to re-engage as soon as he had her attention again. I found these interludes painful and felt relieved when she turned back to him quite quickly on each occasion—that is, just before he could become too disappointed and therefore distressed (she seemed to have a remarkable sense of precisely when this point might be and each time avoided it).

This observational extract is suggestive of all sorts of possibilities—ones that may, or may not, be borne out as the pattern of Fred's relationships with his mother, his family, and the outside world unfold—and the quality and intensity of the kinds of exchange, so vividly described here, can be gauged and reflected on over time. A baby's fascination with the visual effects and changing sounds and rhythms of a washing machine is a common enough sight, but, as it emerges, Fred's chair has been positioned not so much to distract or preoccupy, as an older child might be placed in front of the television, but, rather, in such a way as to be part of a richly shared relationship with his clearly imaginative and intuitive mother. The observer is sensitive to the specificity of the exchange. Fred's ecstasy and fulfilment seem to involve the sense of "taking in", perhaps even "drinking in", a joyful quality of reciprocity and recognition. Fred is expressing his delight by every means at his disposal, a small degree of delayed gratification seeming only to add to his pleasure.

It is clear that when Fred has to share his mother's attention with a third—the observer—some significant psychic events are set in train. The observer finds herself painfully identified with Fred's distress, his disillusionment and disappointment at another relationship intruding. But she is also, nonetheless, able to appreciate that this mother has a capacity to register and understand what is within Fred's compass and to re-focus her attention before its absence extends beyond him. In quite simple, yet subtle, ways we can trace how the minutiae of the observation of simultaneous external and internal events suggest the beginnings of profoundly important patterns of developmental possibility. Movingly, the observer describes how the light seems to go out of Fred's world when he loses the passionate gaze of his mother's involvement. Yet he is able briefly to sustain the absence of the former exclusivity and to reignite the lost pleasure as soon as he refinds his mother, because, as the description makes clear, she knows, and unconsciously times, the degree of frustration that her son can bear.

Here we see, in embryonic form, the beginnings of a baby being able to tolerate the entry of a third party into the primary mother–infant dyad. In Klein's terms, this would signal aspects of the early oedipal constellation. In Bion's, these beginnings might offer evidence of a mother's capacity for containment, her desire reciprocally to get to know her baby, thus allowing him to get to know her, and himself in her, as a step towards himself in himself. Thus the observer's reflections, inward, as she seems to be both with Fred's disappointment and with his mother's capacity to contain his feelings, whatever they may be, enable us to derive a sense of this mother's understanding of her son's mental and emotional capacities. This contributes, in turn, to *his* capacity to tolerate anxiety and frustration and to learn that disappointments need not be catastrophes. One infers that these introjective capacities are already quite developed in Fred and that the gap between desire and satisfaction has long been bridged by a rudimentary form of mental holding, or "rêverie", which the observer is both witnessing and also experiencing and thus learning from. A modicum of anxiety, if contained, is part of getting to know, and thus to deepen, one's own resilience.

This experience of Fred's of having his emotional experiences mentally held and understood has little to do with theories or axioms of infant developmental research, nor with philosophical models. It is not to do with "learning *about* infants". It is to do, rather, with whether, as

Keats put it in a letter to his friend John Hamilton Reynolds, the axioms "are proved upon the pulses" (3 May 1818, in Gittings, 1970, p. 93). It is to do with resisting the blocking of observation by preconception, with being able to register the emotional impact on the self as a guide to the potential meaning for the baby, while also being able to remain constantly open to new developmental possibilities.

To go back to the picture gallery—we can see in this exhibition the consequences of the very varying early experiences of the containment, or otherwise, of anxiety among the young painters described: the range of defensive strategies clearly adopted by the children to express their internal states. It is important to bring these insights to bear on the understanding of adolescence. For we are thinking about parental capacities, familial circumstances, and soon the institutional settings of nursery, school, college, and their working (or not-working) worlds. Inseparable from the external world matters, we need to be thinking about the child's own disposition and very varying capacities to elicit, accept, and manage his experiences and to cope with inevitable fears, anxieties, and frustrations.

A brief extract from the case of a 3-year-old twin, Sammy, brings particularly poignant clarity to the fearful figures that, at times, took "control" of his inner world:

Sammy had a very difficult beginning. He had been born prematurely with several quite serious physical problems which had resulted in his being kept in hospital for two months after his mother and twin sister had gone home. His mother had been very depressed following the birth and had been convinced, for a long time, that Sammy would die. Sammy spent his first three weeks in an incubator and suffered many brief stays in hospital thereafter. He was referred for treatment because of his parents' distress over his nightmares which had begun around the time when his mother had started to wean him from bottle to cup. Scarcely a night passed without his mother having to spend long periods attempting to calm him down and to try to render more manageable the persecuting world in which he would find himself. She described how, when he awoke, he would often seem to experience her as a frightening, rather than as a comforting figure. This increased her own distress. There seemed to be a complete split between the happy, chatty, daytime Sammy and the terrified and tyrannical night-time Sammy. He could now demand his mother's reassuring presence, unlike before when, as a tiny infant, he was not only helpless but frequently physically separated from her as well. He may also have sensed in her an unsurprising difficulty in marshalling an emotional capacity to contain his fear of dying since she was so frightened of death herself.

As time went on and he began to experience his therapist as someone who could bear the naughty, messy, and destructive "boy" as well as the charming and chatty "Sammy", the terrifying nature of his inner world, hitherto confined to his nightmare life, started to appear in the sessions. Violent fantasies began to be played out, usually attributed to the "nasty, biting, crocodile", or to "Louisa", his twin, or to "Howard", one of his soft toys. The play was only very occasionally preceded by the pronoun "I", for Sammy, at this stage, found it almost impossible to take any responsibility for his rage and aggression. Primitive, persecutory fears were expressed that were clearly linked to oedipal anxieties concerning the seduction of the good, maternal figure, who might, at any moment, turn into something bad and witchy. ("There are lots and lots of witches and they'll put the boy into a cauldron and make him into frog-soup and eat him all up.") There were also fears of punishment by other frightening figures who were increasingly represented as one huge, ever-watchful and punitive "God".

But in terms of professionals' work, too, it is very relevant to bear in mind a comment of child psychotherapist Margaret Rustin in the context of, as it happens, the learning experience of the observer of infantile development: "the capacity to observe emotionally powerful psychic phenomena is the basis for knowledge of oneself, and for that contact with psychic reality which is at the core of an authentic personality" (Rustin & Trowell, 1991, p. 244). Such experiences are fundamental to all our ongoing possibilities of professional as well as personal development.

In the foregoing, we can see that Bion's model for the thinking of thoughts is really a model for processing emotional experience which, insofar as it is repeatedly reproduced in the infinite flux of life thereafter, makes a fundamental contribution to the structuring of the personality. Impulse life may thus become bound by thought rather than expressed merely through action and reaction. Initially the mother thinks *for* the infant. Slowly the infant learns to perform that function for himself, so that later the mother, or parent, may think not so much *for* him as *with* him.

I have dwelt at some length on the infantile stage because it is so crucial to setting in place the psychic mechanisms and defences that are central to the structuring of the personality across the years, but especially during the transitional stage of adolescence. It needs to be emphasized that upon the relative "success" of psychic development in any specific phase depends the likely "success" of the next phase. One can see this especially clearly in the way in which the quality of containment in infancy fundamentally affects the capacity to manage, for example, the significant oedipal phase as well—the change, that is, from a dyadic relationship to one that can manage a threesome and, gradually, more. Adolescence is often a time when oedipal dynamics resurface.

Where the internal world is concerned, the thinking of Melanie Klein and some of her analysands was especially focused on the kinds of factors that enable a child to acquire a zest for life, to develop valued and secure relationships, a healthy curiosity, and a strong imaginative capacity. She listened to what young children were talking about and paid close attention to what they expressed in their play. She followed their thoughts, fantasies, and ideas, not only about their daily concerns but especially about inside matters—about what was going on in their own bodies and, in particular, in those of their mothers. As a consequence, she presented an extraordinarily vivid and diverse picture of the inner life of the young child and, by inference, of the baby too. The mind became a kind of internal theatre for generating the meaning of external experiences, one bearing a close relationship to the stuff of myths and fairy tales. Klein became convinced that the individual was shaped from the first less by biological drives than by relationships.

Throughout this book, the emphasis is, as it was in these early days, simultaneously on the observable details of any particular interaction in the external world, and on the possible meaning of that interaction in the inner world of the person concerned. The notion of an inner world is one that psychoanalysts now take for granted, but it is important to be absolutely clear about it for it has so central a place in a book such as this. Psychoanalyst Joan Riviere, describing the Kleinian view, put the matter very clearly:

> Although in psychoanalysis we speak of the inner world, it must be remarked that this phrase does not denote anything like a replica of the external world contained within us. The inner world is exclusively one of *personal* relations, in which nothing is external, in the sense that everything happening in it refers to the self, to the individual in whom it is a part. It is formed solely on the basis of the individual's own urges and desires. . . . This inner life originates at least at birth and our relation to our inner world has its own development from birth onwards, just as that to the external world

has. Thus, our loving and hating of others relates as much (and more crudely) to that aspect inside us as to those outside us. [1952/1955, p. 350]

Much still remains to be known about the boundless mysteries of the human mind. Indeed, it could be argued, as Freud once put it, that psychoanalysis itself is still only in the foothills of understanding "that most marvellous and mysterious of all instruments" (1900a, pp. 768–769). My concern in this book, as in *Inside Lives* (1998), is not so much to *explain* adolescence but, rather, to describe with a measure of precision and coherence some of its qualities and characteristics, ones that have been enshrined in literature and philosophy throughout the ages. But beyond this, I shall be looking to literature to emphasize how important imagination and understanding are, and always have been, to personal growth, how closely related is the capacity to think, to form symbols, and thereby to derive meaning from experience and to express the nature and contours of people's internal worlds. For psychoanalytic approaches all to easily stray from description to explanation, a danger that Wordsworth (1805) well knew and eschewed:

> But who shall parcel out
> His intellect by geometric rules. . . .
> Who that shall point as with a wand, and say
> "This portion of the river of my mind
> Came from yon fountain?"
>
> [*The Prelude*, Bk.1, ll.203–210]

Where adolescents are concerned, it is sometimes hard to keep in mind that there seems to be an underlying drive towards development in every person, and that adverse circumstances at one stage, or age, are not necessarily determinant. The defensive measures that a youngster may need to adopt for psychic survival at one point in his life may bind him to a regressive or self-protective mode or they may constitute a kind of holding operation that can be relaxed in the light of later, more positive experiences. For development runs unevenly and is always inflected by social experience, both in relation to a person's sense of himself and in terms of the expectations of others.

The capacity to develop, slowly to acquire a genuine sense of identity, truly to suffer one's own experience in such a way that it may genuinely be learned from, rather than simply learned about or reacted to—this capacity is rooted in an infinite range of interlocking factors for which psychoanalytic theory provides certain central concepts and descriptive mechanisms. A working and reworking of these concepts in relation to someone's lived experience will offer the basic elements of the developmental picture presented here, a picture that will convey how a youngster's sense-of-the-world, and his view-of-himself-in-the-world, gradually acquire meaning and definition. I shall draw on a notion of the artist Ben Nicholson's that I quoted in *Inside Lives* (1998, p. 4), for it expresses so precisely something of my own sense of shared goals in life, whether we are talking about art, literature, music, psychoanalysis, or the lives of ordinary people. He is addressing the issue of what teaching art is all about: it is, he says, "really a question of discovering the real artistry in a person (every-one has it but often deeply buried) and then liberating this—it is, I suppose, enabling someone (or indeed oneself) to become more fully alive" (quoted in Thomson, 1989, p. 6).

PART II

ASPECTS OF THE ADOLESCENT EXPERIENCE

CHAPTER THREE

Adolescence

Puberty was memorably designated by D. H. Lawrence as "the hour of the stranger" (1923, p. 102), a phrase that will recur in the course of this book. I shall take this powerfully apt description as a metaphor for that developmentally challenging borderland time between childhood and adulthood, the liminal period of becoming what children call "a grown-up", the "adolescens" process of moving towards adulthood. Bearing in mind that that process tends, these days, to extend well beyond 18 or even 21, my present task is to try to clarify the kinds of worlds, both internal and external, that today's youngsters occupy as they negotiate the turbulent and challenging adolescent adventure of self-discovery. I shall be describing the typical preoccupations, excitement, and anxieties of the teenager; the nature of their relationships to the older generation; their characteristic ways of defending against the intense anxiety that attends these transitional years; and the nature and impact of such defences on their relationships and on those around them—their families, their friends, and the adults who are concerned with their education and welfare. Above all, I shall be seeking to establish some clarity as to an issue that lies at the heart of the matter: that of meaning. What does a feeling, mood, action *mean* to the adolescent himself and to those of us who are seeking to understand what life is all about?

There is no doubt but that, for the moment, we have a generation of struggling adolescents. The number of students seeking counselling at university has risen by 50% in the last five years. The suicide rate is rising too, and the already scant mental health services cannot meet the ever-increasing need. In fact, the incidence of self-harm, depression, and suicide, especially among 14- to 15-year-old girls, is currently the highest ever recorded. There are many elements that are recognized as contributing to this serious situation, although none of them is, strictly, causal as such. They represent, rather, some of the reasons why adolescent angst about, for example, identity, gender, self-worth, exam performance, friendships, appearance—whatever recognizable issues there may be—are less caused by external factors alone than exacerbated by them. The external worlds that the young now inhabit are changing very rapidly, perhaps faster than ever before. They are having to contend with the internet, positive or negative, with social media, educational target-driven expectations, unemployment, and the rapidly changing possibilities and hazards of the digital age. All these can add considerably to already existent emotional disturbance. Massive and rapid technological and cultural changes have made possible some of the opportunities of the modern age, but also many of the horrors: cyber bullying, online sexual grooming and violation, virtual reality, gaming addiction, and innumerable other recent phenomena—all deeply destabilizing—greatly add to the toxic mix of adolescent challenges. One might invoke the title to Tony Judt's last and brilliant book: *Ill Fares the Land* (2011). Judt is drawing on Oliver Goldsmith's 1770 poem, "The Deserted Village":

> Ill fares the land, to hastening ills a prey,
> Where wealth accumulates, and men decay.

There is, in other words, no doubt but that socially, politically, psychologically, and ecologically, these are very troubled times. Media commentary, often focusing on the plight of young people, is laden with assertions that describe "us" as, for example, undergoing an "existential malaise", as being gripped by an "epidemic of anxiety". Catastrophic swathes of violence, war, terrorism, starvation, migration, famine, floods, despair, and death are sweeping across the world with a decreasing sense that anyone is in a position, or condition, adequately to control or to respond to them.

In one such newspaper article, "Attackers United by Youth and Driven by Search for Meaning", Emma Graham-Harrison (2017) writes:

Extremist beliefs appeal to people across gender and class, religion and race. . . . But the large majority of their supporters, footsoldiers and lone killers tend to be united by youth, across continents and regardless of motive. . . . Young people tend to be more open to risk than their elders, a tendency highlighted by a range of data from everyday life; adolescents are more likely to be involved in a car accident and much more likely to commit a crime.

Scientists are still arguing about reasons for this behaviour, which may be driven by the chemistry of still maturing brains, or outside factors including lack of experience needed to evaluate risk. But the same factors that influence some young people to hit the accelerator may make others more likely to prepare an attack or travel to combat zones. They are also more likely to be searching for meaning and purpose in life, something that extremist ideology and hate groups can offer, usually through their dark, but simple, world view.

Graham-Harrison quotes Benjamin Abtan, president of the European Grassroots Antiracist Movement, on the attraction for young people of far-right or jihadist groups:

"[They] bring a meaning that transcends the individual, that allows one to raise their head, to rediscover their dignity, to make sense of the suffering around them, and to feel reinvigorated with hope for the future. For young people and others alike, this is an attractive proposition."

This is by no means a new phenomenon. It bears repeating that in the Preface to *Adolescence,* G. Stanley Hall wrote: "Nature arms youth for conflict with all the resources at her command" (1904, vol. 1, p. xiii).

Struggling amidst the turmoil of post-pubescent changes, it is easy for parents to overlook the fact that the difficulties of this age group often go hand in hand with a blossoming of the personality, an expansion of interests and friendship networks, a proliferation of skills, and a pleasure in the degrees of new-found independence, passions, and commitments. Such passions and commitments may be short-lived, or such resolutions changeable, while the adolescent in question sorts out the fundamental problem of what is often portentously called "the meaning of life". In this sense, adolescence could, reasonably, be called, "the Age of Experimentation".

I shall first be exploring what is really going on during these often troubled but equally often creative and rewarding years. In short, what adolescence is. Second, I shall look at the kinds of ways that things can go wrong and why, and at what to do about that.

The present chapter is intended as a general overview of the period as a whole, the different phases of which are taken up in detail in successive chapters. I shall focus, in particular, on how stress may manifest itself and on some of the psychological mechanisms that come into play when a young person is under pressure. Many parents find this age group especially hard to understand or to know how to relate to—not surprisingly, perhaps, since finding a way of being and a sense of self that is significantly distinct from that of their parents and that of their childhood selves is one of the central developmental tasks of this phase of life.

Everyone goes through adolescence at their own speed and in their own way. But in their teens, caught between lost childhood and unrealized adulthood, these young people often experience especially conflictual, bewildering, and challenging times. They are torn between both wanting and not wanting to be understood, between knowing and not knowing what they want. There is no longer a consistent person in terms of what he or she is thinking and feeling, nor of how he or she is behaving. Boundaries are being tested, assumptions questioned, losses endured. The 12-year-old "child", newly out of junior or primary school, is struggling to relate the old world to the new, undergoing often intimidating, though also perhaps intoxicating, rites of passage, clinging to the familiar, fascinated by the untried. By age 16, this "young person" may seem to have abandoned childhood things and to be precariously, perhaps precociously, launched into a personal and social world of immense complexity, but as yet with no clear goals or sense of direction. The central preoccupations are ones of identity—"Who am I?"—and things are happening extremely *fast*.

For these young people, adverse external events can have a particularly destabilizing effect. Parental separation, death in the family, illness, job loss, bullying, internet grooming, all potentially traumatic at any time, may pose specific difficulties and, for specific reasons, arouse especially acute pain, though the manifestations or expressions of that pain may not always be at all easy to decipher or to understand. Entry into puberty and secondary education often represents a kind of protracted crisis, one of separation, possibly involving considerable, though perhaps not obvious, mourning—mourning for lost childhood, lost certainties, lost qualities of parenting, lost dependency. "I don't pine for my Mum any more", said one 15-year-old, well aware of the mixed blessing she was describing.

Although often not recognized as such, the process of adolescence is one of moving into a world where *everything* is in flux. At a time when bodies, feelings, impulses, familiar selves are all changing, these young people are also having to deal with the social changes and with new, exciting, challenging, and anxiety-provoking responsibilities for organizing their lives and thinking about their futures. They are forming new relationships, making friends, facing big decisions. And all this is going on under the sway of the enormous hormonal upheavals of puberty and the resulting intensification of sexual and aggressive urges. The excitement and turbulence are extreme, both thrilling and also by no means always welcome. This, essentially, defines what adolescence is. It is a developmental process of working through endocrinological, physical, psychological, neurological change in the context of the wider social and cultural pressures that Hall so comprehensively describes.

What needs to be stressed is precisely this "developmental" aspect. Although the "hour of the stranger" emphasizes the unexpectedness of many of the personal changes, they are, nonetheless, often ways of responding to anxiety and the strangeness of the unknown that have been in place for a long time. Many parents find it especially hard simply to be a parent during these challenging years, because teenagers, in their efforts to discover who they are and what they really think, will often struggle to dissociate themselves from parental attitudes and values, ones that may well be identified with being authoritarian and/or generally dated and somewhat irrelevant, and to reach for alternative models of being. The familiar and the tried will be being relinquished or rejected before there is anything at all clear to put in their place—hence the confusion that so often prevails. Being able to make sensible choices and to have consistent views, to think ahead and make judgements, is premised on there being a consistent sense of self to do those difficult things. In search of this elusive "sense of self", the young adolescent is usually to be found experimenting with a number of alternatives: trying on one identification after another, rather like outfits of clothing (indeed, the extreme versions of dressing often represent precisely that). These experiments are exciting but also fraught and problematic in a variety of ways that are expressive of swings of mood, disposition, and attitude, not just from day to day but often from moment to moment. The struggle is to discover who they are, independent of the received wisdom of the parental generation, which, at this point, is often felt to be dated at best and, at worst, uncomprehending, diminishing, or, as so often, hostile.

Anna Dartington put the generational differences very clearly:

> Parenting is after all, a management role, albeit in a highly charged emotional atmosphere . . . it is often the case that children are more likely to become aggressive and out of control when they experience their parents as lacking authority and conviction. Parents who feel helpless may lapse into depression, or be subject to impulsive displays of aggression out of sheer frustration. In this way an atmosphere of mutual disappointment and recrimination can easily escalate. [Anderson & Dartington, 1998, p. 15]

It can escalate, that is, into ever more vitriolic and goading verbal assaults, on the one hand, and, on the other, often fruitless attempts at ever more impotent and punitive efforts to control things. Not infrequently, it is precisely the areas of who controls whom that lie at the root of difficulties as one generation succeeds another. As one parent put the problem, in humorous complaint in Shakespeare's *The Winter's Tale*: "I would there were no age between ten and three-and-twenty, or that youth would sleep out the rest; for there is nothing in the between but getting wenches with child, wronging the ancientry, stealing, fighting" (III.iii.59–63).[1]

A brief unpublished clinical example, recounted by Anna Dartington, vividly captures the complexity of such parent–child relationships:

> Luke, 16 years old, is pale and seems agitated as he walks with me to the therapy room. He sits in the seat he usually chooses, diagonally opposite mine. He stretches his arms in front of him, as if trying to squeeze tension out of his muscles, then relaxes them and says that he thinks the police might be after him. I give him a questioning look and he tells me that he has come here directly from school after having had a fight with another boy. A bad fight. I ask him how it happened.

> "He had it coming to him for a long time. He's a wuss. Poncing around the place like some great toff. He's a queer—he likes other boys. I saw him coming out of the classroom at break time with his wussy friends, and he laughed at me, so I just snapped. I walked straight up to him and gave him a giant punch in his silly, mummy's boy face. He fell flat on his back. Then I gave him a kicking. A teacher saw me then and dragged me away. I ran off. X [the assaulted boy] was lying there, moaning like a little fairy. I don't even know if he was unconscious or whether they took him to hospital."

Despite the swaggering bravado in his tone, Luke looks nervous as he tells me this: his hands are shaking. On further enquiry, Anna Dartington learns that:

> "The kid's a wussy little mummy's boy. He gets brought to school every morning by his mummy. I expect she still wipes his bum for him and tucks him into bed every night, too."

As the session proceeds, the therapist finds a way of talking to Luke about what the source of his violence might be, hazarding that it seems, perhaps, more like an act of despair about feeling so in need of "caring attachment and friendship".

Something in the therapist's way of talking to Luke enables him first to mutter "I am alone" and, gradually, to say more about how unloved he feels: "My problem is that my parents don't love me. You can't cure me of that, can you?" And later: "My Mum just shrieks at me or freezes me out, my Dad just doesn't want to know me. All I've got are my mates, they don't treat me like shit, like everyone else does."

Towards the end of the session the therapist talks to Luke about how desperately he wants to be valued and needed but, at the same time, hates his own need for this, as if the need itself is some terrible, humiliating weakness. Luke is by now weeping and trying to conceal his embarrassment.

> His voice quite tight with emotion, he tells me that it wasn't like this always. A few days ago, his Mum showed him photographs of him when he was little: "There was this happy little kid running into Dad's arms in the garden. My Mum was in the background laughing. It was me, but I don't remember it."

The therapist reflects aloud about the experience that Luke has, in fact, had of being cared for and thought about, with love and laughter, as he was growing up.

The exchanges in this session convey so much about the possible sources of the utterly characteristic, often homophobic, racist, sexist, violent enactments of teenage pain and despair and the projection of unspeakably vicious feelings onto a selected other (X, in this instance) or, in particular, into siblings or parents. As we see here, parents are very likely to be "at a loss" as to how to manage such extremities of feeling, whether encountered in themselves or, incomprehensibly, in their very own child or children.

The session described conveys something of the immense distance that has been travelled in this one, fifty-minute, hour.

Quietness again. My impression, though, is that the sharp-edged defensive anger of the early part of the session and the forsakenness of the latter part have lifted.

Turning now to some of the characteristic ways in which young adolescents try to deal with these confusing and unmanageable states, I shall try to evoke some sense of the impact that their various strategies may have on the adults involved. A central question for the adolescent in pain, as for the baby from the very first, is that of whether he will, on the one hand, project the pain in an attempt to get rid of (evacuate) it, or, on the other, be capable of taking in something that can ameliorate it internally. That "something" might, most helpfully, be the receptive mind of a parent who can listen and respond, while, to draw again on the wisdom of Martha Harris, being continent and cognisant of his own infantile impulses or unresolved adolescent states of mind. The first response, the projecting of pain, usually represents a non-thinking response, the second, the internal amelioration, attests to a much more loving and attentive, though not intrusive mode, one that is conducive to thinking rather than acting. When I say, "as for the baby", it should be clear just how often we have to remind ourselves with teenagers that we need to be thinking in terms of very infantile states of mind, ones that may well engender, in those concerned, similarly infantile states—hence the furious family rows that can so painfully erupt.

As we saw in the last chapter, a "normal" regression to very early emotional constellations and a reworking of old passions is central to the adolescent process. Puberty usually brings with it a surge of destructive emotions as well as of loving and lustful ones. A characteristic mode of dealing with painful experiences may well be the one current in the nurturing family—in other words, one that has very likely been established from early days. If this mode is to seek to avoid experiencing painful feelings, or to evade taking responsibility for destructiveness, anger, or, indeed, of neediness and dependency, the troubled teenager may resort forcefully to projecting his states of mind—attributing them to others, getting those others to *feel* them, or to enact them, instead of undergoing the suffering, or carrying out the enactment themselves. These are powerful, primitive communications, and they have a strong impact on the recipients, who can find themselves having to grapple with very unfamiliar or unwanted emotions being stirred in them (see the Appendix for projective and introjective functioning). Those drawing on the projective mode usually find ways of bringing about versions of their own feelings in the families and institutions involved—ones of excessive anxiety, which may very well lead, for example, to premature action rather than to the capacity to hold the feelings and to think about them until they can be better understood. (A heroin-addict patient of mine would regularly miss the last session or two before a holiday break. Early on, I would find myself telephoning the police or the local hospitals. I came to realize that she needed her pain and anxiety to reside in me, and for me to be able to hold such states of loss and abandonment for the duration of the break. For a while, she succeeded in so doing. But she would always return to the consulting room, on time, when the break was over.)

The phenomenon of bullying, whether among children, between parent and child, carer and child, or even teacher and child, provides a good example of these projective processes, in that bullying usually encompasses some degree of investment of unwanted feelings in another or others. This dynamic is fully explored in chapter 7, but a simple, stark example may elucidate what I mean: Jamal was the Year 9 bully. Bigger and tougher than the rest, he would lash out indiscriminately with a punch or a kick, characteristically striding through the locker room, randomly picking up smaller boys or girls and ramming the backs of their heads against the coat hooks. There was only one known source of revenge. In a music lesson, during the singing of the black spiritual, "Poor Old Joe", Jamal had been observed, on one occasion, to be crying. From then on, whenever the others were invited to request a song, they invariably chose "Poor Old Joe", watching, with contemptuous delight, as the tears began to roll down Jamal's cheeks. The song is a nostalgic one about loneliness and loss—loss of a world and companionship that will never be regained. Could it have been that the words evoked in Jamal a profound sense of bereavement? Perhaps he was a refugee and *had* lost what, effectively, was his whole world. Or, perhaps, he was traumatized by his parents' death—again signifying the loss of a way of being and an assumption of security that he felt he would never recover. The point is that we don't know. The obvious link between the stress of some hidden tragedy and Jamal's aggressive behaviour was never made. His pain was left unaddressed, and the sadistic pleasure of the persecuted/turned persecutors at seeing him humiliated continued unabated, just as his own persecution of other children remained unconstrained.

At this stage, shame and humiliation can be very hard to bear. Failing exams, being "mugged", a compromising photo "going viral" may all have a deeply disturbing impact on the adolescent psyche, each being among the many destabilizing experiences that sow despair and desperation at any time. I learned, only recently, about the horror of the "B" word. My own mind flitting to "bullying" or "bestiality", I was told that it referred to failing to achieve an "A" grade in exams.

There are many different modes of defence against confusion and anxiety of the sort that bedevils this age group. One may often encounter, for example, excessive certainty or rigidity of outlook of a quite omniscient or omnipotent kind—"Yes I know . . .", before the other's sentence has been completed. Such a position usually brooks neither modification nor questioning. But the young adolescent may transform at any moment: at one he is the baby, at another the poet, the philosopher, the politician, the invalid, the criminal—confusing, indeed baffling, to self and to others alike. To take only one position or point of view into account at any one time, when a contradictory world is felt ever to be shifting around them, is a common recourse for the troubled, particularly in situations where it is felt that there are no clear or fair positions available. An alternative to this unsettled situation may be a sort of denial—an incapacity to let in the pain, or the various possibilities that there might be for thinking or talking about it (see chapter 5).

Rather as a small child cannot contemplate accepting a digestive biscuit that is cracked, and therefore felt to be completely spoilt, so the adolescent will rail against parents for some slight misunderstanding, whereby, if something is not totally understood, it is totally *mis*understood. The object of criticism, whether one parent or the other, becomes not just a bit stupid, but a complete write-off. This is the stuff of myths and fairy tales—the good mother and the wicked stepmother, the good fairy/the bad fairy. In directing bad feelings towards the other, that other is then felt actually to *be* bad and, significantly, may, as a consequence, even experience him/herself as being so. Attacks of unwonted ferocity and contempt may occur unexpectedly, especially towards parents, and very often an alternative ideal is found elsewhere, perhaps in an older "child", or in a teacher, therapist, or, as so often, in someone else's parents.

In other words, the parental image may be split into two—either between parents (bad/mother, good/father), for example, or *between* parents and others (*my* bad parents/*your* good parents), or between different aspects of one parent or the other. It may, at some level, be felt to be a less painful option simply to hate or blame one parent and cleave to the other than to struggle to maintain the difficult mixture of love and hate towards both and each. When a characteristic mode of being is so closely linked to infantile states, as in adolescence, this capacity (so powerfully described by Melanie Klein—see Appendix) to sustain ambivalence rather than to be drawn into idealization and denigration is at a premium. Being the recipient of idealizing feelings is itself often very hard to resist, and some understanding of the likely processes occurring may be helpful, otherwise the clinician can be drawn into rather unrealistic views of what he or she can actually do—or can't do (being designated "such a waste of time").

This age has a general tendency either to "think" (in the narrow cognitive sense) too much, "in the mind alone", as W. B. Yeats put it, or to avoid really thinking at all, attempting to cope with painful experiences through a variety of what might be termed anti-thinking, action-orientated, or mindless modes. These may be based in the tendency to deny, to simplify, to evade, or to circumvent what is felt to be intolerable pain and confusion. Avoidance of feelings, disparagement of others, belief in the omnipotence or omniscience of the self, acting rather than thinking, over-simplification, excessive or insufficient self-regard—all these are characteristic and recognizable defences against adolescent confusion and pain. The whole gamut of more obvious adolescent states of mind will be part of that same panoply of defences, and, as we shall see in the following pages, there may be a huge range of attempts to expel pain or internal conflict—for example, in the impulse to act rather than to think; to move in groups, sometimes gangs, rather than to risk being an individual; to somatise; to become promiscuous; to split between one person or group and another; to drink or take drugs; or, these days more commonly, to disappear into addictive forms of social networking. Such responses, and many more, can all be ways of projecting pain in order to avoid experiencing it. It is with the pressures and freedoms of the adolescent years that these strategies are significantly challenged, when the containing (as well as restraining) function of the family diminishes and the quality and coherence of inner resources are sorely tested.

As we have seen, these various mechanisms can have an enormous impact on the adults concerned, often touching on (or scraping up against) a variety of psychic Achilles' heels, ones that parents may not, so far, have registered as there at all, let alone as being present and so raw. To be mindful of the nature of the mechanisms and honestly reflective about their impact is both one of the hardest, and also one of the most fruitful, ways of professionally and parentally addressing the muddles in which these young people find themselves.

In order to evoke, in a bit more detail, something of the characteristic contours and emotional tenor of the world of the adolescent, I shall describe what a number of them had to say about their own states of mind—comments collected during a random day's work in a CAMHS (Child and Adolescent Mental Health Services) Department.

First, a 17-year-old girl: "I can't bear mental pain" was her initial remark during her first assessment session for psychotherapy.

Her arm, covered with scratches and scars, told a desperate story. They offered evidence, in concrete and physically searing terms, of her incapacity to think about her experience or to tolerate it. They betokened, rather, her impulsive need to attack her own body, as if that could assuage her unbearable states of mind.

A 16-year-old boy: "I just feel angry. All I want to do is hurt somebody else."

A 14-year-old anorexic girl: "I feel like I'm a complete loser. Basically, I hate what I look like. I'm fat and ugly. I don't smile much—only when I smoke or get drunk."

A pregnant 15-year-old: "I didn't feel wanted at home. I blame my Mum. I was always rowing with her and her new boyfriend. I suppose I just wanted someone to love me unconditionally, someone I could love too."

A 17-year-old boy: "I just felt different from everybody else, so I got in with a bad lot. I wanted to belong somewhere, we stole mopeds and smashed them up. The adrenalin did make a difference at the time and I'd probably do it again. Everything is such a mess now."

An 18-year-old girl: "I wake up in a panic most nights. The exam pressure is impossible. I just want to cry all the time. It's hopeless, I just can't work or sleep."

Each of these statements is, in its own distinctive idiom, an eloquent expression of the intensity of adolescent pain and confusion and of the often unstoppable urge to act. The girls, it will be noted, tended to do so against themselves, the boys against an external person or thing. The gender difference is already stark—the girls were preoccupied with intellectual pressure, depression, body image, lack of self-esteem, and separation anxiety taking the form of a fear of rejection.

The boys tended to project their pain elsewhere; the girls to attack and undermine themselves. All the statements describe responses to unmanageable states of mind. As it happened, these young people were seeking help for their difficulties, but the sorts of problem that they described will be familiar to most adolescents. Such extreme states are of the nature of the adolescent experience itself—they come with the label "normal".

To address the sorts of troubled, even destructive, behaviour that often typifies adolescent states of mind more generally is to pose a very difficult question for parents or professionals of the matter of degree: when does self-exploration become abuse or addiction; when do care and restraint become obsessionality; when does a degree of contempt and self-hatred become self-mutilation; when does the supportive group become the subversive gang in which the individual personality becomes subsumed under negative group values of an unconstructive kind? When does withdrawal from the characteristic mêlée become a worrying degree of boredom, listlessness, and apathy? When does anxiety about sexual identity become promiscuity or, indeed, homophobia or gender dysphoria? When do slightly controlling food fads, particularly around body image, become serious eating disorders? When does the tendency to hard work become an inability to enjoy oneself'? When does ebullience become mania and caution depression? In each case, there may be very fine lines between ordinary adolescent processes and perplexing issues that go deeper. Finding a way to discriminate between the two is a perennial problem, as much for the adolescent as for those concerned with their welfare. Moreover, it must always be borne in mind how frequently a troubled adolescent is fielded as "the problem" when that problem actually lies in some other aspect of the family dynamics.

An introductory chapter such as this cannot conclude without a more positive note on an adolescent characteristic that is not encountered much in the consulting room—that is, a sense of humour, for humour is often a quality that becomes especially evident during the teenage years. This is a time when "being funny" can fill many functions and take many forms: it may be wry, dry, ironic, clever, it may be characterized by idiosyncratic expressions, whether of wit or self-mockery; it may constitute a bid for popularity; exaggerated or jokey expressions of camaraderie, some defensive, some excluding, some posturing. But the bottom line is that it may simply offer frequent evidence of a kind of generous ebullience among members of this age, one that is often so at odds with the more usual epithets of lazy, self-preoccupied, rude, selfish, oppositional, and the innumerable negative characteristics that attract so much adverse attention. The clever wisecracker may well have developed an ability to get away with things by making one parent laugh at the expense of the other who may, perhaps, be struggling to hold the boundaries. Shared humour can mobilize sibling solidarity in the face of parental discipline; understatement or over-exaggeration may make a painful situation more tolerable by charming the opposition. Oddly enough, this was Aristotle's view too. Hall (1904), nominating Aristotle as offering "the best ancient characterization of youth" (vol.1, p. 522), quotes a long passage from *Rhetoric* that rings so true even now. Aristotle ends: "Finally, they are fond of laughter and consequently facetious, facetiousness being disciplined insolence" (p. 523).

The matter can be summed up in instances that did, in fact, appear in the consulting room. I draw on Anna Dartington's description of what we might call T-shirt humour (Anderson & Dartington, 1998). Shortly before the end of treatment, a 17-year-old, Mario, offers her a "statement" of self-parody that she felt certain he knew would be a powerful and reliable communication of his slowly acquired self-understanding and a recent capacity to let go of grievance. Having arrived at the session in a rather suggestively striking T-shirt, Mario told her the very good news of his parents allowing him to go to the university of his choice and to be based with his grandparents in his country of origin.

During the session, nothing was said about the unusual T-shirt. But when he turned to leave, Mario paused at the door, and his therapist could see the words on the back: JOHN FELT LIKE A LOST SOCK IN THE LAUNDROMAT OF OBLIVION. He left "with a wry smile"—Mario's way of saying "thank you".

Another patient, Zoë, apparently sometimes wore a T-shirt expressing "a gentle parody" of her ironic stance on her own fears and need to think more objectively about herself: LACK OF CHARISMA CAN BE FATAL, her T-shirt read. Apparently, adds Anna Dartington, the most popular T-shirt at the time referred to the first album of the British rock band Oasis. "It simply reads DEFINITELY MAYBE and" she says, "as far as adolescents are concerned you cannot get clearer than that" (pp. 21–22).

More than at any other developmental stage, during adolescence the young person is stirred by the concatenation of internal forces in the personality, physical changes in the body and brain, and specific pressures from the outside world. As I have attempted to show in this introductory overview, the ways in which all this is negotiated are rooted in very early developmental processes. These, in turn, significantly depend on the extent to which states of anxiety have been variously modulated, modified, or, alternatively, evaded from the first. Subsequent experiences will have a significant bearing on this picture of things, but much depends on the extent to which frustration can be borne, enactment can be understood and held in check, thinking can occur, and mental pain can be tolerated—all of which capacities are beginning to be established in the course of the internal structuring of the personality in the very early days.

It must by now be clear that adolescence is, indeed, not a state, it is a process—a process of becoming. It is a time of challenge and discovery for all: "the hour of the stranger".

Note

1. All quotations from Shakespeare's plays are from the Arden Shakespeare editions.

CHAPTER FOUR

Managing the transition: puberty and early adolescence

[M]an is not meant to remain a child. He leaves childhood behind him at the time ordained by nature; and this critical moment, short enough in itself, has far-reaching consequences. As the roaring of the waves precedes the tempest, so the murmur of rising passions announces this tumultuous change; a suppressed excitement warns us of the approaching danger.

Jean-Jacques Rousseau (1762, Book 4)

In a sense, the whole of human life is one long transition. It is about the differently weighted and freighted developmental journeys across the years: pre-birth to birth; infancy to latency; latency to adolescence; adolescence to adult; adult to old age; and the final transition to death itself. "Liminal" or "threshold" states of mind and body are what we are all having to manage all the time. Yet, as I have suggested, there are some phases of the journey that are especially stark in their significance for young people, and almost certainly for those who care for them, be they parents, foster parents, kinship networks, teachers, or, of course, psychotherapists.

"Transition" at any age or stage spells or suggests, in effect, instability, loss, change, uncertainty, the unknown: the shift from something familiar, and therefore relatively safe, to something foreign and potentially threatening. It is not surprising that many societies develop complex rituals to express and to manage it. The period of adolescence *itself* is one long transition. Puberty is, perhaps, the most momentous of all the many momentous changes occurring in the course of the life cycle. For during *this* transition, there are greater and more rapid physiological, endocrinological, and neurological changes occurring than at any other stage of life except in the womb. These changes carry with them new, untried psychological states—hence, the difficulty, and the absolute necessity, of understanding what is happening, variously, between the ages of 10 and 14 years—the crossover from childhood into adolescence via puberty. In simple terms, managing such a transition on the part of the adult world has a lot to do with understanding what it is all about, and, educationally as well as personally, what kind of impact it might have on the models of learning hitherto recognized, even relied upon, and on the personality hitherto, also felt to be reasonably known and relied upon.

Any crossover is bound to entail an awareness of the loss of past things and an apprehensive excitement, as well as dread, about what is to come. The known has to yield to the unknown. We need to be bearing in mind the different ways in which these young people may be reacting, both emotionally and cognitively, to what is happening to them and to how they are responding to this extreme developmental challenge—that process in which, as I suggest, loss figures so prominently. For this is the kind of loss of which the impact and meaning is often only slowly assimilated into the personality, and then with considerable struggle and pain. It is not just untimely actual and evident loss, which may cruelly be visited, unbidden, on a child or young person at any time: bereavement, for example, or parental separation, or, in these present and parlous times, job losses in the family, the sudden change from a secure assumptive childhood world to financial insecurity and massive disruption, sometimes entailing the alarming experience of an unexpected change of school or locality. Externally, such losses are all too real, but I am mainly referring to the less visible, yet deeply formative, losses associated with the course of all ordinary development: the loss of focus and attention when psychic disintegration threatens; the loss of an all-comforting presence when loneliness and a sense of abandonment loom; the loss of parental mindfulness when the stresses and anxieties of the adult world obtrude; the loss of the breast, actual or metaphorical, when mental and emotional sustenance—the very stuff of survival—is felt to be wanting; the loss of courage when some testing time overwhelms; the loss of an honest response when truth is needed; the loss of self-respect when just standards are forsaken; the loss of faith in parents in the face of disappointment; the loss of trust when dissimulation is sensed; and, perhaps ultimately, the grinding fear of the loss of love.

All such losses are part of the fabric of life, of what it is to be human. We have to learn to manage them. They may, in good circumstances, ones where there is sufficient insight or support, be emotionally processed, indeed metabolized, so that they can become assimilated within the personality and, as a result, can actually contribute to the individual's emotional growth and development. But they leave their mark nonetheless.

Robin Anderson and Anna Dartington (1998) put the matter very clearly in the Introduction to their book *Facing it Out.*

> By the time children arrive at puberty, most of them have by some means or another achieved some kind of balance, but this balance depends on the world being relatively stable both internally and externally. Puberty and what follows are quite the opposite. The work of adolescence can be compared with Freud's description of the work of mourning in "Mourning and Melancholia" (1917e). The ego is required to examine every aspect of the lost object—the lost relationship—to pick up each particular aspect of the relationship, explore it, remember it and face the loss in order to let it go. If the adolescent is to successfully achieve adulthood, he must re-negotiate every aspect of his relationship with himself and with his external and internal objects in a new context—this activity is what we often refer to as *the adolescent process.* It is like a review of the life that has been lived so far. [p. 3]

Faced with such losses—ones that are likely to present themselves, one way or another, in the ordinary fabric of any child's day-to-day life—we might speculate on a range of self-protective measures that a youngster may be drawing on just to get by, some obvious, some less obvious. One child may, for example, seem to be exaggerating the difficulties. Another may take flight into manic behaviour, even hyperactivity, often linked to a "no-entry" mentality (Williams, 1998) of finding it difficult to take in anything thoughtful. A third may retreat into self-deprecation, easily overcome by fear of failure, perilously challenged by anything less than perfection, whether physical or academic. Or, indeed, a fourth may take emotional refuge in intellectual achievement and over-performance (the dreaded "B" word) at the expense of the many other developmental tasks of the age group. In relation to this last, attention needs to be given to the very varied picture of what, for the individual child, these results and achievements are really all about. Is the driving force the desire to please or appease parents, for instance? To satisfy personal aspirations and ambitions? To surpass others? To keep states of anxiety and inner turbulence at bay? Or is it something more about self-discovery, the love of learning, the pleasures and joys of trying and doing well, the enhancement of self-esteem?

Patterns of defence may have become established very early on in a child's life, significantly affecting the quality of the kinds of learning that can take place, whether from books or from life, but some may be perceived as consequent upon the difficulties of navigating a path through the choppy waters of self-discovery. A 21-year-old Oxford graduate comes to mind. Having achieved a first-class degree at Balliol College, he was heard to say, "that's the last thing I'll ever do for my Dad". He became a carpenter.

To emphasize the link between early forms of nurture and later development, I shall again draw on a statement by Freud (1933a). Although he is not talking specifically about adolescence, the metaphor is very apt:

> If we throw a crystal to the floor, it breaks; but not into haphazard pieces. It comes apart along its lines of cleavage into fragments whose boundaries, though they were invisible, were predetermined by the crystal's structure. [p. 59]

The notion of planes of cleavage affords a way of thinking about the underlying operation of forces that often only become apparent later on, especially so in adolescence—when the stress of whatever undertaking it might be reveals cracks and fissures, vulnerabilities and weaknesses, that, although they may long have been present, have not been manifest hitherto. In developmental terms, the nature of these underlying forces predominantly relates, as we have seen, to the baby's early experience, particularly to the extent to which mental and emotional states were held and understood from the very first. It is these forces that shape people's inside lives, that influence the sorts of internal picture that they build up of their parents, ones that, as we know, may bear little resemblance to the external realities.

As I have suggested, two very significant determinants of the nature of this inner world include the quality of the original mother–baby relationship and, later, the way in which a third "term" is introduced into, and becomes part of, that first dyad. In one of her last papers, Klein (1959) wrote conclusively that, "nothing that ever existed in the unconscious completely loses its influence on the personality". She observed: "our mind, our habits, and our views have been built up from the earliest infantile fantasies and emotions to the most complex and sophisticated adult manifestations" (p. 262).

In short, all developmental transitions in life are coloured, defined, perhaps even determined, by early issues of love and loss, for each one involves losing, because leaving, the previous known self. This may bear on why learning to walk can often be long resisted, as if, despite the extraordinary achievement, it feels too risky to lose, forever, being a crawling person. A degree of mourning as well as excitement must always accompany so major "a step" in life. So, too, will a degree of mourning accompany all subsequent changes in life: the inevitable weaning, the first day at playgroup, at primary school, secondary school, college or university or the outside world of work, or of being without work.

Having traced something of the developmental picture—both the inside and the outside stories—of 10- to 14-year-old youngsters, I shall address the particular vulnerabilities of this age group in terms of the varying quality of the internal resources that each individual young person has built up during his short life. These resources may aid and support them through troubled times, or they may be ones that will let them down, perhaps even propel them towards much more dubious sources of pseudo-security—the extremes of which can take the form of a whole panoply of defensive measures. For example, as we shall see, there often develops a safety-in-numbers mentality of ganging up on others in a persecutory and anti-developmental mode, so different from the kinds of supportive groupings that can, equally, so often take place at this age (chapter 6). Or, they may take the form of what looks like quite the opposite—an anxious, over-industrious, competitive youngster; or an unsociable isolate, a loner, one who doesn't fit in and for whom the private space behind a closed door, alone with a television or computer, on social media, WhatsApp, YouTube, or computer games can offer a sometimes helpful (if temporary) place of safety.

The basic and often baffling question for all is what is really happening during these early years of transition. What lies behind many parents' fearful, furious, frantic, irritable bafflement, even intimidation, at the fact that the child whom they thought they knew and the child whom they are now encountering seem to bear so little resemblance to one another. Anna Dartington (personal communication) quotes the mother of a 14-year-old boy:

"He was always a happy-go-lucky kid and never had any problems with things like writing his thank you letters but suddenly he has become a monster. He won't wash, he won't get up on time and has become a militant vegetarian."

Dartington comments, "I am not quite sure what this mother meant by militant vegetarian, but I heard it as 'refusing *my* food'." She goes on: "The developing scepticism of the 15- to 18-year-old seems to concern itself primarily with the unveiling of hypocrisy in all its subtle forms." As Meltzer (1973b) once described it, "The great difference is that while the small child thinks his godlike parents know secrets, the adolescent knows that his clay-footed parents have not found them" (p. 159).

There is, however, one crucial difference from actual early states of mind for post-pubertal children, and that is that as adolescents they do now possess the mental and physical ability to act on their feelings, urgings, and fantasies. They are now in the "deep end": able to give and take away life itself—to impregnate or to have babies, to harm or kill themselves, to inflict actual damage on others, on their parents, and on their surroundings. This new-found potency is both exhilarating and also absolutely terrifying. Life and death issues are quite literally around during adolescence. As Winnicott (1971) put it:

> [G]rowing up means taking the parent's place. *It really does*. . . . In the total unconscious fantasy belonging to growth at puberty and in adolescence, there is *the death of someone*. [pp. 144, 145]

> [G]rowing up is inherently an aggressive act. And the child is now no longer child-size. . . . [S]omewhere in the background is a life-and-death struggle. [pp. 144, 145]

Where such considerations are concerned, the culture of the school can, in good circumstances, often be extremely important, for, in some schools, a positive culture would include an awareness of, and sensitivity to, the trials and tribulations of this particular transition, despite the "meeting-of-targets" pressure. In that parents are often as much in the dark as the child about what is going on, the school culture and attitude towards learning can have an important role that includes being advocates for the youngsters, particularly those on whose shoulders rest, as is all too often the case, extremely high expectations. Very many individuals long remember the name of a particular teacher by whom they felt especially helped and understood. By shocking contrast, driven to distraction by such a melee of internal contradictions, one 13-year-old tried to hang himself; too intimidated to talk to his parents, he had told a teacher—and was expelled.

Although versions of the pressures and complications that often erupt in early adolescence may have been rumbling for some years, their stark and extreme expression will usually begin with the transition that we are now addressing, puberty, and often again, later, towards the end of school life. At this early point, a reactivation takes place of the emotional and impulsive states that were, in a general sense, suspended or "hidden" during what used to be called, eponymously, the "latency" period. As the pre-pubertal child begins to mature sexually, his reactions, fantasies, thoughts, and passionate urges become caught up in a maelstrom of unresolved, and often seemingly unresolvable, conflicts. The rising levels of sexual and growth hormones lead not only to the development of sexual organs and secondary sexual characteristics, but also to greatly increased, though highly variable from individual to individual, sexual and aggressive drives, often with powerful accompanying fantasies and mood changes. The body changes rapidly. It changes in shape, in smell, in texture, and, obviously, in size. Menstruation begins, as does the production of semen. Boys develop bodily and facial hair, voices start to alter, and genital excitability often becomes insistent. For girls, the physical and emotional changes can be a source of pride, but the alterations of shape and size often feel not just strange but rather horrifying (see Harriet's description in chapter 12). Renewed aspects of conflict—for example, between the conscious thoughts and unconscious impulses attached to these new physical sensations—are partly mentally and partly chemically fuelled.

The developmental picture suggests that whether or not these conflicts may be felt to be manageable and thinkable about will depend both on the quality of the early containment of infantile impulses and feelings on the part of the primary caretaker and also on the degree both of the stability achieved during the latency years and of the internal and external pressures on the young person in terms of personality and life events.

Very often the conflicts are experienced as "too much", and as having to be got rid of, or extruded, from conscious awareness. As we saw in chapter 3, the psychoanalytic picture is that old infantile conflicts are being reworked (in the context of these biologically renewed genital drives), as a regression takes place in the direction of early infantile desires, needs, and terrors. There now emerge conflicts and intolerable frustrations that test the quality of previous containment and internalization in terms of how well the child is able to manage the newly felt power of his emotions. Pubertal changes can set in train what seem like major personality changes, often to the consternation of all, but they are also highly variable in relation both to different intensities of hormonal charge and to social and familial pressures. For when the strength of internal structures is being so severely challenged, the external environmental ones acquire enormous significance, in terms of whether they are supportive or further undermining. The degree of coherence and harmony, be it in peer groups, in school life, or in the family, is crucial to the availability, or absence, of some kind of broader containing structure within which these confusing and troubling dynamics may be addressed and negotiated. Let us look at a brief case study:

> Michael, aged 13, was physically very mature. Recently he had "discovered girls" and began indulging in, and much enjoying, extensive "show-off" behaviour. A teaching assistant found him in a passionate embrace behind the bike sheds with Rosie, aged 12, with whom he had become infatuated. What are those in responsibility to do about this situation—the reality of which seems now to be filtering down into the ever-younger years?

The issue was well recognized by a psychoanalyst in the thirties, Siegfried Bernfeld (1938), when he wrote:

> Puberty occurs in a certain body, but that body lives in a definite time, at a definite place and under concrete social and cultural conditions. The pubescent child is surrounded by people who have clear ideas about how he should behave. The means he chooses to overcome the situation aroused by the increased amount of libido, may either be in harmony with these prerequisites or may contradict them. Adolescence may be compliant or rebellious—it is a process not a state. [1938, p. 258]

These comments are especially pertinent now in what has been called, the "age of compression". But I would like to offer a brief clinical example to stress the extreme confusion that characterizes this transition—mature one moment, infantile the next, sexually predatory one minute, terrified the next—and so on.

The swiftness with which things can change, back and forth, was brought home to me by a recent description from the psychotherapy session of a 13-year-old boy, Jay. This was the first meeting after the Christmas holiday break, and his therapist noted that her young patient seemed suddenly much taller and with a noticeably lower tone of voice and bigger hands than she had been aware of before. He denied the significance of the missed sessions over the Christmas break and reverted to a characteristically latency-type of play that had been on the wane before the holiday. This rather repetitive and mindless activity had long been a source of satisfaction for Jay.

> He created a target by placing the bin on a low shelf and then aimed a sponge ball at it from the farthest part of the room. He successfully lobbed it in the first time and was delighted. It was like the slam dunk of a tall basketball player. He tried to put the target in various, more difficult, positions, but the options were limited. Eventually he stopped, sat down, and began fiddling with the ball.

A few minutes later, as his therapist noted, Jay, for the first time, took out his phone and said that he would play her his favourite song.

> A nasal male voice sang about wanting to get back with his girlfriend and missing her and wanting things to be how they were. There was a repetitive electronic beat and it felt both sentimental and trendy. Jay seemed to abandon himself to the music as he swayed and, on occasions, waved his arms. Towards the end of the session he reverted to his more latency preoccupations, wanting to play repetitive games of noughts and crosses and to avoid talking about the area of obviously intense feelings that he had just demonstrated.

With Jay we can see that the confusing engagement with adolescent states of mind is both exciting to experiment with, but also something, at this point, anxiously to be fled from into the relative safety of a developmentally earlier state of mind. Early adolescence, as we have seen, is a crucial time of inevitable turmoil and confused identity, often peaking at age 14 or 15. "Crucial" is an important word, because undergoing and coping with turmoil and confusion is, of itself, a necessary aspect of the process. For while the very stress of this degree of psychic disruption and dislocation may often propel the young person into various behavioural and emotional states that can be disturbing and a worry to self and others, equally, weathering the storms may be significantly character-building. The problem is that, for many, "normal" manifestations of early adolescent confusions are so hard to tell apart from what they may dramatically, or insidiously, become—that is, disturbed and "pathological" ones.

What needs to be stressed is the inextricability (as Hall stressed in *Adolescence* all those years ago), at this point of transition, of sexuality and character formation, and the ways in which that inter-relation itself links to the range of different identifications with which the adolescent is experimenting. At puberty an attempt is made to break out of the constrictions on sexuality imposed by the earlier latency organization and to achieve a sense of sexual potency. But, in the early days, this attempt usually feels not only compelling, but also very alarming. For the boys, it may result in anxieties about potency itself—expressed in a whole variety of different ways: by behaviour typical of what may be called the "phallic swagger", for example, or by a kind of know-all pseudo-maturity, or by withdrawal from the threat of intimacy by way of an intensification of latency splitting and unadventurousness instead, often bordering on the obsessional.

For girls, as suggested, the challenge of sexual development is often expressed in extreme awareness of bodily appearance: issues of looks, especially weight, and major problems of depression and self-esteem. The digital age brings with it an extraordinarily intense focus on physical appearance, absence of privacy, and intrusive curiosity. A splitting between different parts of the self often occurs. It is not so much that the internal world, as a whole, is being externalized and played out, as in the structured games and hierarchical pecking order of the primary school child, but, rather, that the general certainty, however precariously upheld, of that earlier period dissolves into confusion about good and bad, adult and infantile, male and female, and so on. As we saw with Jay, shifts between one state of mind and another can be very rapid and often inexplicable. The youngster may, for example, be cooperative at one moment, recalcitrant the next, unable easily to acknowledge that the person who undertook the task and the person who failed to deliver was one and the same—namely, himself.

In this context, the significance of the group comes to the fore. The childhood years, perhaps never as stable as the epithet "latency" suggests, are now definitely, as we have seen, unsettled, and the young adolescent becomes attached to a group-orientated subculture in which peer relationships acquire enormous significance. As we shall see (chapter 6), at this time of stress and change, the young adolescent group can often begin to perform an extremely important holding function. As family bonds start to loosen, social life to extend, and feelings of uncertainty and confusion to intensify, the company of friends may be sought to enable the young person to sustain some kind of relationship with the different aspects of the personality, ones with which he may temporarily be having difficulty integrating into the previously known childhood self—feelings, fears, and impulses that are dimly recognizable from early development but also frighteningly unfamiliar. Group members often come together in flexible and changing combinations in which the various individuals represent different aspects of each others' personalities, whether attributes or deficiencies, which may be desired or repudiated. When these different aspects of self are located in the group, the young person can remain in touch with them, as somehow belonging to himself, while not being excessively troubled by them. Group life—often, these days, constructed online—can, when benign, provide these young people with social ways of sorting out who they are. The seemingly inexhaustible appetite for conversation and social networking, with "trying out", or experimenting with, different versions of the self and of others' reactions to that self, may well become intensely fascinating to all concerned. Moreover, the invaluable ingredient of humour is often involved, as a bulwark against taking themselves too seriously. Yet members of the "pack" are less often found hanging around coffee bars and fast-food outlets than alone in their rooms, more compelled by social media than by person-to-person contact.

The impact of the external culture is particularly strong during these early adolescent years. To take but one example: increasingly intense psychological confusion is already being engendered in the primary school child by the fact that, for largely environmental and dietary reasons, physiological puberty (not emotional) is occurring at a younger and younger age. For many, this can be acutely troubling. Girls who find themselves at a different stage from others in their peer group can feel weird and distressed. Some, on the other hand, feel proud and at an advantage. The market has not been slow in recognizing this. Juliet Schor (2005), a researcher into youth marketing techniques, points out the trend of "age compression"—"taking products and marketing messages originally designed for older children and targeting them at younger ones" (p. 55). The 8- to 12-year-old "tweenager" is now being selected for "tweening" as young as age 6. The pressures to grow up fast are becoming more and more insistent, and experience tells us that the more unstable the pre-pubertal years, the more difficult it is to negotiate the age of transition, or to hold on to any secure notion of what "growing up" really means. Everything feels out of kilter.

The dilemmas and difficulties of a 14-year-old, Christine (whose case I have drawn on before in *Inside Lives*), will give some sense of the problems of coming to terms with, and processing, many of the typical conflicts faced by her age group. Christine was referred for assessment as a result of pressure from Social Services, from her school, and from her mother (her father had left when she was a baby). She had been stealing. The objects stolen—a wedding ring, earrings, a watch, and, in the last incident, a large sum of money—belonged to the family, specifically to her mother and grandmother. Christine had spent the money on grown-up, sexually alluring clothes which she had ostentatiously worn in what seemed like a clear invitation to be found out.

On first meeting in the waiting room, Christine was indistinguishable from the six friends who accompanied her. They were all dressed in the then fashionable 501 black jeans and heavy Doc Marten boots. "My friends come with me everywhere" were Christine's first words in the consulting room, after she had shyly and smilingly identified herself and reluctantly walked up the corridor to my room. Her second comment was that she was only there because there was a worry that the police would have to be involved. She said that she had stopped stealing, so there was really no longer any problem. Again she smiled winningly.

The account that followed made it clear that what was being "acted out" by the stealing constituted a constellation of characteristically early adolescent issues. Christine described how she had been accused of causing arguments between her mother and her mother's boyfriend of three years, Paul, who had recently moved in unexpectedly. The arguments were about Christine's habits in the home, particularly her tendency to wander around in a state of semi-undress, to which her mother objected—"totally unreasonably", Christine thought. "She's probably jealous because she's becoming a fat old bag" (her mother was a trim 34-year-old at the time). Christine outlined her plans to move out, to get a flat of her own, to do it up, and to have a baby. But, she added, suddenly tearful, she would have to have her Mum behind her if she did something like that, "I couldn't do it alone". It was as if she was suddenly aware of how practically and emotionally unrealistic her plans really were.

Her mother was described as, alternately, in tears about "losing my daughter, my little girl" and furious about her daughter's indiscipline and moodiness. The oedipal issues, perhaps starkly present for the first time now that Paul had moved in, were fully apparent. Each member of the family was having difficulty in adjusting to the new situation and in recognizing what was really going on, and why. The struggles were made worse for Christine, in particular, by fears of growing up, of separating, of becoming a woman, finding a job, hoping for a partner. She was clearly worried about leaving her childhood behind at a time when she was suddenly having to relinquish the exclusive relationship that she had enjoyed with her mother for so many years. It was not only the containing function of the family that was being threatened, but also the more loosely containing structure of the group, because the friends who had accompanied Christine to the waiting room were a year older than she and were about to leave school.

Christine did not feel that she herself was a problem ("I don't know what the fuss is all about"), but, rather, that she had been "fielded" as the difficult one because of her mother's unhappiness and Paul's anger: "We'll have to throw you out if it goes on like this," he was reputed to have said to her. These rather selective sequences and comments were part of a bare fifty-minute session. On the surface, it was an ordinary sort of discussion with a rather likeable, but troubled, young adolescent. Yet it represents many of the problems, preoccupations, reactions, and defences that are so characteristic of this age. It encompasses, for example, the experience of renewed oedipal anxieties, centring on jealousy, exclusion, and competitiveness. It focuses on a particular presenting symptom, "delinquency". It relates to worries about separation. It clarifies enmeshment in the all-girl group, one that probably went along with the delinquent enterprises, yet also seemed to provide a still much-needed supportive structure. It highlights the oscillations between infantile and adult attitudes. It points out the splitting of the same figure (the mother) into good and bad. It reveals typically unrealistic fantasies ("I want to buy and decorate my own flat and have a baby"). It emphasizes the anxiety about sexuality—and so on.

It is striking that Christine started stealing soon after her mother's boyfriend moved in. At puberty, stealing is one of the most common manifestations of "acting out". It may represent any one of a range of meanings: perhaps of restoring what is felt to have been lost, here a mother–daughter relationship. It may be aggressive—that is, to deprive someone else of a treasured possession out of primitive envy and rage, or of precious things (her mother?) of which the person herself feels deprived and consequently impoverished. In Christine's case, there may well have been feelings of guilt and a desire for punishment in relation to her attitude to Paul. Was this, in other words, a protest? Or was it a statement about something having been stolen from her to which she had a right (the commitment symbolized by the wedding ring was something that she now felt she lacked)? Was the problem one of anxiety about her own attractiveness (it was feminine things that were stolen—a ring, a necklace, a purse, clothes, watch)? Was there also a jealous attack on her mother and a desire to take her partner away from her, a desire enacted by the flaunting of her own sexuality? Whatever the specific reasons, there was clearly a general anxiety about change and growing up, about losing relationships on which she was currently counting.

Christine was worried about being excluded from the newly formed family and about having to leave the safety of school (despite the fact that this was, in her case, still a year away). She told her therapist that going into the Army had seemed a rather good option for her, in that it entailed a tight, disciplined organization and "something interesting to do all the time". It was evident that she idealized this potential structure just as she idealized the alternative and equally unrealistic goal—namely, to have her own flat and family. Perhaps the unconscious idea behind this latter plan was that she could continue to have her infantile needs met by entrusting her own baby (self) to her mother. She wanted her mother to remain her mother and not be a sexual partner to Paul. Thus she set herself up in competition (she wore no underwear beneath the tracksuit). Christine was terrified of rejection and therefore behaved in ways that would provoke it ("We will have to put you in care"). She was both fiercely independent ("I want to leave home and get my own flat"), and at the same time childishly dependent ("I want my mum behind me and to bring up my baby at home").

Christine was trying to cope, in early adolescence, with a number of problems that aroused in her (though not consciously) feelings and anxieties about abandonment, exclusion, and separation and about being surpassed and relegated to second place. She was unable to contain either the implications and threats of her present predicament or the echoes of the past which those threats conjured up. She did not have a family setting within which her feelings might easily be registered and understood, nor was she herself, at this point, able to communicate her distress in ways that could be heard. She failed to understand that there might be other emotional priorities in the family besides her own. She was worried that she could not count on her mother's continued emotional support for her daughter's growing feminine independence and need to establish a secure relationship of her own. Christine felt impoverished and uncertain about such loving resources, and her insecurity led her to steal the symbols of commitment and femininity—that is, the concrete representations of feared emotional deficit.

At this early stage an extraordinary range and diversity can be recorded of adolescents' responses to the predicament in which they find themselves. But it is not so much the details of these various strategies for evading mental pain, or, less commonly, for actively seeking it out, that are of primary interest here. Rather, the question is one of the overall picture of the early adolescent situation and its function for the developing personality. While the description of Christine's difficulties in coming to terms with the pressures described are especially typical of her age group, they may also make their appearance at any subsequent stage in life, when the prevailing state of mind favours action rather than thought and provokes infantile rather than adult responses. For adolescence is indeed a process, and its outcome, at whatever stage, fundamentally affects, as already suggested, any future capacity to engage with life's vicissitudes.

CHAPTER FIVE

Models of learning

A s we have seen, a child's capacity to develop and grow internally is closely related to the kind of learning that has been going on from the earliest phases of his life. Depending on the predominant task, or function, of the phase in question, different models of learning will come into play. In primary school, for example, a child may both need, and enjoy, the sense of an extension of skills and an amassing of information. At adolescence, this kind of learning may seem to run counter to the more imaginative and creative capacity of beginning to think for oneself. But, underlying such shifts of emphasis between one phase and another, there is a further fundamental distinction. It is the one that Yeats so impressively describes as being between the thinking that goes on "in the mind alone" and that which occurs "in the marrow-bone". A similar distinction, as we shall explore in this chapter, pervades Bion's work: he described a central difference between learning "about" things and being able to learn from the experiences of the self-in-the-world.

Thus a chapter on "learning" belongs at the heart of a book about adolescence, a book focused on the ordinary ways in which a person may grow up—internally as well as externally. I find it significant that these reflections on "learning" were also at the heart of the version of *Inside Lives* first published two decades ago. For this emphasizes the point being made throughout these pages—namely, that the "inside stories" take shape and develop in ways that may be strongly affected and fuelled by external circumstances, but they are more significantly driven by internal forces and dynamics that are embedded deeply in the very make-up of the human mind. The aim was then, and is now, to differentiate between the sorts of thinking and knowing that contribute to character strength and the capacity to think for oneself, and those that encourage the mere proliferation of qualifications and expertise—the "learning" that may measure external success without increasing internal growth. Of concern are not so much matters of social goals and priorities, but the most specific and personal of issues: the kinds of identification to which a child has been drawn from the very first.

In over-simple terms, the question may be posed, in ways that I shall clarify: do the child's primary identifications seem to be of an adhesive, a projective, or an introjective kind? There will, of course, be constant movement between these. But in any one child, it is usually possible to discern the underlying tendencies towards any one mode over another, despite shifts and changes. It is the predominance of one of these modes over others that determines whether learning takes place by way of imitation, of a mimicking, parroting adhesive kind; or by the child's anxiously seeking to be someone that he is not, projectively acting in role, or even experiencing the self as if actually *being* the other; or by the child's resiliently seeking understanding by engaging with his own experience of a secure, inner sense of self, derived from a capacity for introjective identification with good, sincere, and thoughtful qualities of mind.

The importance of the link between these broad types of identification, and the different learning modes that are embedded in them, is that such a link both characterizes and illuminates fundamental developmental processes. The present task is to try to explore the origin and nature of different kinds of learning and the possible consequences for the personality when one mode takes precedence over another.

The following dreams of three adolescents may lend definition and clarification, in however schematic a form, to the different kinds of identification in question. In the first example, the adhesive mode seems to have predominated from early on and seriously to have inhibited development. In the second example, a more projective mode would also seem significantly to have impeded emotional growth. The third example, by contrast, offers some evidence of early adhesive and projective tendencies yielding to a more introjective capacity, with a consequent enrichment of the personality.

The first patient, John, was 19 when he began therapy. He was the son of a successful writer. His dream will be seen to characterize the type of identification in which it may look as though development is occurring, but, in fact, that development is very superficial, offering little genuine internal support. John's primary identification was one of slavish observation, imitation, and mimicry of the social behaviour and appearance of those to whom he was close, particularly his father. He described himself as dressing, speaking, gesturing, and behaving exactly like his father. It was as if he needed to be somehow stuck on to the older man's skin, surface-to-surface. He adopted his parents' tastes, their way of life, their interests and goals. He was frequently overwhelmed with panic at the idea of having to make an independent choice. Not surprisingly, when he began therapy his personality seemed rather shallow, as if two-dimensional. At this point his state was one of total dependence upon the thoughts and views of those to whom he attached himself.

John had survived his mid-adolescent years by appearing to be mature, although perhaps excessively self-preoccupied, lacking *joie de vivre*, and without much genuine feeling for others. His behaviour seemed to be socially adaptive at the expense of any internal development. He had had no meaningful sexual relationships or friendships and appeared to have very little capacity to think for himself, getting through the educational system by rote-learning and a parroting technique of the "in one ear, out the other" variety. This method left him with little feeling of confidence in having any knowledge of his own, with the result that the knowledge that he did acquire made no lasting impact on his personality. He was a teenage isolate, presenting to the world a rather fraudulent appearance of stability, one that, on the whole, attracted little attention from the adults concerned. He only came to anyone's attention when he started becoming seriously depressed at the point at which his age meant that, educationally at least, he had to take steps to separate from his family. Separation was felt to be both traumatic and damaging, not only to himself but also (at least in his mind) to the individuals from whom he was having to tear himself free. (He became morbidly preoccupied at this time with the idea of his father's death.) The characteristic defence against this kind of primitive sense of being torn apart is familiar in Esther Bick's (1968) notion of a "second-skin" defence: a muscular, sensory, or vocal means of holding the personality together externally, one that can develop from early infancy in the absence of any internally secure psychic "containment". In John's case, the mode seemed to be a muscular one.

He was a brilliant sportsman, as his father had been, but in no other area of his life did he excel. A requirement of any response beyond the most clichéd and conventional provoked anxiety.

The following dream epitomizes his predicament and focuses his aversion to exposing himself to the painful process of growing up, with the attendant anguish of separation and the risk of change. In the dream,

> *I was a child, gazing at a Harley Davidson motorcycle* [with associations closely linked to his father] *which stood on the summit of a mountain, outlined against the gorgeous hues of the evening sky. Between me and the bike, which I desperately wanted to reach, lay a dark mountainside. I would have to ascend a steep, drizzly, and foreboding road, winding its way towards the top. I had a powerful sense of wanting just to be "raised up" so that I could simply "be" the motorcycle.*

John longed, in other words, just to *be* his father, to be grown-up like him, having eliminated the alarming and hazardous, winding, and foreboding adolescent process. He wished to evade the risky business of separation which he would have to undergo in order to become himself. His adhesive mode of identifying had put in abeyance any genuine growing-up. His unconscious desire was to bypass the problems of adolescence, or, rather, perhaps, to deny the adolescent state of mind in favour of a pseudo-adult one; to deny, that is, the function of adolescence in the process of maturing into one's own—as opposed to a borrowed—identity. The fact that, in the dream, he was still a child suggests that the nature of his learning process had, from early on, blocked the path to becoming *himself*, as opposed to being a look-a-like version of his father. While outwardly nearly a "grown-up", inwardly he had hardly begun.

The second patient, Simon, a bright young medic, was accustomed to doing well in his exams and was predicted to "go far". He had an interesting dream on the eve of his finals, in the days when students still wore white coats and carried stethoscopes around their necks.

> *I turned up to the exam room and realized that I had come without my white coat or stethoscope. I was also aware that I had lost my copy of Bion's* Learning from Experience.

Simon was troubled by the dream, the meaning of which became clear when he arrived at a later session very angry and upset. He had failed his finals and would have to re-sit the following year. We spent the session making links between his pre-exam dream and what he felt to be his shameful results. With time, it became possible for him to acknowledge how prescient his dream had been, for it indicated the extent to which he was, in fact, in touch, unconsciously, with the reality that he did not yet merit the trappings of being a doctor when he knew really that he had not yet sufficiently learned from his experience actually to *be* a true doctor. Rather, he realized, he had been parading his medical "know-how" on the exam paper without really believing it. An extra year of hard therapeutic work enabled him to grow up on the inside with his "real" self, rather than to attempt, on the outside, to get by with his "clever" self.

The third patient, Tom, had, in the course of his long treatment, begun to move from the kind of adhesive mental state that John was in, through the more projective mode that characterized Simon's learning and functioning, and beyond, to a more "mature" capacity to form intimate and loving relationships with others. I shall briefly draw on two of his dreams here, ones that are explored at much greater length in chapter 9. As with Simon, the first dream of Tom's therapy eloquently described his internal predicament:

> *I was trying to play tennis on an indoor court of which one of the walls was missing. Every time I threw the ball up to serve, it hit an unnaturally low ceiling and bounced back at me prematurely, making it impossible to set the ball in play.*

This dream seemed to describe the frustrated experience of a baby of a depressed mother, who, as it was later learned, was soon to become schizophrenic, when her son was 2 years old. It suggested a very early experience of a lack of containment on Tom's part (the missing wall) and of the hopelessness of his attempts to communicate. His projections were felt to be prematurely pushed back at him (the unnaturally low ceiling), as if bouncing off the surface of his mother's unreceptive mind. This made it impossible for him to set in train the normal processes of projection and introjection in the game of life.

A much later dream of this same patient described an internal situation that was very different from the frustrations and insecurities of this early indoor-tennis-court–self. The dream gave some indication that a process had imperceptibly been occurring in which Tom was able to take in, and make use of, a thinking and holding quality in his relationships—a process that had previously been impossible for him. He had started to progress from his initial adhesive and projective tendencies towards a more even balance between projective and introjective modes. He had begun to engage with, and suffer, his own experience rather than fleeing to his old habits of premature certainty, or to any of the readily available forms of mindlessness in which he had been inclined to indulge. In the dream,

> I was in a house that was solid, well-built, and rather beautiful. I seemed to be staying with a group of friends, not my old drinking companions but college friends whom I did not yet know very well but whom I liked and who seemed serious about what they were doing. Among them was a particular woman who had a name similar to yours, Margaret [someone who had often, in terms of looks, attitude, and qualities been associated with me]. The atmosphere was relaxed. I found that I was unusually unstressed, able to talk, to be myself. At one point I was riding a motorcycle. I stopped to fix an unsafe chain with one of my friends.

This final detail, he interjected, was very different from his early motorbike dreams, and indeed experiences, ones that had been reckless and often out of control: his bike had been constantly in need of repair, and he was often in danger of putting his own life and those of others at risk. By contrast, in this dream he felt in control, "I don't mean in a bad way, but somehow able to pursue my own endeavours. It was a good feeling, sort of hopeful. I think that maybe I'll come through all this." He then completed his account of the dream:

> I spent the night in the house alone, my companions seemed to have gone elsewhere. In the morning, I discovered that the young woman had also spent the night in the house, but without my knowledge. I wished that I had known that she had stayed, but I also felt very good that she was somehow there with me, there whether I knew it or not.

Tom acknowledged that the "containing" house seemed much more solid than those of previous dreams and that he was oddly at ease with the figures within. The motorbike-riding had the feeling of self-expression and individual spontaneity, by contrast with his former self-destructive, "gang-like" activities. But, most important and illuminating of all, was the description of the young woman/analyst figure who was somehow there with him, whether he was aware of her or not; present internally as a companion and a resource "in the mind". He described her as having qualities to which he aspired and in the light of which he felt humble: ones of integrity, loyalty, helpfulness, and friendship. The dream suggested that, at least some of the time, Tom could feel that he possessed these qualities himself, that within his now more solid house/mind, there was a very different structure from the tennis-court area where he had previously been trying to "play out" his life, in the absence of any obvious source of containment.

These patients' dreams have been drawn on as representing, albeit schematically, the different modes of identification under discussion. Although each may indicate the predominance of one particular state of mind, there is always a certain fluidity, and a person may be constantly shifting between one or the other mode. The dreams offer evidence of very distinct types of learning: with John and Simon, ones that had been in place from early times; with Tom, one that he was able to develop beyond in the course of his analytic experience. In external terms, we are familiar with the ways in which emotional factors may adversely affect a child's capacity to take things in and to learn, whether in the most general sense or in specific cognitive ways. Less familiar is the complexity of the interaction between what might be called a learning ability and a learning capacity, that between "thinking in the mind alone" and "thinking in a marrow-bone". As we have seen, an individual may show ability in the acquisition of particular skills, be it with figures, words, computers, sports, exam-passing, but the difficult question always remains: that of whether, in simple terms, these abilities, over time, contribute to the personality as a whole—the singing of a "lasting song"—or whether they are developed either as distinct from, or at the expense of, other parts of the self.

A shy latency child, whose mathematical ability had served her well in terms of gaining her status and supporting her fragile self-esteem, may find, in adolescence, that that particular carapace begins to limit her emotional development. The turbulent and imaginative flowering of her inner self may be inhibited by an understandable tendency to hang on to what wins approval and makes her feel safe. Indeed, as we shall see, it is often only during adolescence that the degree to which an early use of intelligence, as a defence against genuine thinking, may become apparent. As at any age, work may become a way of avoiding intimacy and evading engagement with painful and conflictual emotional reality.

* * *

Psychodynamic thinkers, along with progressive educationalists, have long striven to define and encourage the child's capacity to learn in a way that is associated less with narrow educational attainment and socially visible qualities and more with the enrichment of a person's creative potential. Conventional success and inner development need not be at odds with one another, but it is important to determine for whom, and for what, the success is sought before welcoming it with any special acclaim. Historically, psychoanalysis has always concerned itself with matters of learning and thinking, but the focus has impressively changed over the decades to the point where theories of thinking have now rightly become central to our present ways of understanding the individual as a whole person.

With Freud, thought, or the ability to think, was, roughly speaking, regarded as a way of bridging the frustrating gap between the moment a need is felt and the point at which the appropriate action satisfies it (1911b). By contrast, Klein's early concerns centred on much broader and more personal matters of a child's education: on intellectual inhibition and emotional blocks to learning. She was interested in how psychoanalysis and education might together contribute to the blossoming of the personality in all its dimensions. She and her friend and colleague Susan Isaacs (who, for several years, ran the progressive Malting House School in Grantchester) wrote about the way in which intellectual and creative capacities are inhibited, in particular, by anxiety and also, quite specifically, by the repression of sexual curiosity (Isaacs, 1948; Klein, 1921, 1923, 1931). Their view was that the child can only learn from engaging with his or her own real experiences and that the educator should seek to support those experiences rather than to stand in the way of them.

Underlying these views was a notion that the child's need to know and understand the truth about himself and his experience of the world (initially represented by the mother's body and mind) was an impulse so fundamental that it almost amounted to an "instinct". Klein called it the "epistemophilic" impulse or instinct (1928, p. 188). She thought of it as originating in the infant's unconscious desire to fathom the contents of the mother's body, and she introduced a central distinction, one that later acquired significant dimensions: a distinction between intrusive curiosity, stimulated by a voyeuristic need to "know" in order to master and control, in contrast to a more enlightened desire to understand—something more akin to a thirst for knowledge, in the interests of growth rather than of mastery.

These ideas raised questions as to the degree to which learning and finding-out would encourage, or inhibit, the developing self;

whether learning would be in the service of the genuine growth of the mind or would function as a defensive prop for the more timid self; whether or not, at root, learning was an emotional experience. Such questions became fundamental to Bion's way of conceptualizing these matters. His theory of thinking (1962b) put emotionality at the psychoanalytic heart of things. Learning of the kind that properly contributed to development (by contrast with mere cognition) occurred primarily through experience and not through increasing the stock of knowledge. He pointed out that, in certain states of mind, "having" knowledge can become a substitute for learning. It may often be the case that a kind of mental law of "unequal development" occurs, one in which there is an inverse relationship between "brains" on the one hand, and a deeper kind of thinking on the other; between an intellectual ability to manipulate concepts of, say, truth, meaning, or virtue, and the emotional capacity genuinely to understand and espouse these things. If knowledge is acquired in the interests of potency rather than insight, that knowledge may function in the psychic economy rather like a material possession. Wherever this happens, knowledge will run counter to any genuine quest for understanding. Much rests on the motive—what is being sought in the process of acquiring knowledge, and what is being avoided.

Bion designates the distinction between these different modes of mental functioning as that between K, a thirst for knowledge, and –K, the mental state in which experience is stripped of its true meaning and knowledge is treated as a commodity: it is superficially attractive but has no lasting nor growth-promoting influence. The model that Bion draws on as a prototype for learning, as we have seen, is the feeding relationship between mother and baby, taking into account both the disposition of the baby and the mother's state of mind, or capacity for "rêverie". These issues reach back to earliest times. They relate to the way in which anxiety has been registered and responded to from the first. They relate to the kinds of identificatory mode that have been established. The dominant emphases of these modes may be significantly altered in the light of later experience and in relation to a range of environmental factors. Yet important patterns are laid down in these early days, patterns that, in simple terms, may be defined as stemming from the nature and quality of the relationship between baby and carer.

Bion (1962a) proposed the term the "K link" to signify a relationship of mutual dependency and benefit, one whereby both mother and baby could grow emotionally. Just as the baby who has been talked *to,* by contrast with talked *at,* is better able to begin talking himself, so too with complex mental processes. The baby's capacity for taking in sense impressions develops in relation to those same capacities within the mother, and with that capacity comes an awareness of the nature of the outside world and of his experience of it.

> Learning depends on the capacity for [the growing container] to remain integrated and yet lose rigidity. This is the foundation of the state of mind of the individual who can retain his knowledge and experience and yet be prepared to reconstrue past experiences in a manner that enables him to be receptive of a new idea. [p. 93]

Bion saw this "container–contained" relationship between mother and baby as representing an emotional realization of a learning experience that becomes progressively more complex as it constantly recurs in different forms throughout mental development, finally encompassing the possibility of whole hypotheses, and scientific deductive systems (pp. 85–86).

As we saw in chapter 4, the mother's capacity to contain the projected infantile fears (the contained) renders the original anxieties more manageable: "During their sojourn in the good breast they are felt to have been modified in such a way that the object that is re-introjected has become tolerable to the infant's psyche" (Bion, 1962a, p. 90). Or, more precisely: "The breast in K would moderate the fear component in the fear of dying that had been projected into it and the infant in due course would re-introject a now tolerable and consequently growth-stimulating part of its personality" (p. 96).

When something interferes with this early linking, or mutually communicative capacity between mother and baby, a quite different process can be set in train, one that, if it occurs too often or too extensively, is ultimately in the service less of understanding than of misunderstanding, as represented by –K. This active "misunderstanding" is the product of the experience described in chapter 4. At times, the emotion to be projected is felt to be too toxic, or the projection itself too forceful, and/or the mother is, for whatever reason, unreceptive. At these times, the projection is not understood by her and the content of it is experienced by the infant as being forced back into him, together with that non-understanding aspect of the "breast". As Bion put it, "The infant who started with a fear [that] he was dying ends up by containing a nameless dread" (p. 96).

The emotion that brings about this "denuding" of meaning is thought of, psychoanalytically, as a primitive form of envy. The baby has hostile and destructive feelings towards the object/breast, which is felt to have what he lacks. For example, the breast is felt to be feeding itself, and leaving him hungry; or the breast is felt to be the source of good feelings, but these feelings are being withheld rather than freely given. This emotion of envy is incompatible with growth and learning. It is the source of particular problems subsequently manifested (especially, perhaps, during adolescence) in assertions of superiority, or in finding fault with everything, or in hating a "new development in the personality as if the new development were a rival to be destroyed" (p. 98). The effect of this kind of process, which may *look like* learning, is, in fact, to destroy rather than to promote knowledge. The process is often tinged with "moral" superiority, one of the characteristics, Bion thought, of *un*-learning (p. 98).

The degree of the toxicity and of the intensity of the projections relates to the baby's response to frustration, the frustration that naturally belongs to any experience in which need is not immediately gratified. If the baby/learner is intolerant, there will be a tendency to try to evade the pain of absence, of uncertainty, or of not knowing. One way of doing this is to project all the more massively and insistently, to the point where so much of the self is felt to be in the other that an illusion arises that there is actually no difference between the two—that is, between the self and the other. When there is no experience of twoness, neither separation nor envy need to be felt, but, equally, no learning can occur. Bion suggests that an alternative way of avoiding the pain of frustration is to turn to fantasies of omniscience and omnipotence, as substitutes for the dreaded experience of being starved of food for thought. "Knowing" thus becomes something that consists of "having" some "piece of knowledge" (a misunderstanding frequently echoed in political debates on education, and sustained by the "mastermind" model of educatedness). This is quite different from what is meant by K—that is, a capacity that resides in the more complex and arduous process of "getting to know" something, supported by being able to tolerate both the sense of infinity (that there is always more to know) and of doubt (that is, of being able not to know).

A characteristic of a particular kind of omniscience, one that stems from the lack of a sufficiently holding and integrating experience between baby and primary caretaker, is that there is a tendency to substitute for the complex ethical discrimination between truth and falsehood a dictatorial affirmation that one thing is morally right and another is wrong. A potential conflict then arises, as Bion points out, between the assertion of truth and the assertion of moral ascendency.

In such a case, there is an attempt to avoid the painful business of moral conflict and uncertainty by the unthinking imposition of moral certitude, always a hindrance to genuine learning.

The infant who is capable of tolerating frustration is able, in the absence of the needed breast, to draw on his own resources, if only very temporarily. The baby substitutes for what Bion calls the "no-breast", something that amounts to embryonic thought. That is, he draws on something of his own to tide him over, thus, in Bion's view, initiating a very early kind of thinking and learning apparatus. These resources result from having had an experience of a mother who, at least some of the time, is herself able to bear anxiety and frustration: from the opportunity, that is, to take in, from the first, that particular function of her personality. If he has neither a dispositional capacity to bear frustration, nor the experience of adequate maternal rêverie, the baby will attempt, all the more forcefully, to get rid of whatever it is that the physical/emotional system feels unable to digest or metabolize.

A further hindrance to learning at this very early stage, and one that is also a feature of the –K link, stems from the fact that, in difficult circumstances, the baby's predicament will be one of having to take back inside him not only his own feelings left unmodified, but also that part of his mother's mental state which was incapable of receiving those projections. The baby thus has lodged within him instead of an understanding object, a "wilfully misunderstanding object—[one] with which [he] is identified" (1962b, p. 117).

These early interactions were offered by Bion as "models" for thinking and learning processes. As such, they enable a fundamental differentiation to be established, whether for individuals or for groups, between the kind of learning and thinking that is in the service of the growth of the personality, and, by contrast, the kind that is opposed to growth, favouring, instead, aspects of character that obstruct development—superiority, for example, or dishonesty, or moralism. When the "K" mentality predominates, the group is enhanced by the introduction of new ideas or people and the atmosphere is, as Bion says, "conducive to mental health" (1962a, p. 99). By contrast, under the sway of the –K mentality, a quite different kind of functioning emerges, one that Bion would refer to as the "lying group", who are dominated by envy. In such a group, new ideas and new people are stripped of their meaning. The group feels devalued by any source of interest or significance that is not generated from among its members. As a consequence, it becomes no longer viable as a group. The essential diehard obstinacy of many group processes rests on an inherent resistance to change. Change is felt to threaten the group's survival. Change puts the group under pressure to integrate aspects of character and functioning that are felt to be more comfortably kept elsewhere, held off in the other person, in the other group.

K and −K connote fundamentally different kinds of linkage between self and other, whether in individual or group relationships. The individual's capacity to learn is determined both by the kinds of internal dynamic already discussed, and also by the modes of learning dominant in a particular family and culture at any specific time. Indeed, in any situation, qualities of learning will be significantly influenced by the attitudes of the teaching group—that is, by whether that group promotes or discourages honesty in the individual. Especially in an educational setting, creative thought may be undermined by the stirring of feelings of inferiority and defensiveness, by the push towards certainty that obscures further penetration into the area of the unknown. Perhaps not surprisingly, very little has changed in this respect over the centuries (chapter 10), as we can see in George Eliot's description in her last novel of her character Daniel Deronda's disillusionment when he first went to Cambridge:

> But here came the old check which had been growing with his growth. He found the inward bent towards comprehension and thoroughness diverging more and more from the track marked out by the standards of examination: he felt a *heightening* discontent with the wearing futility and enfeebling strain of a demand for excessive retention and dexterity without any insight into the principles which form the vital connections of knowledge. [1876, p. 220]

As we have seen, the kind of thinking that will be going on in any one learning situation is based on processes for which the mother–infant relationship offers the prototype. The degree to which an individual can retain his own capacity for thinking rests, to a great extent, on the nature of the learning that has been possible from the first. It rests on those earliest defences against psychic pain, defences that are inevitable in the experience of life, at whatever stage or age. It also rests, as already suggested, on the predominant identificatory modes that will have developed in the attempt to resolve the central conflict between need and frustration and, ultimately, between love and hate. We return to the original question: does the baby in pain try to expel that pain by seeking to rid the self of it by projecting it into a containing object, or does he have the capacity, and the opportunity, to introject an experience that can ameliorate the pain internally? The first kind of identification, the adhesive one already outlined, is particularly visible when it comes to describing different learning processes. As we have seen, this mode of being tends to occur defensively when the three-dimensionality of a containing experience is lacking and, instead, a two-dimensional sticking-of-the-self-onto-the-other develops. In the absence of an internal structure, an external one is felt to be essential to survival. The result is that as little feeling of separation as possible is suffered, and very little learning can take place. Insofar as learning does occur, it tends to be based in the memorizing, and rote-methods that characterized John's educational experience.

It is, perhaps, becoming clearer just how complex is the relationship between cognitive and emotional learning and their underlying mental states. The issue is not simply that emotional factors affect the individual's capacity to think, to learn, and to understand, but, rather, that the capacity genuinely to take things in, and to use them to develop a truer picture of the-self-in-the-world, is rooted in very early experiences. These different modes of learning often acquire especially clear distinctiveness only in adolescence.

This question of the types of learning that contribute to development, and those that undermine it, links the Kleinian picture of the instinct for knowledge to Bion's conviction that every individual has an unconscious desire to seek truthful experiences in order to know the self; a belief that people are fundamentally truth-seeking. Truthful experiences are, in his view, food for the mind. Lying experiences are its poison. In some ways, the positive and negative aspects of Klein's "epistemophilic instinct" look very similar to Bion's formulation of K and –K. Klein traced a close connection between the early acquisition of knowledge, on the one hand, and sadism and anxiety on the other. She suggested that the epistemophilic instinct initially arose in the context of the child's anxious desire to explore the nature of his immediate world, represented, in these earliest times, by the inside of the mother's body. When the baby was feeling frustrated and needy, this exploratory desire was motivated, in phantasy, by negative impulses, envious ones perhaps, to destroy, to control, or to take possession by eliminating feared rivals. The main stimulus was thought to be one of anxiety-driven voyeuristic curiosity. Slightly later, in Klein's view, the baby begins to harbour a curiosity that is more akin to a thirst for knowledge than to a compulsion to "know about" things. The desire is to understand both the self and the other, to explore the self in the mother's mind. Such an exploration takes place through the kinds of projective processes that are in the interests of understanding rather than of disavowal. The discoveries made can be re-introjected and drawn on for knowledge of the self and for further understanding of the outside world. The first kind of investigation is profoundly inimical to genuine learning. It encourages a mentality that regards knowledge as a thing to be "had", to be possessed, usually for ambitious, rivalrous, competitive, and self-serving purposes. It carries with it many pitfalls, in that it stirs fears of fraudulence and provokes crises at moments of success when, for example, internal qualifications are feared to fall short of the external acclaim.

* * *

Several brief examples may convey a sense of the importance of discerning both the quality of learning that is really going on, and also its precise function for the personality, in relation to the motives and goals that underlie it. The examples each have their own particularity, but they are not age-specific in any precise way. They may be taken to represent recognizable aspects of the different kinds of learning under discussion, whatever the actual developmental stage or age of the children and young people described.

Maggie was 2 years 6 months old. She had been struggling hard to come to terms with the existence of her little brother, Roy. By temperament she had always been rather brittle and nervous, in contrast to Roy's easy and relaxed disposition. Her relationship with her mother became unsettled, indeed stormy, after Roy's birth, and she drew markedly closer to her rather bookish father, who, in turn, delighted in his daughter's precocious intellect and her new-found fondness for him. On this particular occasion, Maggie was finding it especially difficult not to interfere with, and obstruct, whatever it was that Roy was trying to do. She would insistently "upstage" him with her superior abilities, especially her manual dexterity. Undaunted in the face of her contemptuous comments, Roy would doggedly pursue his projects. Observing, with growing frustration, Maggie's repeated sabotage of Roy's attempts to fit different-shaped wooden blocks into their respective holes, their mother fiercely remonstrated: if Maggie continued to behave like that she would have no jelly for tea. Only momentarily crestfallen, Maggie immediately turned to her father and asked if they could "play schools". She sat, as if at a pretend-desk, while her father asked her a series of questions. To a casual observer, the questions seemed startlingly sophisticated for such a young child: "What is the name of the Prime Minister?" "What is the flag of Great Britain?" etc. Maggie answered most of the questions perfectly, much to her father's delight. But when she made a mistake, she became excessively aggrieved and vociferously challenged her father's probity.

This simple example describes, with great clarity, the way in which Maggie needed to acquire intellectual skills to help her to combat the sense of being displaced by her charming little brother. She turned to factual knowledge to boost her confidence and to enable her, in phantasy, to win her father over to his clever-little-girl, and, in so doing, perhaps to persuade herself that being daddy's favourite intellectual companion was somehow preferable to her mother's attention to "baby" things. The greedy gathering of facts and information was being drawn upon to assuage her longing for the special position that she had occupied as her mummy's only baby. Ultimately, sucking up to clever-daddy, though perhaps only temporarily effective, could function as but a flimsy protection against the painful feelings of her wounded and displaced self. We may feel the force of a discernible risk that her parents would derive amusement and intellectual gratification from Maggie's big-girl-self and that her baby-self would be overlooked rather than understood. She needed help to integrate these infantile feelings into a sense of herself as a true, rather than a performing, person.

* * *

Mental performance is frequently mistaken for mental health, and the desperate feelings behind the cognitive functioning are often lost in social and educational acclaim. Two highly achieving adolescent girls were referred for psychotherapy: Sandra was capable and brilliant but anorexic and mute; Claire had won a scholarship to Cambridge but was prone to frequent bouts of tears and inexplicable distress. It emerged that both of these clever and troubled girls had suffered serious losses at around the age of 5 years: Sandra's parents had separated; Claire's little brother had died of meningitis. Both sets of parents described how wonderfully the girls had behaved at the time and what a shock it was to discover that they now seemed so distressed. Not surprisingly, it soon became clear that both Sandra and Claire had taken refuge in academic prowess as a way of not engaging with their intolerable sadness. Each had sought to spare her parents further anguish by "managing" her own grief, through intellectual success. Their unconscious anger, guilt, and rage, possibly even triumph, were "taken care of" in the socially acceptable realm of competitiveness and achievement. This turned out to be at the expense of an integration into their personalities of aspects of themselves that, at the time, they could not bear. Each found it necessary to disown her distress and attribute it elsewhere (in both cases, as it happened, into a troublesome and recalcitrant younger sibling).

The contrast between these different states of mind is well caught in George Eliot's description of the difference between being egotistically enclosed within a set mental attitude on the one hand, and being able to form a sense of connectedness with all ordinary human existence on the other:

> It is an uneasy lot at best to be what we call highly taught and yet not to enjoy, to be present at this great spectacle of life and never to be liberated from a small, hungry shivering self—never to be fully possessed by the glory we behold, never to have our consciousness rapturously transformed into the vividness of a thought, the ardour of a passion, the energy of an action, but always to be scholarly and uninspired, ambitious and timid, scrupulous and dim-sighted. [1872/1965, p. 314]

These lines from *Middlemarch* draw the threads of this chapter together. And it is not surprising that Freud is recorded as having given his bride to be, Martha Bernays, a copy of *Middlemarch*. The kind of learning that contributes to the growth of the personality is that which engages with life passionately and honestly, if painfully. It is a learning that encourages change, one that inspires growth and supports a person in thinking for himself and thereby becoming more genuinely himself.

During adolescence, the capacity to pursue such learning may waver or feel only sporadically possible. It is rooted in the nature of the identificatory mode that has predominated from the earliest days, but it is also sensitive, thereafter, to the complex relationships between internal motivation and social expectation. As the foregoing examples have shown, shifts may constantly occur between the kind of learning that remains "scholarly and uninspired, ambitious and timid" and the kind that stirs aspiration and further endeavour. During adolescence, these shifts between –K and K can become more pronounced, but these youngsters are usually still at a stage when, with help and increased security, they may settle at the more flexible and positive end of the spectrum.

CHAPTER SIX

Groups and gangs

A t no point in a person's development across the life cycle is the character, quality, and overall expression of group life more formative and significant than during the adolescent years. Having to begin coping with the experience of the "hour of the stranger" involves not only the turbulence of a newly physically and emotionally unintegrated personality, but often includes a physical destabilization too, an unsettling of what had been felt as the body's "centre of gravity" (Tabbia, 2017, p. 95). With the passing of the binding force of latency–obsessionality, and of the holding function of the family, comes the dispersal, or splitting up, of the self—a function that now requires an alternative group structure to hold together those parts of the self and to prevent further fragmentation.

As Martha Harris (1976) puts it,

> Adolescence may be seen as a period during which the containing function of the family disappears and has to be replaced externally and eventually internally in the personality; when the young person has to proceed through a disintegration to a new integration as an independent adult. During the transition the adolescent group may be seen as performing a second-skin holding function. It is a period when old infantile conflicts have to be worked over again in the light of new, intense genital drives which test the quality of the internalisation of previous object-relations and identifications. [p. 123]

The group, in other words, may be performing, to draw on Bion (1970), a positive "exo-skeletal" function as an alternative to the holding function of the family until the endoskeleton, or internal backbone, is more firmly in place (p. 23). In this way, the group may have an integrative and protective role too: that of a kind of network, one of holding the different parts of the personalities involved together until the more distinctive aspects of their respective identities begin to emerge. As already mentioned, it is not uncommon for the different members of the group to carry specific characteristics of those split-off parts of the rest of the group—for example, the clever one, the jokey one, the scapegoat, the promiscuous one, and so on.

There may also be a safety-in-numbers dimension to the group formation. It can function as protection from the fears of isolation that are so often an accompaniment to the confusion of those new and bewildering feelings that can frequently accost the young teenager with a sense of being "unlike the others". All manner of confusions swirl around: about gender identity, about adult and infantile feelings and strivings—ones now scarcely recognizable to the hitherto "known" personality. The youngsters find themselves stranded in a totally unfamiliar place. Disguised as a group member, the sense of isolation is sometimes assuaged. The fear of difference can be the driving force towards the imperative to be "like" the others, in terms of dress code, accent, taste in music, and so on. The acute self-consciousness about appearance, as the body, inexplicably and often horrifyingly, takes on quite different characteristics of size, smell, texture, proportion, can be felt to be masked by similarities of style. Consequently, the groups, at this early point, tend to be gender-specific as a defence against strange and unwanted sexual urges or aversions being stirred by the hormonal and endocrinological explosions (discussed in chapter 4) of the age.

A last but important general point needs to be made about these sorts of group formations: joining a group does not necessitate being against parents. A member is allowed to disengage from the family to join a group that fosters development, just as a group member may ally with parents if it is felt that a friend may be in trouble—be it in relation to not eating enough, to excessive work or exercise, to drug-taking, depressive anxiety, addiction to social media, or whatever. Some years ago, I met with a clear example of these two mentalities in contrasting encounters in the waiting room of a CAMHS clinic.

On the first occasion, I walked into the waiting room to pick up the referred patient—a 15-year-old youngster. I encountered eight or ten girls, identically dressed in the code of the time: Doc Marten boots,

501 jeans and hair tightly pulled back in pony tails (very like the first encounter with Christine, in chapter 4). After a moment's bemusement on my part, one of them shyly put up her hand: "I'm the one you're looking for, the others came with me to make sure I actually got here."

Shortly after this, I found myself in a not-dissimilar situation. I came to see a 16-year-old "girl" who had been referred for excessive drug use and depression. There was now a familiar scenario awaiting me: a similarly clad group of girls, but one somehow more threatening in their collective attitude than on the previous occasion. After a long pause, one of them stood up and said, rather challengingly, as she pointed to one of her friends, "It's her you want. Either we all come or nobody comes."

In these very different presentations, there are some recognizable defensive characteristics in common. The importance of "likeness"; the ironing out of differences; the necessity of "fitting in", whatever the hidden qualms. These are all responses to the mental and emotional flux of the age-group: the fluidity of moods and states of mind consequent upon the momentous pubertal changes (chapter 4). When you feel that you are losing your "centre of gravity" and everything about you is changing and scarcely in control—disturbing as well as, perhaps, exciting—simply looking like "the others" may be of enormous comfort. There is a safety-in-numbers mentality, sharing the same styles and attitudes. So, with the two sets of friendship just described, we have external uniformity, although with very different conscious and unconscious motives. In the case of the first encounter, the priority is to make sure that the troubled young friend actually gets to her session. The second grouping is there to obstruct their friend getting the help she needs. The "obstructing" may have a number of background reasons: envy of her getting special treatment; anxiety lest the help somehow results in her leaving them; worry about a hole appearing in the shared carapace of their dysfunctional lives together, such that the entire group might be threatened with disintegration. It could be for any, or all, of these reasons, and for many more. The point is that the first group is about fostering development, whereas the second is, ultimately, though almost certainly not consciously so, about exerting anti-developmental pressure.

Bion (1961) made an important distinction between two such modes of group functioning. He would have designated membership of our first "waiting-room" companions as a "Work Group", one of mutual cooperation in the fostering of development, and the second, as a "Basic Assumption Group". By this latter, he meant a group constellation of which the ostensible purpose is undermined by unconscious sabotaging mechanisms, peculiar to group functioning generally, but not necessarily taking precedence over the group that has a clear task and a purpose. He designated three dominant forms of such "basic assumptions" as being based on "fight or flight", on "dependence", and on "pairing", leading to Messianic hopes, "be it person, idea or Utopia" (p. 152). In early adolescence, these kinds of grouping, both external and internal, often function as an unconscious defence against change, against intimacy, pain, and the fear of loss and also as a "basic-assumption" escape into thoughtlessness and destructive enactment.

The question that these contrasting scenarios pose is, basically, that of the origins, nature, and functions of the groupings and gangings so characteristic of the adolescent years, especially early on. All, as I have suggested, do, in their very different ways, provide a crucial form of emotional holding and containment during the ferment of adjusting to puberty and to the rocky road of transition towards adulthood. For many, the general maelstrom can be especially intense and problematic in the early teenage years, when the significance of finding some kind of individual as well as group identity is often so hard and so evident. Some groupings, as we have seen, have a generally integrative function—that of helping to keep the different parts of the personality together. Others have a more disintegrative one, encouraging further splits or conflicts between one part of the personality and another. In the most general terms, group membership, benign or malign, is usually, at this stage, to do with sorting out at least a "sense" of identity. As we have seen, a distinctive uniform or dress code, or even mode of transport, is usually involved. The group can provide safe places where different aspects of the personality can be, as it were, "tried on", can be played out and kept in touch with—developmental, in other words. Alternatively, by contrast, it may provide unsafe and anti-developmental places that exert a negative force on the individual, as true of family groups as any other. Indeed, as we shall see, it tends to be in the culture of the characteristic family relations that the contrasting leanings, predominantly towards work groups or basic assumption groups, are often rooted.

We can see something of this in a historical anecdote—a recognizable situation that has stayed in my mind since I first heard it some years ago. It is about the impact on two 10-year-old football fans (fans being members of a large group that could be described as forever shifting between group and gang cultures). The two lived next door to each other. Thierry Henri is to leave Arsenal. Sam is described by his mum as having been very upset that morning. He'd come downstairs clutching a figure of Henri and crying bitterly that he was leaving the team. For Sam, being a fan of a successful player in a successful team made him, too, feel successful, and Henri's departure made him feel a reject, a failure, according to his mum. He wept with a sense of loss and sadness.

By contrast, his friend next door was said to have torn down all the Arsenal posters from his wall in a rage and joined the "gang" who booed Henri off the pitch after his last game. Little Sam struggles to contain his grief with the help of his mum. His enraged friend participates in an ugly enactment—idealization slipping to denigration in a trice. The sense was that Sam had long enjoyed a particular kind of understanding from his thoughtful mum, one that had modulated his potential blame and fury in a way that his friend could not manage.

At the heart of things, as far as these individual or group phenomena are concerned, is the fate, from the beginning, of the angry, aggressive, sadistic, and frightened feelings common to us all: how securely and consistently that original emotional "centre of gravity" was established. As we have seen (chapter 4), it has its roots in the extraordinarily complex relationship between mother and infant from the first, even before the first, in terms of what might be called the culture of foetal experience. This crucially includes, as Maiello (1995) has described, the mother's state of mind, her voice, her words, her mood, to be followed, post-birth, by her passionate gaze and emotional receptivity. The psychoanalytic picture of the human psyche is that there are many facets to everyone's self-destructive and healthy parts, perverse and creative ones. In reasonable circumstances, the destructive side can be contained, understood, and, in a sense, neutralized by the healthy part. In more difficult circumstances, that destructive part is felt to threaten both the self (with consequent fears of fragmentation and confusion) and/or the person or people who are primarily loved.

"Reasonable circumstances" are those in which the baby's initial environment, that of the mother or caretaker's mind, is one that has the capacity to take in, to tolerate, and to understand the baby's ordinary communications of distress, anger, and fear, as well as those of gratification and love; the mother who, in the language of the Attachment theorists, can be responsive and attuned to the baby's cues and signals. The frustrations and anxieties of infantile helplessness in the face of hunger, loneliness, or the fear of dying, and the respective efforts to communicate such states by splitting and projection, are feelings and mechanisms that are common to all. Babies, like adolescents, are, by temperament, "easy" or "difficult", with varying capacities to tolerate frustration. What makes the difference, characterologically and developmentally, is the mother's/ parents' ability to cope with such intense and often toxic communications, the capacity to withstand them—or, by contrast, to feel excessively angry, helpless, or desperate in the face of them. Of crucial importance is being able to comprehend, by way of internal resources (gradually acquired from, and experienced as, internal parents), what are often felt to be hostile attacks so that they can be thought about, modulated, and thereby rendered meaningful.

We need to consider what some of the early factors may be that will tend, later on, to propel an individual towards one kind of grouping rather than another. For that, we must look to early experience, both physical and emotional. For example, an incapacity on the part of parents to bear mental pain of an anxious, frustrated, and fearful kind, or its usual form of expression in anger, may leave the infant struggling with his own feelings left unmodified, or, worse still, augmented if the mother's sense of rage and inadequacy is, as all too often, pushed back into the frightened child. In this predicament, there are all sorts of options open to the child. Some will cut off and develop a kind of pseudo-independence, too fearful to risk seeking, and failing to find, the needed response. Others may try to project all the more forcefully, mentally battering away at what is experienced as the resistant surface of the mother's mind (often tragically being physically battered in return, as the mother, unable to cope with the infantile desperation, tries to get rid of it back into the baby). Yet others will split their feelings, keeping good ones for one relationship and depositing bad ones elsewhere.

An example of these early dynamics is to be found in chapter 7 in a brief example from an infant observation that may serve to bring together, in a suggestive rather than deterministic way, some of the threads that I have been pursuing. I draw on these earliest years in relation to Ernest Jones's paper, "Some Problems of Adolescence" (1922), in which he describes the way in which, during puberty,

> a regression takes place in the direction of infancy . . . and the person lives over again, though on another plane, the development he passed through in the first five years of life. . . . [I]t signifies that the individual *recapitulates and expands* in the second decennium of life the development he passed through in the first five years of life . . . [pp. 39–40]

In other words, old conflicts, especially those of infancy and of oedipal struggles, are being reworked (in the context of new genital drives), conflicts that test the quality of early containment and internalization.

Different ages and stages have different ways of expressing inner disturbance and anxiety. Let us look, for a moment, at an historical vignette: as we have seen, with adolescents, the evacuation of unbearable feeling tends, early on at least, to be expressed in groups rather than as individuals. I shall offer a brief example from the transcript of a prominently reported trial for the manslaughter of an adolescent boy by a gang of his peers. On leaving the youth club in a small rural town on a Friday night, 16-year-old Nick was set upon. Four youths beat him up and then, apparently in rage and frustration that their victim was carrying no valuables, dropped him over the parapet of a bridge above a fast-flowing river. "I can't swim", Nick screamed as he clung to the brickwork. His attackers stamped on his fingers until he let go and dropped into the water beneath. He was washed downstream and drowned.

Perhaps in the external contours and features of this bookish, bespectacled lad, who couldn't swim, the others feared encountering aspects of their own vulnerable and inadequate internal landscapes, aspects that they wanted to attack and get rid of. Perhaps the absence of instant gratification (no money) stirred violent impulses that had to be enacted because they could not be managed internally. Perhaps all sorts of things. We do not know. But what one of the boys said at the subsequent trial provides a clue: "I went along with the others, we lost all human feeling . . . we wanted *him* to be hurt, frightened, and alone."

On the opposite page of the same newspaper, there was an account of a Nazi war criminal who, himself scarcely more than an adolescent at the time, had been instrumental in the rounding up and killing of hundreds of Jews in Lithuania. After serving a long prison sentence he was interviewed: "What do you feel about it all now?" "Look, I spent fifteen years inside, that's it. I was obeying orders." "Do you have any regrets?" There was a long pause and then a shrug. "The interesting thing was—you pulled the trigger and people fell down."

What we hear in these two chilling accounts, one domestic, one world historic, is something about the separation of action from thought, of behaviour from meaning and consequences. The issue both for the gang of boys and for the Nazi war criminal was not so much, "what have I done?"—a question that relates to the recognition of individual responsibility and to a possible capacity for guilt and remorse, but, rather, "what did they make me do?"—a much more paranoid, persecuted, remorseless, and alienated state of mind.

In relation to groupings and gangings, it is during adolescence, as I have suggested, that the flight into group life, so characteristic and often so developmentally helpful at this age, can take on a much more sinister gang-like flavour. The "gang" is adept at co-opting the more destructive parts of the personality to sign up for the job description of being partners in crime. All groups, at times, exert intimidating pressure on their members to do things that those members would not have ventured to do as individuals. But that is a different matter from falling in with others *because* they seem to express the more timid or vicious parts of the self and to reproduce an atmosphere of fear and oppression, particularly attractive to those who have been intimidated and oppressed themselves. Just as the baby explodes with the "fury" of unmet need if he feels uncontained, so too does the adolescent who is contending with pubescent versions of those same infantile struggles. The gang-like mentality invites a kind of collective sanction for the expression of destructive feelings or attitudes that are hard, individually, to keep in check.

If we go back to the example of the murdered boy, we can see how the lads concerned collectively suffered intolerable rage and frustration. They wanted, physically, to expel such insupportable feelings by getting rid of the actual person, the one who, they felt, had caused their discomfort and frustration. They threw him into the river, for the moment unconcerned that he was unable to swim and would surely drown. Here we can see that each boy is acting, mindlessly, in the gang of peers in a way that he would be unlikely to be able to alone. In other words, there is a kind of confluence of projections leading to a rush of enactment. The power of that confluence wipes out the capacity for individual thought and judgement. This horrible incident exemplifies the emotional situation in which if, in infancy, there is a low capacity to bear frustration, or if excessive frustration is enjoined upon the infant or young child, the absence of the containing mother is felt as a present persecutor and does not allow thought to occur. The anxiety is experienced as overwhelming. It has to be got rid of by an omnipotent enactment.

The gang-like expressions of these intolerable feelings were first explored by Herbert Rosenfeld (1971) and Meltzer (1973b), in terms of the notion of an internal gang. In a chapter on gang dynamics, Gianna Williams (1997) outlines the theoretical frame of reference on which she is drawing. She cites the work of Freud, Rosenfeld, Meltzer, Joseph, and Steiner, in particular. For example, in his paper on "Identification and Socialisation in Adolescence", Meltzer (1973a) describes how, in some cases, the types of groupings that adolescents are attracted to may be a mirror image of an internal cluster that contains the destructive parts of the self, better defined and designated as a "gang" (p. 52). He enlarges on this idea in "Terror, Persecution and Dread":

> Where dependence on internal good objects is rendered unfeasible . . . and where dependence on a good external object is unavailable or not acknowledged, the addictive relationship to a bad part of the self, the submission to tyranny, takes place. An illusion of safety is promulgated by the omniscience of the destructive part and perpetuated by the sense of omnipotence generated by the perversion or addictive quality involved. [1973c, pp. 105–106]

This "destructive part" is described by Rosenfeld (1971), as by Meltzer, as an internal gang:

> The destructive narcissism of these patients appears often highly organised, as if one were dealing with a powerful gang, dominated by a leader, who controls all the members of the gang to see that they support one another in making the criminal destructive work more effective and powerful. [p. 174]

Williams emphasizes how Rosenfeld stresses that the essence of the gang formation is to join forces in order to perform "criminal, destructive work". He highlights, she suggests, the tight grip it has on other parts of the personality in order to maintain the "status quo". In other words, the binding force of the gang is its destructive aim. The gang gets together under the guise of offering protection to its members, but its primary task is to do damage. The group, by contrast, is often permeated by very hurtful dynamics, such as making outsiders feel excluded, but it does not get together *in order* to hurt.

Two further brief examples may clarify some of the ways in which a young person's development, in terms of properly managing to move forward and own their potentially adult capacities in the external world, were constantly obstructed by the internal pull back into the kinds of perverse states to which, during their adolescence, they had seemed to become in thrall. As Williams and I point out in a joint article, "Reflections on Perverse States of Mind", one that seems all too relevant in the current social and political climate, "the addictive quality of perverse states of mind can be more easily observed when patients make their first attempts to disengage themselves from the domination of an internal 'Big Brother'" (Waddell & Williams, 1991).

As we make clear in our frame of reference for this article, perversity here has no connection with descriptive aspects of sexual choices but, rather, with a kind of negative caricature of relationships, as if in service to the Ministry of Truth in Orwell's *1984,* where "War is Peace"; "Freedom is Slavery"; "Ignorance is Strength".

Such mental processes were evident in the dream material of two young patients, each intelligent, creative, and committed to trying to secure outwardly respectable positions in society as well as meaningful intimate personal relationships. They were, however, constantly threatened by persecuting anxieties and internal charges of fraudulence and deception. Each maintained a relatively conventional exterior, yet each was persecuted by dreams and fantasies that belied the conformist crust.

The characteristic mode of defence of Andrew (an 18-year-old lab technician) against the pain of separation, of intimacy, of the experience of "littleness", and, especially of the struggle for change, lay in homosexual fantasies and dreams, usually of a part-object or of an anal kind. The nature of the internal conflict had been clearly expressed in a number of early dreams and was typified by the following:

> I was imprisoned in a dark house. Every time I attempted to escape over the horizon to life, light, and freedom, I was pulled back by a gang whose leader's name was "Cave".

This "leader" was linked, by association, to a character in the pop music world who was said, as a child, to have enjoyed pulling the wings and legs off insects—a detail that had particularly stuck in Andrew's mind.

A similar constellation is evident in the dream of another patient, Beatrice (a 19-year-old student), the setting for which was, as she put it, a *"Nineteen-Eighty-Four*–type building".

> The building—a huge barn-like structure, cavernous in its interior—was the headquarters of a Big Brother organization under whose watchful eye uniformed people laboured in the fields and orchards nearby. I found myself, unexpectedly, at a distance from the main group, somewhere down a grassy track, enjoying the beauty of the evening. I suddenly became aware that, inadvertently, I had nearly escaped. Terrified that the alarm would be raised, I ran, slipping and sliding back up the muddy track to H.Q. There I was met

by my own big brother [a man who had, in fact, exercised a tyrannical hold over her in childhood, and as an internal figure, continued to do so]. *I was terrified.*

Andrew's "dark house" and the pull back into the cave/claustrum (Meltzer, 1992), and Beatrice's return up the muddy, slippery track, distinctly indicate the ganging up of destructive aspects of the personality against the part that was making a bid for freedom, light, and beauty. Andrew's associations to the gang leader, Cave, revealed a clear link, for him, between himself and a version of pop culture, as he experienced it, in terms of slavish adulation and mindless group behaviour. In being similarly controlled by a mass-media propaganda machine, this scenario was not dissimilar to the *"Nineteen-Eighty-Four"* context of Beatrice's dream, albeit slightly more disguised. What characterized the two dreams was a perception of the unthinking nature of large-group phenomena. Moreover, the sadomasochism—explicit in Andrew's torturing-of-insects associations and implicit in the dominance/submission axis of the *1984* world—relates these dreams to a tendency towards a kind of internally perverse world. Each clearly intensifies the painful struggle in the individual between forces of philistinism, cynicism, and perversion and those that could be described as being on the side of the life.

Further to clarify the distinction between a group and a gang's characteristic mode of internal world functioning, I shall again draw on the case of Simon (discussed in chapter 5), who was an 18-year-old medical student when referred. Simon had, for some time, suffered a variety of anxieties: he became panic-stricken in the company of male consultants; he was terrified of any kind of sexual contact with women; he suffered acute discomfort about the fragility of his massive intellectual defences and about his general incapacity to form intimate relationships. But, as he told me at the very beginning of treatment, it was one dream, in particular, that had significantly influenced his decision, finally, to seek help.

There was a huge, pink, snail-like creature in the corridor of the Obstetrics and Gynaecological unit of the hospital where I work. Inside the creature's large, fleshy tail, articulated as if to form some sort of tunnel, was a group of male students playing and cavorting in the cavity. With alarmingly seductive laughter, they exhorted me to "come in, it's fun in here". Inside, it was exciting and disorientating with a flavour of rather perverse enjoyment, as at a children's funfair. The atmosphere began to make me very anxious and I suddenly found myself panicking. I tumbled out and rushed along the corridor, finally tunnelling my way into a lecture theatre. Here I took up a position behind the projector where the consultants/professors usually stood.

Reflecting on the dream, Simon described a clear sense that he was being invited to enter a womb-like object. Although he himself did not refer to "desecration", his narrative certainly conveyed some such feeling. The "group" that he depicted was of a kind that gets together in a disrespectful and mocking way. "There was somehow an atmosphere of damage", he said, "of doing violence, of manic excitement in a place where unborn babies were developing towards a readiness to enter the birth canal." He remarked on a feeling that such a group would be more likely to kill life than to nurture it.

Simon also described himself as often feeling claustrophobic, in the grip of the sort of anxiety that can accompany the gang mentality that was holding sway over the students' activities in the fleshy cavity. He managed to extricate himself from what seemed, in this first part of the dream, to evoke something of what lay behind his terror of sexual intimacy. The second part depicts another of his worries, which, this time, he is less able to avoid. When he positions himself behind the projector, we see his tendency to enter another type of identification, this time as an intellectual defence against being too in touch with his own foetal self, a self that had so much still to learn. The fact that he is at the podium and not in the student audience highlights the way in which, in this state of mind, he discards his actual predicament for the delusion of belonging with the superior figures whose status and knowledge he so wished to possess.

As treatment progressed, this delusion became linked with a belief that he was more conversant with psychoanalytic theory than was I, his therapist. Although there was a degree of genuine interest and constructive curiosity associated with his avid reading and thinking on the subject, it was also clear that, at times, this hunger for knowledge became contaminated by a greedy and intrusive quality of being excitedly inside me, or inside my mind, in a way that bore similarities with the gang cavorting in the snail's tunnel-like interior. We can see that becoming a professor/lecturer represented not so much a progression but, rather, a way of getting inside, through a different kind of tunnelling, and *into* the persona of a male authority figure, as if he belonged there. In linking the content of this early dream to a more recent one, we may chart a distinct shift in Simon's mental organization. In the second dream,

I was a member of the "staff group" at a hospital where I had recently worked. Oh, it wasn't really the staff group. No, it was not a staff group, it was a patient group. In this patient group there was a consultant in charge, a big man, associated in my mind with an atmosphere of buggery, of a primitive and sadistic nature, as enacted in an old film I had watched last night, Deliverance. The consultant seemed somehow to be failing, quaking; there was an evanescent quality about his uncertainty and his shadowy presence. I had a clear feeling within the dream that the group represented parts of me. There was a sense of expectation about the arrival of a second consultant who would have strong and generous qualities of understanding, attentiveness, and, as you would say, containment and perception.

Indeed, as Simon described these qualities, he conveyed a sense of potential (soon to arrive) identification with a genuinely parental, even therapeutic, figure, combining aspects of maternal and paternal attributes that, in the earlier material, he had found it difficult to recognize—for example, in describing the snail as female and emphasizing the masculinity of the lecturer/professor. Previously, he would keep his parents carefully divided—even dreaming of being in bed between them and seducing one away from the other—although he was not absolutely certain about which way round the seduction was occurring.

In the first dream, there is a corridor between the maternal and paternal representations—they are separated—while the "Simon" consultant in the second dream is perceived as a parental figure, combining paternal and maternal aspects. The sense was that Simon was becoming more closely in touch with smallness in relation to the senior figures, as clearly indicated in the second dream. He realizes that the group of which he was a member was one of patients and not, as he had at first thought, of staff. Second, in thinking about this dream, he himself described, with great insight, I thought, something he called a "dismantling" that he felt was taking place in himself. He clarified by referring to removing the hard mantle of a beetle so that the softness and vulnerability inside might be risked, felt, and fully experienced. It seemed that what was being slowly "dismantled", in the therapy, was his self-protective, intellectual membrane/skin/shell, which, if taken away, would leave exposed the more fragile, tender, even timorous, parts of Simon's personality. The two dreams, together, show a growing capacity on Simon's part to be dependent on an admired figure, one able to carry the responsibility of parental concern for his infantile parts, very different from the former sadistic and intrusive qualities of the more tyrannical consultant/authority figures whom Simon had admired and subserved, while covertly holding in contempt.

The shift between these two dreams does, indeed, mark the beginning of a "dismantling" of the infantile delusions of adulthood and a move towards a capacity to be a dependent patient with much to learn, less about psychoanalytic and medical theory than, truthfully, about himself. At this point, Simon felt, appreciatively, that the analysis constituted a way of being "delivered" from the inhibiting and destructive part of himself and guided towards a capacity to take in some kind of genuine food for thought. This was in stark contrast to the perversion of the "delivery" setting of the first dream. For there, no live babies were being born: instead, a gang of male medical students was desecrating and attacking the maternal figure and, by inference, the very capacity to bear babies.

I have been describing the progress from an infantile, narcissistic organization, characterized by splitting between genders and projective identification with superior figures, to a more integrated and modest adult capacity to appreciate, and be in touch with, nurturing internal figures. This account is in danger of oversimplifying a characteristic and hoped-for development in the vicissitudes of adolescent experience. In fact, over time, constant oscillations occur between these different states of mind. I am thinking, in other words, not so much in terms of linear development through and beyond these adolescent years, but, rather, of repeated shifts and conjunctions between various and varying mental organizations and states of mind.

Betty Joseph (1982) puts this picture very succinctly:

> Such patients feel in thrall to a part of the self that dominates and imprisons them and will not let them escape, even though they see life beckoning outside. . . . The point . . . is . . . that it is not only that the patient is dominated by an aggressive part of himself . . . but that this part is actively sadistic towards another part of the self which is masochistically caught up in this process, and that this has become an addiction. [p. 451]

In the past, both Andrew and Beatrice had tended to carry out their adolescent learning by way of rather primitive identificatory processes—either through conformity with professional status (with Andrew, the scientist/position-in-the-lab-pecking-order) or, as in the case of Beatrice, with actual family members. The relationship between surface accommodation and covert sadomasochism is clear in both cases.

Different aspects of these two patients' material demonstrate how the links of relatedness, theorized by Bion as links in Love (L), Hate (H), and Knowledge (K) (see chapters 5 and 9), were constantly opposed by a pulling away from the freedom of individuality, intimacy, and aesthetic sensibility into the mindlessness of group conformity (whether internal or external), in the guise of respectability, social rank, and status; or, into the gang mentality of "Newspeak" and two-dimensional cultural forces. All these processes function, ultimately, in negative modes that are more characteristic of anti-linkage, anti-thought, anti-knowledge—in short, –L, –H, –K. Bion fleetingly referred to this mode as a kind of "negative grid", a mental and emotional constellation that in effect represents a system for generating "lies"—that is, as functioning in the service of misunderstanding and anti-thought. These lies constitute, in Bion's view, the poison of the mind. The implications of this theoretical position, a kind of *terra incognita* at the time, are still being mapped out in further clinical exploration and, indeed, in large-scale social and political enactments. Clearly, it is the links between these intrapsychic processes and the social and political sphere that must always be emphasized, especially in the age group under discussion. In these last two examples, we encounter the risk, for these young people, of the groupings and gangings, so characteristic of the adolescent years, failing to find some kind of resolution. There may be multifold reasons, both internal and external, for these developmental difficulties. There may be over-intense fears of loneliness, or of exclusion, persecution, anxiety about sexuality and intimacy, about separation and identity. But it should also be stressed that the various paths across this often treacherous territory can continue to wind and twist well into so-called adulthood, though often with a gradual resolution taking place along the way.

CHAPTER SEVEN

The psychodynamics of bullying

> If you leave a lot of boys to their own devices, in a brutal age, themselves brutalised by rude surroundings and rendered aggressive by violent discipline and often harsh childhoods, you will get bullying. You get it sufficiently without all these. The bullying in these centuries was inevitable, continuous and fiendish.

Jonathan Gathorne-Hardy (1977, p. 60) is writing about a particular aspect of the public school phenomenon. "There are horrific accounts", he says, "from all centuries, but it is clear the eighteenth and early nineteenth centuries marked a climax. Boys killed each other" (p. 60).

In quoting this forty-year-old, yet also very contemporary, account, I wish to establish, from the first, that the phenomenon of bullying is the product of an extremely complex picture of external and internal events. Albeit in an historical, class, and gender-specific context, the issues raised in the quotation are central to any present exploration of adolescent development. Axiomatically, at least in external terms, the bullier must have an object or person to bully. There is a dynamic relationship in which, aggravated or fuelled by external circumstances, aspects of the personality are played out—never without some toll, and sometimes with tragic consequences.

As Gathorne-Hardy suggests, bullying among children and young people cannot be separated from wider social, cultural, and political circumstances. For the subject could be said to encompass everything from a stressed mother yanking her child away from a shop toy, "If you touch that again I'll slap you"; to a domestic row; to relationships at work; to structures of class, racism, and sexism; to religious and tribal warfare—indeed, to any kind of oppression in which, by means of power, violence, cruelty, or perversity, one side persecutes another, whether as a group or individually. How does one understand the evils of the human heart, of all our hearts, and what kinds of factor render one individual vulnerable to the co-opting of his impulses, whether towards being a perpetrator or a victim, and another able to contain and withstand?

This chapter overlaps with the previous one about groups and gangs but stresses, in particular, the possible determinants of the bullying mentality and its consequences, whether in the individual himself, or in the victim. In childhood and adolescence, there are factors that contribute to these destructive forces in quite specific ways. It is often the case, as we have seen, that, at puberty, early vulnerabilities and frailties are re-stirred and have to be managed anew. Moreover, during the teenage years, pressures towards conformity, on the one hand, and individuation, on the other, are often at their most complex and most absolute. Anxiety about identity arouses an acute intolerance of difference either in the self or in the other—the seedbed of group identity, if benign, or of gang or mob mentality when the shared purpose becomes that of cruelly bolstering the ego at the expense of others. People will toe the party line or succumb to the leader in relation to gang attitudes and behaviour that as individuals they would completely eschew.

It was at Eton, we are told by Gathorne-Hardy, that the terrors and indignities visited upon the boys surpassed description. Lord Chatham stated that "he scarce observed a boy who was not cowed for life at Eton" (Gathorne-Hardy, 1977, p. 66). Less cowed than omnipotent and vengeful, Percy Bysshe Shelley was among those whose lives were fundamentally coloured, or rather scarred, by his experiences at his prep school (aged 10) followed by Eton at age 12. His biographer, Richard Holmes (1974), vividly and painfully describes the "Shelley-hunting" that went on, particularly virulent in the face both of Shelley's refusal to cow-tow to his "fag masters" and in response to his personal "wild and marked peculiarities" (p. 19).

Insubordination and appearing *different* were a fatal combination. Holmes recounts the game of "nailing", in which "a muddy football was kicked through the crowd" waiting in the cloisters for supper and was "shot as hard as possible at one agreed target. Frequently this was Shelley" (p. 20).

> The particular name of some particular boy would be sounded by one, taken up by another and another, until hundreds echoed and echoed the name. . . . The Shelley! Shelley! Shelley! which was thundered in the cloisters was but too often accompanied by practical jokes,—such as knocking his books from under his arm, seizing them as he stooped to recover them, pulling and tearing his clothes, or pointing with the finger. [p. 20]

This will be all too recognizable to many—though less so, perhaps, Shelley's response. "The result", we are told, "was . . . a paroxysm of anger which made his eyes flash like a tiger's, his cheeks grow pale as death, his limbs quiver, and his hair stand on end" (p. 20).

Shelley's subsequent hatred of organized authority and of social conformism would seem to have had a lot to do with these years, but so, too, did his own outbreaks of anguish, anger, and violence that were to recur in later life. The wildness of his contemporaries' excesses might seem more akin to aspects of the boys' behaviour in Golding's *Lord of the Flies* (1954) than most of what would be described as bullying these days—although, of course, scorchings and killings, and now knifings and acid attacks, are all too prevalent.

My initial emphasis is on *predisposing* factors, ones that focus less on an attempt to establish direct or specific causal relations (e.g., violent films or videos, abuse, social media, online enactments, etc.) than on the necessity of looking at a constellation of possible underlying psychodynamics. Why, for example, did Shelley respond with tigerish rage, when another child might have withdrawn in an agony of depression and silent anguish? How is it that any child has the resilience to withstand baiting and name-calling? How is it that he has the internal capacity to hang on to a secure sense of self in the face of mockery or torment? Is resilience inborn, or is it acquired? If the latter, what kinds of factors might generate or nurture such a quality? There are no easy answers here. A child's disposition plays a central part; so, too, does the nature of the *parents'* childhood, *their* experience of being parented and thus of parenting; as does the family culture, its support network, the social environment, educational provision, financial resources, and so on. What needs to be explored is the extremely complex relationship between all these external, and especially internal, factors in the matrix of communication between the child, the adult, and the outside world from the very first.

Why is it that some are cruelly bullied at school and others are not? Or, why is it that, once bullied, some, like Shelley, come through it with a hatred of cruelty and authoritarianism and others with a deep propensity for it? Why does one individual identify with the bully, another with the victim? How does one account for these different identifications, for the contrast, for example, between Ralph and Jack in *Lord of the Flies*? An interesting detail in Golding's compelling story is that Jack and his band of the most vicious and murderous hunters were, before the crash, all members of the choir. What might be the implication of this detail? Perhaps having previously been shored up by the external structures of conformity and deference, these boys were especially unable, *in extremis,* to engage with, and contain, their own more deadly impulses. Without an externally enforced prohibition, or a parental source of containment, their lack of internal restraint gave rein (as with the Eton scholars who similarly lacked any adult supervision) to the most primitive and perverse practices, ones bred of anxiety, fear, and hatred.

We are talking about something much more complicated than the fact that, with notable exceptions, those who have been brutalized tend, in turn, to brutalize, overtly or covertly. One of the most basic defences against pain is to identify with the aggressor, as Anna Freud (1958) made so clear. But the nature of the defence adopted depends, importantly, on a number of other issues.

In terms of predisposing factors, I want first to offer a familiar story of a very generalizing kind, one that touches on some of the wider social and environmental influences already mentioned, and on the kind of impact these influences may have on the individual personality, especially when they resonate with, or stir up, unresolved internal struggles. I then look at some examples in more detail, in terms of intrapsychic phenomena, drawing on developmental psychology and psychoanalytic theory to venture some understanding of what may underlie this alarmingly intractable problem.

Just as the Second World War began, a young woman, Gladys, and her young man, Arthur, were married. She had had a miserable childhood and was passive in the face of the emotional deprivation enjoined on her by her envious and bullying mother. Gladys was committed to trying not to reproduce the same situation with her own children. Arthur had also had a financially and emotionally deprived childhood but was less cowed by it, having compensated for lack of attention from his well-meaning but overworked parents by becoming a scholarship boy and separating early from expectations of familial intimacy and peer-group culture alike.

Their first child, Christopher, was born during the Second World War Blitz. Arthur was by this time away fighting, and his new wife found herself alone with a small baby as the bombs fell on central London. At the end of the war, a second child was born, Mary. Christopher was thus doubly deprived. His father, a stranger, had appeared and claimed his mother, who had then, as was customary, sent her little son away to an unfamiliar nursery for ten wretched days and had mysteriously produced a rival baby girl who seemed to get all the attention. He returned home from the nursery a ball of tempestuous and jealous fury, never to forgive his sister for being born, nor his parents for the betrayal. His anger raged unabated until, in despair of controlling his persistent bullying and delinquent enterprises, and worried about his capacity to learn or take things in, Gladys and Arthur sent him away to school at age 7, in the belief that institutional England would provide the disciplinary structure he needed. (In fact, they later learned that their son suffered intense physical abuse at this school.) They had little experience of the relationship between containment and constraint, between structures of understanding and structures of repression. Nor were they aware of the renewed and ever more ferocious attacks on their young daughter during the school holidays. They later discovered that she had been terrorized into silence and had submitted to quite terrifying bullying, in thrall to Christopher and his local gang of fellow-persecutors. As far as her parents knew, she was happy, popular, successful; her brother unhappy, troublesome, and a failure. Both children married bullies. Both marriages failed.

Some interesting elements emerge from this outline. It turned out that Christopher's problems did not begin when his sister was born. His mother later described to Mary, by then her confidant, what a difficult baby he had been from the first, and how ill-equipped she had felt to handle him, her first baby, alone and terrified in war-torn London, with no experience and no emotional support. She recounted how he had never seemed to want any emotional contact, even as a little boy, never hugged nor cuddled, never seemed to miss her, was always "fiercely independent"—such a contrast to her daughter, who seemed a perfect baby from the very beginning. "He was such an alien little creature, but I felt at home with you from the moment I set eyes on you," Mary had reported her mother as saying.

It seems likely that Christopher may have been what Attachment theorists would call an "insecure avoidant" child—one, that is, who, having experienced a miss-matching in the parenting relationship in his early months, might, at age 1 year, manifest the kind of response witnessed in Mary Ainsworth's famous "Strange Situation" experiments (Ainsworth & Bell, 1970). When left by a mother with an unknown experimenter for three minutes and then totally alone for a further three, some children in the experiments showed no overt signs of distress; they tended to ignore their mother on reunion and remained distant, watchful, and inhibited in their play. This was in contrast to a more "secure" child, who was distressed by separation but able to be comforted by the mother on reunion and to resume play; it was also in contrast to the "insecure ambivalent" child, who was distressed, could not easily be comforted, clung and pulled away simultaneously, both seeking and rejecting contact and unable to pursue any exploratory play.

These conclusions followed from a year's observations, in the children's own homes, of the responsiveness and attunement of the primary parent (usually the mother) to the baby's needs and communications. Not surprisingly, the ambivalently attached children were found to have mothers who tended to intrude on their children when playing happily and to ignore them when in distress—who were inconsistent, in other words, in their responses. The "secure attachment" is rooted in an experience of active, reciprocal, and responsive interaction with the caregiver, the quality of which seems more important than the quantity. The "insecure avoidant" child was observed to have a relationship with the carer of a kind that was not so much one of neglect as one in which there was a marked mismatching of cue and response. It might not be, for example, that the baby was not picked up and carried enough, but that the request of outstretched arms to be lifted would be consistently missed. The child would be picked up when he was otherwise engaged; cries of anxiety would be interpreted as those of hunger or rage; smiles would be overlooked; distress ignored.

Statistics based on longitudinal studies are impressive in tracing the characterological and behavioural outcome of these differently classified 1-year-olds, and such research-based studies offer interesting corroboration with the picture of development with which psychoanalytic practitioners have long been working. The "securely attached" child, like Mary, has more positive social perception, a capacity to concentrate, to learn, and to play creatively and appropriately and to manage separations and loss. In contrast, with a child like Christopher, who seems to have been a more "avoidant" type, the incidence of social and behavioural problems, and of withdrawal and poor impulse control, is much higher.

This is not to say that there may not also be considerable variability. Dispositionally one child will manage adverse experiences better than another. Moreover, it is important to be neither blaming nor deterministic. A depressed or excessively anxious mother who is unable fully to respond to her baby initially may well, with changed circumstances, manage much better with her toddler. The input of another relative, childminder, or nursery school teacher may also affect things quite fundamentally. But, in significant ways, the nature of these very early dynamics establishes a primary mode of being. This may be variously modified, or confirmed, even hardened, by later experience, but the first year constitutes a foundation—establishing a number of predisposing factors that have a lot to do with the way in which subsequent events are managed.

At the heart of things, as far as the bullying/being bullied axis is concerned, is—as I put it in chapter 6—the fate, from the beginning, of the angry, aggressive, sadistic, and frightened feelings common to us all. The psychoanalytic picture of the human psyche is that there are many facets to everyone's "self"—destructive and healthy parts, perverse and creative ones. In reasonable circumstances, the destructive side can be contained, understood, and, in a sense, neutralized by the healthy part. In more difficult circumstances, that destructive part is felt to threaten both the self (with consequent fears of fragmentation, misery, and confusion) and/or the person or people who are primarily loved.

To reiterate, what I mean by "reasonable circumstances" are those in which the baby's initial environment—that of the mother or caretaker's mind—is one that has the capacity to take in, to tolerate, and therefore to understand the baby's ordinary communications of distress, anger, and rage, as well as those of gratification and love; the mother who (to go back to the categories of the Attachment theorists) will be likely to be responsive and attuned to her baby's cues and signals. The frustrations and anxieties of infantile helplessness in the face of hunger, loneliness, the fear of dying, and the respective efforts to communicate them by the mechanism referred to as "projection" (in the earliest days, by screaming, defecating, vomiting, crying) are feelings and mechanisms common to all. Babies are by temperament "easy" or "difficult", with varying capacities to tolerate frustration.

The capacity of the mother to have an intuitive understanding of her baby's states of mind, at least some of the time, is thought of by Bion as that of being able, as stated earlier, to sustain "a state of rêverie". To remind and repeat: the baby's feelings are responded to in such a way that he gradually derives a sense of self, a dawning awareness and understanding of the nature of impulses and emotional experiences, out of which process, little by little, there develops an ability mentally to hold such feelings for himself. Thus the baby slowly acquires that very capacity for containment that was initially the function of the mother. A bit later, containment becomes the function of others too—both parents, perhaps, or the wider family. Still later it is complemented by the peer group, if it is a largely positive one, or by the school, the workplace, or the community. The degree to which the individual acquires and strengthens the capacity to undergo and contain his own emotional experience depends significantly on the respective cultures of these settings and their impact over time.

An incapacity on the part of parents to bear mental pain of an anxious, frustrated, deprived, and fearful kind, or its usual form of expression in withdrawal or anger, may leave the infant struggling with his own feelings left unmodified, or, worse still, augmented, if the mother's sense of rage and inadequacy is, as so often, pushed back into the frightened child. As we have seen, in this painful situation, one recourse for the child is to split his feelings, keeping good ones for one relationship and putting bad ones elsewhere (often more recognizable later on when, for example, the "good-as-gold" child at home becomes the terror at school, or, as with Christopher and Mary, the one child remains the "goodie" at the expense of the other "baddie"). Intrinsic to this unhappy situation is the problem that a child who consistently projects bad and destructive feelings towards, or into, a parent who cannot contain them and thereby modify them often believes that parent to have become the embodiment of those aggressive impulses, and subsequently the child internalizes a persecutory and guilt-inducing figure who is felt constantly to challenge and undermine any good impulses or finer feeling. This is an internal constellation that later became thought of as the "ego-destructive superego" (Bion, 1962a, pp. 97–98).

With close observation, it is often possible to detect a situation that seems, intrapsychically, to enact processes very similar to interpsychic phenomena. Different aspects of the self vie for supremacy in a kind of internal family feud, just as, in the external situation, different children come to represent, or identify with, their allotted roles. Such a dynamic seemed to obtain in Gladys and Arthur's family. Christopher was the bad boy who constantly ruined everything, Mary the good (though suffering) girl who walked off with all the prizes. The cost to the authentic personality of each was immense—though it took longer to make its appearance in Mary's case because of being concealed by her social and academic success. It was her unhappy marriage to her brother/bully/husband and the fact that her son also became a bully that belied her otherwise successful and coping exterior. One can see quite clearly, though perhaps in over-schematic form, the functioning of the splitting and projection that I have been discussing in this family. As I said, both Christopher and Mary married bullies: the one, perhaps, in an attempt to rein in his own impulses and identify with a hitherto split-off victim self; the other as a continuation of a sense of self which, despite being persecuting, relieved her of any responsibility for her own aggressive impulses. The destructive aspects of Mary's personality that had been located first in her brother and then in her husband, leaving her innocent, albeit somewhat unsure, were now manifesting themselves in her son's problems of bringing the two sides of himself together in some kind of personal integration. These were problems that Mary had never herself resolved. The point about this example is that had the dynamics described been recognized earlier, there might have been some hope of release from the otherwise seemingly overdetermined cycle that played itself out later on.

An example from an infant observation may serve to bring together, in a suggestive rather than deterministic way, some of the threads that I have been pursuing, ones that often reappear in exaggerated form during the adolescent years. I draw on early infancy not only because of its established importance as the foundation for later development, but also as a model for the child's later relationships—be those with family, school, work, and so on.

These observations of a mother–infant interaction took place over a period of two years for an hour a week in the family's home. The mother was thrilled with the arrival of her first child, Joshua, and the observer recorded many instances of intense and intimate "conversations" between Joshua and his mother, to the deep delight of each. For present purposes, however, I shall draw attention to an aspect of the relationship that was noticed on the very first visit and was to be repeated in different ways many times thereafter: the mother's acknowledged difficulty in tolerating any kind of pain and distress in her baby ("I couldn't bear it if he cried"). Fortunately, Joshua cried very little, but whenever he showed a tendency to whimper he was instantly distracted. His needs would always be anticipated lest he suffer a moment's frustration or anxiety and express that in any angry way to his mother. Delightful, passionate, moving though this early relationship was in many ways, there was a striking absence of any traffic in pain.

Joshua seemed an extraordinarily accommodating baby—he willingly accepted the constant substitution of material objects for sustained emotional presence when anxiety threatened. It was the observer, at this stage, who felt the unacknowledged pain most intensely. Joshua's experience seemed to be one of having discomfort continually anticipated and deflected before he could suffer it, thereby being deprived of the important developmental process whereby anxiety aroused by a bad experience might be relieved by the mother's capacity, through her receptiveness to the unconscious projections, to modulate that pain, to tolerate it, process it, digest it, in such a way that it could become manageable later on, by her son too, and thus help to build his resilience.

This is where our immediate story begins—in the details of one observation, conducted when Joshua was about 5½ months old. The observer arrived to a scene that she was to witness on many subsequent occasions: Joshua, red-faced and angry, was, for the first time, crying, as he turned away in desperation from the spoonfuls of squashed banana that were being fed to him with calm and loving insistence by his mother, until he had finally "swallowed it" all down. The observer was surprised by the mother's out-of-the-blue remark that possibly she was not conceiving because she was still feeding Joshua. This was the first mention of an intended second pregnancy. By the following week, Joshua had been completely weaned—or, it could be said, the breast had been summarily removed in the aftermath of his having, apparently aggressively, bitten the nipple. In this observation, Joshua, crying hard, and not apparently tired, suddenly and dramatically fell asleep in the middle of his feed.

Joshua's mother seemed momentarily shaken at the sight of his head slumped on the feeding tray. He was clearly in some kind of crisis. His relationship with the breast had been suddenly terminated in the context of his parents' attempts to conceive (he still slept in their bedroom) and was apparently precipitated by what was experienced by his mother as oral sadism, in biting the nipple, an "act of aggression" that his mother could neither understand nor tolerate. He was unwittingly a witness to parental intercourse, subject to his mother's attention now being focused, in part, elsewhere (the next baby), and lacking, meanwhile, a containing and available mental space into which to put his anxiety and murderous rage (though still provided with plenty of objects to help to deflect it).

Aware of his mother's ever-present, but impenetrable, smile, Joshua may have been further confused by not being able to fit his felt experience to his perceptions of her. At this point, it was no longer possible for Joshua to sustain his efforts to spare his mother, and himself, pain by continually allowing himself to be distracted from his bad sensations, fear, and confusion. It seemed that this traumatic experience of maternal absence intensified things to the point that his feeble internal resources and lack of any learned way of dealing with anxiety were truly exhausted. Usually so accommodating, his bursts of unwonted anger met with no answering response and he simply gave up, cutting himself off from the painfulness of it all by going, suddenly, to sleep.

During an observation a year and a half later, the following incident occurred. His mother described Joshua as having a "crush" on ladybirds, an ironic expression in the light of what subsequently emerged. It was explained that there had been a lot of ladybirds in his room. Apparently he liked spiders and ladybirds in particular, but would often be heard to whisper, "Kill spider", and was discovered secretly to have "crushed" many of these creatures, both spiders and ladybirds, between his fingers, "murdering" them in the privacy of his room. During his mother's narration, Joshua was sitting with his back to the adults, singing "Rock-a-Bye-Baby" all the way to the last lines:

> "When the bough breaks the cradle will fall,
> Down will come baby, cradle and all."

What is interesting in this example is the discovery of the relationship between Joshua's surface accommodation to his mother's mode of being and his covertly sadistic behaviour. It would not be surprising that, if Joshua's normal aggressive tendencies continued to be met with incomprehension or punishment, he might either take to bullying other children as well as insects or identify with his victims and become himself the bullied one. The expression of angry or destructive feelings is, literally, inadmissible in this family. His mother, who could only tolerate the ideal baby, rejected the real baby. Joshua was left to cope both with the bad feelings and with the guilt of having them. He feels, perhaps, a bad person, one who deserves punishment for his wish to enjoin his sadistic impulses upon others.

But the situation is still more complicated. The picture is not simply one of bad feelings that are denied expression towards one person being split off and lodged in, or directed at, a substitute. For it is observable that the dominance of the bad self over the rest of the personality often has a kind of excited or addictive quality, with perverse undertones of a kind that suggest sadomasochism and not just aggression. Where bullying is concerned, we may be fairly sure that sadomasochism underlies it. The Joshua who is crushing the ladybirds is also struggling with the experience of being crushed himself, finding an external representation for his victim self which he remorselessly or playfully tortures in order not to be in touch either with the pain of feeling abandoned, or feeling separate, or with the sense of betrayal when his mother turns away from him to an interest in a new pregnancy. Another way of describing the situation is that he is trying unconsciously to get rid of his own hurt feelings into someone or something else and to get *them* to feel things instead of *him*; or, indeed, that he is trying to communicate how hurt he feels by getting somebody else or, something else, to feel that hurt, so that they might understand *his* hurt better.

A childhood reminiscence where the link was especially explicit will confirm the same point. Mr Smith was remembering being evacuated during the war, along with a group of 7-year-old-boys, to a household in a remote part of Yorkshire. As time wore on and the boys' unacknowledged unhappiness and homesickness increased, they became convinced that the landlady, or foster mother, was giving all their rations to her much-loved cat, which, in their view, she pampered excessively. One day the boys decided to kidnap the cat and drop it over the local viaduct, which they did.

This simple and sad story suggests several possibilities. The boys' experience of separation did not seem to have been adequately thought about by the adults (they were being given a good home, weren't they, and kept out of danger?). The boys turned the pain that they were passively suffering into an active cruelty. Perhaps they were trying to get rid of that source of pain by despatching it far out of reach—an attempt to kill off the inner gnawing—the hunger for food and love. Perhaps some were punishing the mothers and younger siblings left behind—in danger but at least together, represented by the foster mother and her cat. When asked by a bigger boy why they had done it, they believed their own answer. "But [the cat] was eating all our rations!" As a further defence against pain, Mr Smith had converted this awful event into an elegant story, often told alongside the one about the bottle of malt extract, packed by his mother, in his suitcase, having broken and leaked all over his few clothes. He had nothing to wear but the garments he stood up in. Too frightened to mention it, he had hidden the suitcase under the bed. It was some weeks before the increasing smell could no longer be overlooked, and the suitcase was revealed with the clothes covered in a ghastly green, slimy mould. Mr Smith's eloquent narrative is, perhaps, akin to the way in which adults can boast about their past distresses and thus become out of touch with the pain of them—resulting in the "it never did me any harm" approach.

A poignant story may bring together the way in which deep early sources of hurt and grief characteristically resurface at later times of stress or vulnerability. What turned out be a brief clinical intervention in the life of an unhappy teenager, Amy, clarifies the sadomasochistic dynamics already mentioned—ones that are surprisingly common, though seldom recognized, in many unhappy school settings.

Amy was 14 when she was referred to a CAMHS department by her GP. Her parents had taken her to the doctor because of her depression and friendlessness, arising, it was thought, from being severely bullied at school. The bullying had been going on since she started secondary school, three years earlier. She came to be assessed for psychotherapy, and I offered her four preliminary consultations.

The picture Amy presented in the first meeting was typical of a victim of bullying. With a pale expression and tense with pain, she described, in detail, the agonies of the name-calling, the isolation, the ganging-up, laughter, teasing. We spoke at length about these painful experiences and then about other aspects of her life. She wanted to tell me about her younger brother, who had been born with spina bifida with a hole in the heart. He had died eight years earlier, when Amy herself was 6 years old and he was 3. She spoke of terrible feelings of grief at the loss of this little boy of whom she had been very fond. She felt pained that his death had not, understandably, been talked about in the family at the time. It seemed that her parents had not been able to express any upset, in Amy's presence, nor to explain to her exactly what had happened. Although she was young at the time, she said that she remembered every detail of the night her brother died and of how, since then, she had felt that, "he is always with me in some weird way". She described how she would talk to him "in my mind". She had not been allowed to go to the funeral.

She also wanted to tell me about her guilt for sometimes having had bad feelings towards her brother, and even, occasionally, for having hurt him—by shutting his fingers in the door, for example. For a long time, she had believed that his death had had something to do with her. What emerged towards the end of this poignant session, and in the course of the following few, were two significant things: Amy felt both that she had no right to be a happy and popular girl if he was dead, yet also very anxious about the angry and destructive impulses that she sometimes felt in herself.

A psychodynamic understanding of these feelings would suggest that the unconscious adoption of the victim role, however dreadful for Amy, at least protected her from guilt and triumph in relation to her dead brother. It might also be inferred that the angry, destructive impulses that she mentioned and her fears about their part in her brother's death, might have had to be projected into other children, leaving her with a persecuted, though ultimately less tormenting, victim-self. Whatever the specific underlying meaning of what she was saying, it was striking that, in the second meeting, and more especially the third, Amy reported her situation at school as somehow better. She also described herself as beginning to feel that her brother might have wanted her to be happy. It was as if she felt released from having always to be the unhappy one. She said, with a shy smile, that the most bullying group of girls had invited her to join them in a work project. In the last session, and now with a quite different and much happier facial expression, Amy announced that one girl, who had been among the cruellest of the bullies, had invited her to be her special friend.

When I asked her to what she attributed these dramatic changes at school, she volunteered that she felt that, "since coming here I must have begun 'coming over differently'". She reflected that that seemed to have something to do with my thinking with her about what her little brother had meant, and what he does mean to her, and to the fact of being listened to and understood when she talked about things that her family could not bear to hear, or would have found irrelevant to what was making her unhappy.

From the GP's referral, it was clear that her parents were very concerned. They had come over as worried and thoughtful, but as unlikely to make the possible links between their daughter being bullied and past losses. One of the details that emerged in the fourth session with Amy was that things were also better at home. Her mother had, apparently, tended to get excessively cross with her daughter for bullying her little "replacement" sister. Amy said, thoughtfully, that this probably happened not only when she herself was feeling especially bad because of school, but also because her little sister had been born after the death of her brother and she, Amy, could not bear *her* being there instead of *him*. She said that she resented her sister for never having known him nor how much it had hurt when he died.

Amy's situation improved so much in the course of the consultations that I decided not to recommend her for ongoing psychotherapy. I told her that I would see here again in a month's time and we could review things a month after that. I also suggested that a colleague might see her parents, if she, and they, felt that this would be helpful, in order to offer some opportunity for them to explore their concerns and to reflect on their own loss and on their relationship with their daughters. Amy felt that her parents would welcome such an appointment and also that she herself might then be able to ask them what their version was of what happened the night her brother died. She seemed to realize that when there are issues in the family that are not fully known, but are deeply felt, it is especially hard for a child to come to terms with, or understand, a traumatic experience. She felt that the whole family might be helped as a consequence of her own clearer understanding of her difficulties.

In the event, her mother came alone. Having reported that Amy was "a different person" since coming to the clinic, she focused attention on her younger daughter and was enabled to begin to think about the links between this little girl's troubled and provocative behaviour and her and her husband's own unresolved grief. She acknowledged that they had had terrible difficulties in mourning their son's death and in accepting their younger daughter for who she was herself, rather than relating to her as her brother's replacement. Both parents came to the next two appointments, after which this case was closed.

This account, although very schematic, may, nonetheless, point to the ways in which the horrors of bullying, with its terrible immediacy, so often have their origins in past emotional dynamics—in a lack of containment in the family setting, for example, or in early feelings of loss, of inferiority, of guilt or rage which may have become destructively re-enacted in the bully–victim scenario. Amy's thoughtful responsiveness brought unusually swift relief both to her and, through her, to her family.

We can see from this painful, though in many ways more hopeful, account how these kinds of bullying interactions constitute ways of attempting to deal with mental pain and with aspects of the self that are felt to be unwanted or unacceptable. The individual can either disown and attribute elsewhere the vulnerable self, and persecute it externally, or disown a bully self and take up a hapless and helpless victim position in relation to denied aspects of the personality that come to be represented by the persecutors. Very often these different, and often largely unconscious, parts of the self are so polarized in their contrast to the more familiar sense of identity that they are simply unrecognizable, not felt to be part of the personality at all, neither wanted nor sought after. Or, alternatively, sometimes there can be a kind of pseudo-integration that gives the illusion of stability but is often belied either by tantrums or bursts of sadistic rage of alarming intensity or by equally intense bouts of depression and, not uncommonly, self-harm. Indeed. it could be that in some cases being bullied can itself constitute a form of self-harm.

The bully and the victim represent different aspects of the sado-masochistic bind, which is why so often it is those who have themselves bullied who can best understand what it means to be a victim. The superior, derisive, and envious aspects of the bully, together with his contemptuous behaviour towards the victim, are often transparent representations of the bully's own fears or fantasies of being mocked by a superior figure who makes the person feel small and contemptible in turn. Such feelings become temporarily assuaged when attributed to others and guilt is avoided by finding some ostensible justification for the cruelty—usually based in external differences; in weirdness, for example; in some idiosyncrasy or weakness; most generally in the fact of being perceived as not belonging in some way.

Another moving example of bullying being related to an experience of loss, or of being cut off from an emotional base, is to be found in Bion's autobiography, *The Long Week-End* (1982). His understanding, in later life, of the function of containment in the development of the personality must surely be related to his own bemusement and fear, as a child, of the uncomprehending and incomprehensible adult world, first in India and then in the English prep and public school systems.

The 8-year-old Bion struggles alone to try to think about his impending separation. His parents seem emotionally unable to help him with his fears. He is to be sent away from India, from his home, the only one he has ever known, to this mysterious place, "England", which, even more confusingly, was also called "home". "It made me sad like everything else . . . growing up, being a big boy now, England . . ." (p. 20).

My mother just stroked my cheeks and dreamt without fear but with sadness. I couldn't stand it.

"Moth-er! You aren't sad are you?"

"Sad?" She would laugh. "Of course not! Why should I be sad?"

Well, why should she be sad? I couldn't think. It was ridiculous. Sad? Of course not!

But she was. [p. 21]

Later, when the monsoon came, I found she was curiously blind about *that*. "What rain?" I asked, not hopefully, as I stood before her "soaked to the skin" as she called it. It made it worse that she was laughing—inside.

"You're laughing," I said. "No," she said, looking very stern. So she wasn't sad; and she wasn't laughing either. [p. 30]

Shortly after this:

When I found myself alone in the playground in the Preparatory school in England where I kissed my mother a dry-eyed goodbye, I could see, above the hedge which separated me from her and the road which was the boundary of the wide world itself, her hat go bobbing up and down like some curiously wrought millinery cake carried on the wave of green hedge. And then it was gone.

Numbed, stupefied, I found myself staring into a bright, alert face.

"Which are you—A or B?" it said. Other faces had gathered.

"A", I said hurriedly in response to the urgency I felt in their curiosity.

"You're *not*! You jolly well say "B"! You know nothing about it!" This was only too true.

"B", I said obediently.

"You dirty little liar!" said the first one. Appealing passionately to the rest, "He just said he was 'A', didn't he?" That I had to admit.

"You can't go back on that", said the advocate of B. "You must say B or you'll be a beastly little turncoat!" he cried heatedly.

"All right, I'll say B"

A fight developed. I heard the first one shouting, "He *is* a beastly turncoat; and a liar anyway. We don't want him. Do we chaps?"

The crowd had grown to formidable proportions, say six or seven.

"No", they shouted.

The mysterious row turned out to be about whether Bion should belong to School House A or to School House B, which were, of course, rivals.

At last the ghastly day ended and I was able to get under the bed-clothes and sob.

"What's the matter?" asked one of the three boys who shared the dormitory with me.

"I don't know", I wailed. He seemed sympathetic. He considered the matter for a moment.

"Are you homesick?"

"Yes." At once I realised what an awful thing I had done.

"No, B", I hurriedly said. He got into his bed. This time the day *was* over.

I learned to treasure that blessed hour when I could get into bed, pull the bedclothes over my head and weep. As my powers of deception grew I learned to weep silently till at last I became more like my mother who was *not* laughing and was *not* crying. It was a painful process. [pp. 33–34]

This poignant excerpt gives further evidence of the characteristic of bullying mentioned in chapter 6: that it very often occurs in groups, or, rather, in gangs. Bion spent some of his early adult life writing on group processes—in particular, the unconscious, irrational components that inform group functioning and subvert their more conscious and rational aims and values. Later in his life, along with Rosenfeld and Meltzer in particular, Bion began thinking of the same processes as informing internal life. Just as individuals gang up together, usually, as we have seen, out of insecurity in the face of feeling excluded or different, or out of confusion about who they are and where they belong, or in states of fear and desperation, so aspects of the personality can seem to be ganging up together too, deriving some precarious sense of identity and safety from keeping out any overt traces of weakness, uncertainty, or vulnerability. Whether we are thinking in terms of internal or external gangs, the main objective seems to be one of maintaining a dominant position either by inducing in others, or by leaving discarded or marginalized, parts of the self—feelings that are too painful to bear. They are ones that are not felt to be integratable into the personality without excessive disruption to whatever fragile sense of psychic equilibrium there may be.

Adolescents are particularly prone to these groupings and gangings—not all of which, it should be stressed, are malign. For, as we have seen, the fragility and changeability of the growing personality lends itself, especially at this time when the containing function of the family is diminishing, to a "safety in numbers" mentality. A sense of integration is often achieved by different group members representing different aspects of each personality in a relatively fluid and experimental way. This can be especially so, as I have suggested, in early adolescence when struggles to come to terms with the upheavals of puberty are particularly intense and problematic. If uncontained at the appropriate times, the raging, vengeful, sadomasochistic, infantile impulses that are being renewed at this stage may readily find expression and confirmation in a bullying persona, with or without gang backing. Much depends on the individual child's resilience—that is, on the degree to which a capacity to contain and a feeling of being understood has begun to be established in the earliest years. During adolescence, identity is threatened and a selfish, omnipotent façade often obtains, especially if fuelled by actual losses or tragedies. Precisely because of this kind of fluidity, the bullying phase will often pass, as with Amy, or it may become more covert, depending on the internal and external factors under discussion.

The sight of an 8-year-old boy standing alone in the playground, having just said goodbye to his mother (and indeed to what for him was his whole life—his home and country) must have elicited in every small member of the pack of Bion's new contemporaries similarly painful feelings—if they could have allowed themselves to experience them. Away from the pack, one individual boy was able to offer solace at bedtime—was Bion homesick? But in the playground, instead of a sympathetic word or hand on the shoulder, they all descended, baying, mocking, co-opting—with not an adult in sight to supervise, gather up, or understand. "Looking back on that appalling period of my life", Bion writes, "I do not feel, as I did then, that it was my fault; nor the fault of my contemporaries, or the local school authorities. The parents, staff, all were caught up in a web of undirected menace" (p. 47).

It is with the notion of "undirected menace" that I shall conclude this chapter, for one of the difficulties in thinking about bullying is that it is not as circumstantial or as cause-specific as it would be convenient for us to believe. Identifying specific causes not only encourages a belief in specific solutions, but also risks introducing a blame culture. This is not to say that we should not be seeking means to manage the problem and to reduce its virulence. This is essential, but we must *also* address the underlying dynamics and understand something of the predisposing factors, both personal and cultural. It is all too easy for us to say of ourselves, or of our parents, or parents of themselves, that they should, or could, have done something differently—the "if-only" culture.

In conclusion, the capacity to withstand destructive experiences—that is, *resilience*—is lodged in early development. The bullies will effectively go on "killing" others, the victims kill themselves. The seeds of the phenomenon lie deep in the culture and deep in the individual psyche, a psyche that needs support and care and a responsiveness of a particular kind from the earliest days—appropriate support, care, responsiveness, containment, indeed supervision—which are only possible in a society that does not turn a blind eye but *really* values children and young people and also values parenthood. The emphasis has to be on overseeing and not overlooking, at every stage of the mysterious and complex process of growing up. And yet how hard this is to do. The following quotation from Margaret Atwood's classic study of the nature and impact of bullying, *Cat's Eye* (1989), poignantly and subtly catches the way in which even the bravest and best-intentioned quail and even fail. Yet I felt that here, too, there is more than a touch of resilience.

> "When I was little and the kids called me names, we used to say, 'sticks and stones will break my bones, but names will never hurt me,'" she says. Her arm goes vigorously around, mixing, efficient and strong.
>
> "They don't call me names," I say. "They're my friends." I believe this.
>
> "You have to learn to stand up for yourself," says my mother. "Don't let them push you around. Don't be spineless. You have to have more backbone." She dollops butter into the tins.
>
> I think of sardines and their backbones. You can eat their backbones. The bones crumble between your teeth; one touch and they fall apart. This must be what my own backbone is like: hardly there at all. What is happening to me is my own fault, for not having more backbone.
>
> My mother sets down the bowl and puts her arms around me. "I wish I knew what to do," she says. This is a confession. Now I know what I've been suspecting: as far as this thing is concerned, she is powerless.
>
> I know that muffins have to be baked right away, right after they've been ladled out, or they'll be flat and ruined. I can't afford the distraction of comfort. If I give into it, what little backbone I have left will crumble away to nothing.
>
> I pull away from her. "They need to go into the oven," I say. [p. 186]

Note

An earlier version of this chapter was published in 2002 in *Free Associations,* Vol. 9, No. 2, pp. 189–210.

PART III

CLINICAL PICTURES

CHAPTER EIGHT

Assessing adolescents: finding a space to think

E xploring adolescent difficulties with a view to possible therapeutic treatment involves attempting to engage a troubled, and
often confused, individual in beginning to think—to think in
a very specific and probably unfamiliar way. Beginning to think can
itself be an alarming process. It necessitates learning about oneself.
"'They' all hate learning—", says the psychoanalyst in Bion's final
Memoir, "it makes them develop—swell up" (1991, p. 438), pregnant,
that is, with a new idea, a new birth/thought in the mind.

It is often at adolescence that the issue of different kinds of learning and thinking, and their implications for development, take on
particular clarity. The emotional ferment stirred up by puberty
and its complex aftermath is one that adolescents find themselves
worryingly and often unexpectedly caught up in. Inner conflicts and
anxieties are aroused, which many seek to avoid, if at all possible. As we have seen, some seem to stop thinking independently
altogether and submerge themselves either in the shared mentality
of group-life, and/or in activities that can be literally mindless or
self-destructive—drugs, alcohol, substance abuse, or the often quite
addictive worlds of social media. At the other extreme, some may
try to rely on cleverness and cognitive acquisitiveness as a mode of
defence against facing and thinking about new, turbulent, and often
contradictory feelings—as a way of avoiding intimacy and evading

engagement with the "agitation of inexperience", as Pushkin put it (Copley, 1993, p. 57).

What we are often witnessing when adolescents have come to the point of seeking help is the failure of the systems of defence to which they have been turning to assuage their inner turbulence. These strategies may have worked, more or less, hitherto, offering temporary camouflage for, or respite from, the more troubled elements of their personalities. But extra pressures—those of exams, for example, or abuse, illness, bereavement, bullying, loneliness—may test the increasingly shaky holding-structures of family or group, or of what can be the relative safety of school life. A crisis may be precipitated: a suicide attempt, panic attacks, self-mutilation. Disturbances may develop: in eating, in working, or in relation to others. It is with the pressures and freedoms of the adolescent years that the familiar defensive strategies are significantly challenged, when the containing (as well as restraining) function of the family diminishes and the quality and coherence of inner resources are tested.

In the Tavistock Clinic's Adolescent Department,[1] in which I worked for many years, what is called "Assessment" follows an initial "Intake" decision to accept the referral or self-referral of an adolescent as someone who, in principle, might benefit from the services that the Department can offer. The assessment sessions, usually up to four, offer the troubled young person an opportunity to engage in a thinking process; to assess the degree of motivation in seeking help and the impact of beginning to look at private or hidden things; to explore the capacity to sustain the scrutiny; to bear the possible discovery; and to risk the change. This can be described as a *process*— one that may dispense almost entirely with case-history–type procedure and focus, rather, on a "thinking together" that takes the facts into account but also introduces an unusual way of working that may bring with it further disturbance, as well as relief. Bion's somewhat aphoristic comment that pain is more easily borne if it can be thought about is by no means entirely convincing to this age group. But the "process" in question may offer a space for examining the anxiety and ambivalence that usually accompany a request for help, and it may contribute to determining whether the fear of change is greater than the bid for relief and for emotional freedom.

The contrasting assessments of two young women, Sarah, aged 19, and Anne, aged 16, may lend some specificity to the "process" under discussion. Both girls had become a concern to those around them and a considerable worry to themselves. The following account offers a detailed description of Sarah's assessment and a more general overview of Anne's situation. Each young woman was intelligent, attractive, and deeply troubled.

Of initial importance to the assessor is to try to establish whose the problem really is—parents? school? self?—and why now? Sarah's difficulties became disabling around the time that she gained a place at university, and they steadily intensified thereafter. Towards the end of her first year, she wrote to the Department:

> I have been feeling increasingly depressed over the past few months. I have been suffering from very low self-esteem, feelings of hope-lessness and lack of concentration. I cry constantly and am often so agitated that I cannot even sit down. . . . I feel desperate and my work is suffering. I would be grateful for any help you can offer.

It emerged that Sarah's tutor had suggested that she contact the clinic, and the suggestion was followed by a phone call from him. We were told that Sarah, one of their brightest students, was approaching end-of-year-exams. She was in so bad a state that it was feared that she might not be able to sit them. Could we see her as a matter of urgency?

The process of assessment may itself provide a much-needed form of "holding" for a student whose anxieties and fears are felt to be terri-bly pressing and who may find it very hard to wait for a response. Was this simply an exam crisis, or was it, as so often, a situation in which, at whatever age or stage, the extra pressure of exams was exposing unresolved conflicts of a quite different kind?

I saw Sarah the following week. Tall, stylish, gentle, and seemingly mature, she smiled diffidently as she sat down in the consulting-room and immediately began speaking. "I don't know what's happening. I get into these terrible states when I'm alone. I don't know who I am. I can't think. [*Long pause*] I sometimes want to die." I acknowledged the significance of what she was telling me, but felt that I should also let her know about the structure of the assessment process on which we had embarked. So I explained to her that we would have up to four meetings, one a week, to try to understand her alarming experiences and to think about how we could best be of help. Perhaps she would like to tell me a bit more about herself. Hardly prompted, and with beguiling articulacy, Sarah recounted her life situation. Two years pre-viously, her father had, totally unexpectedly, walked out. The impact on Sarah, her mother, and her younger brother was devastating. Sarah described her mother's continuing inability to come to terms with the abandonment. She detailed her mother's rage and desperation and Sarah's own role in trying to calm things down, in taking charge, supporting, caring-for. She had functioned, as I suggested to her, as if she felt that she herself held total responsibility for the emotional well-being of the whole family. Unlike her younger brother, who was described as being very straight-forward about his feelings ("he won't do or say anything he doesn't want to"), Sarah found it impossible to show that anything was wrong. On the contrary, she appeared to take everything in her stride.

A picture began to emerge of Sarah as thoughtful, reasonable, hard-working, popular, and kind. She loved her mother and didn't want to worry her with any of her own problems. She kept in regular contact with her father but wouldn't talk to him about her feelings. She described her friends, and in particular her boyfriend, David, in glowing terms. David was said to be loving and brilliant and to have a wonderful, warm, and supportive family.

This account took a long time. I felt that I was up against an impenetrable barrier of niceness, tolerance, generosity, and common sense. There was no self-idealization, just a troubled, caring, and extremely likeable young woman. And yet there were the panic attacks, terrors, anxieties, impulses to die. We talked about these contrasting experiences of herself and about how difficult it was to relate the one to the other. Sarah's sense of herself appeared to be so rooted in her "good-girl" exterior that I was concerned about how she could possibly engage with whatever it was that lay underneath. To do so would seem to be so risky for her, in that her very success, personally and intellectually, could well be dependent on keeping such things at bay—a problem that is very common when adolescents first seek help.

I talked about the fact that Sarah had clearly thought quite extensively about all the stresses and pressures, shocks and sadness in her life. It seemed that the source of the frightened state in which she found herself lay in an area of herself that she neither knew about nor had access to on a conscious, day-to-day basis. Unusually for an assessment, I found myself wondering aloud about her dreams. She replied that she had a sense of having many vivid dreams but that she didn't usually remember them. "Oh, hang on a minute", she said, "I had a really odd one last night. Shall I tell it to you?"

I was in a warehouse-place where a lot of workers were having a meal. I had an ordinary cup of tea in my hand, which was fine. But then, for some reason, I found myself holding a much bigger bowl. It contained cold tea. It was unpleasant and full of those crystalline Continental sugar-things—very sweet; not what I would normally drink. A friend came and sat down. I heard myself saying, "I hate my father". There was another student at a nearby table: "You shouldn't speak like that about your father", she called out.

Sarah looked at me puzzled. "It's very strange, because I don't hate my father." We thought briefly about what seemed, in the dream, to be two contrasting versions of herself and of her in relation to her parents, both internally and externally. There was the ordinary, nice-cup-of-tea Sarah, whom she felt she already knew intimately. But there was also the much less ordinary and less pleasant Sarah, the bowl/container of cold, artificially sweetened substance, perhaps with some connection to her mother (who had Continental origins). There was both the Sarah who hated her father and the good-girl Sarah who immediately censored any such hostile or angry feelings.

This was, indeed, a significant dream to have had on the eve of her first assessment session. Whatever the precise meaning of the details, it did alert Sarah to the existence and nature of feelings that were "foreign" to her conscious self. "It's very interesting," she said, as she got up to go, "I've never thought about things in this way before."

In the subsequent sessions, Sarah's dreams constituted rather marvellous expressions of her anxieties and of her predicament. They seemed to offer a kind of running commentary on the process of assessment itself, as experienced on both a conscious and an unconscious level. In terms of the quantity of dream material, these sessions are not typical of this kind of assessment encounter. But they do epitomize a process that can make it possible to derive a sense of what might underlie an adolescent's presenting problems and what capacity there may be to engage in psychotherapeutic work, and with what intensity (in terms of the number of sessions per week). To what extent, for example, did Sarah's dreams—whatever might be understood of their content—represent an early-established transference relationship both to the setting and to me? Were the dreams *themselves* versions of the "good-girl" Sarah, versions that offered to the mother/therapist a nice, therapy-dream-cup-of-tea? Or were the dreams expressions of the seriousness of Sarah's desire to engage with her inner preoccupations?

She came to her second appointment, a week later, saying that she had been feeling much better. Exams had been "okay", although she had stopped thinking at some point during Chaucer. She was now concerned lest she might feel better, but only on one level.

"Unless I understand what's going on underneath, something may burst through again at some later date." Smiling a bit sheepishly, she said that she had remembered some more dreams: "They seem completely mad and probably don't mean anything." While being mindful of this suspiciously cooperative side of Sarah—somehow giving me, as well as the rest of the world, what she thought was wanted—it also seemed that the bringing of the dreams represented a serious attempt on her part to examine aspects of herself that she felt she could not understand alone.

I began to feel that Sarah's attitude was trusting rather than appeasing. She had obviously done considerable emotional work on herself, as well as intellectual work on her exams, since the previous session. She conveyed a sense of courage that commanded respect. Nonetheless, since I could not continue seeing her myself, and had told her so in the first session, I felt concern lest Sarah expose more of herself than she could quite manage (not an unrealistic concern, as the third session was to prove). In this second session, Sarah brought two detailed dreams. The first described her as being, as she put it,

> Somehow inside and outside at the same time. I felt inside a warm, lighted restaurant part of a supermarket with plenty of goods on the shelves and a friend to talk to, and, at the same time, outside—in a dark, cold, continental square where a group of students, all strangers, were sheltering behind flimsy, polystyrene boards. There was no protection from the wind and the rain. On top of one of the boards that an older woman had set up to surround a statue in the centre of the square, a plastic cat had been placed. It was a child's toy that this woman had perched oddly on the edge of the structure.

Scarcely pausing, Sarah went on to describe a further dream. "This one is *really* weird," she said with a smile:

> I was on a beach with two friends, beside a swimming pool. Together we were playing a sort of quiz-game in which a speech from a Shakespeare play had been changed around and I had to determine which play, character and speech it was. [She could no longer remember the exact words, which had been clear in the dream itself, but she did know that it was a speech of Iago's from *Othello*.] I noticed that there was a little man, rather elfin-like and dark, jumping around all the time, talking incessantly and somehow getting in the way, in a rather menacing manner. But it did seem that it was only me who was being bothered by him and not my friends. Then I was in a Laura-Ashley-type bedroom. These same two friends were sitting on one of

the beds. The décor was, if anything, excessively tasteful—rather stylish, but without much character. On the window-sill was a huge and lovely bowl of flowers—daffodils and tulips—into which I was trying to arrange some giant, coloured children's pencils, as if they, too, were flowers.

It was difficult to know on what level to take up this mass of material, and in how much detail. On one level, the dream seemed to indicate how quickly Sarah had taken to the idea that it is possible to live in two worlds simultaneously—an external and an internal one—and that each of these worlds might have its own, very different, culture and characteristics. One of her worlds was well-stocked: there were friends; there was care, concern, intelligence, food—goods of all kinds. The other was much harsher, with fragile defences against destructive emotional blasts. The defences offered only a semblance of protection, either from the different and unfamiliar aspects of herself (the student strangers), or from the curious statue in the square. In this setting, the only woman mentioned was someone who had placed a child's toy on top of the inadequate, protective barrier—as though this peculiar, or eccentric, child-part of an adult had something to do with the lack of genuine shelter and the extreme feeling of exposure to the elements.

I felt a strong sense of the danger, for Sarah, of entering this bleak and unfamiliar region of her mind, one that was in such contrast to the restaurant/supermarket part, where "goods" of all sorts could be readily acquired and consumed. It seemed that this other area was not one where any protection had been experienced from a parental, or especially a maternal figure. Was this, perhaps, the doubting, fearful side of the beginnings of an ambivalent transference? The only woman in sight had built a flimsy barrier around a statue—as if trying to preserve a monument (a marriage? a husband?). Possibly these childish objects connected to the continental sugar-crystals (provided by her mother for adults' coffee) which, as a child, Sarah had apparently eaten, like sweets. Possibly this child/adult confusion linked to Sarah's own effort, in the second dream, to try to fit child-like things—the coloured pencils—into the bowl of flowers, *as if* they belonged there. There seemed to be an attempt to preserve the attractively decorated room of her mind without having to recognize dysfunction, conflicts, undigested childish parts—wanting, rather, to mix up those parts, the bad and the good, so that the ensemble would be like a "bowl of roses". The dream itself was already throwing doubt on whether this area really was quite as pretty as Sarah conveyed. It had the rather saccharine quality of mere prettiness, not the depth of actual beauty.

Keeping both the transference and her actual feelings about her external parents in the background, our discussion centred on the Iago part of the dream, and what that might reveal about Sarah's engagement with the psychotherapeutic process. One might suggest that her ability to recognize the Iago speech could indicate the beginning of a capacity to distinguish in herself some envious and destructive impulses—ones that had previously been concealed or projected. These impulses were now presenting themselves to Sarah as unwelcome aspects of her personality, sowing panic and confusion—perhaps related to that dark, elfin-man jumping up and down and insistently intruding into her more ordered, friendly, beach/swimming-pool self—bothering only Sarah and not her friends ("they didn't seem to notice").

As the disparate and curious elements were explored, Sarah responded in unexpected terms: "It's odd that you should say that, because this week, for the first time, I got very angry with my boyfriend. Strangely enough, I felt really pleased." She grinned, "I didn't really show it, it was just the experience. . . . I've always thought David's so wonderful, I could never find fault with him, and that made me feel wound-up about being good enough. Perhaps I was too clinging and dependent. Feeling angry made me kind of delighted. It was weird." Sarah went on, "I used to get on with everyone and wasn't ever at all critical, but I was sitting in the exam-room this week, not really thinking, just staring out of the window, and I felt 'I'd just like to slap them all'." Sarah sounded angry but was, in fact, smiling.

I linked these angry impulses to her first dream, the dream in which she heard one part of herself saying that she hated her father, and another part immediately censoring that thought. There also seemed to be a link to the second dream in which there was a woman who was trying to protect a statue with obviously inadequate and childish materials. There was a lot more anger and resentment, and indeed jealousy, lurking around than Sarah could easily accommodate in the more attractive, tolerant, and pretty areas of her mind. "Well," she said tentatively, "I probably *am* angry with my mother for not getting over it"—"but she's a very good mother", she hastened to add. "We get on really well." She paused, and again her tone changed, "But when she's upset or cross . . . that's *it* [implying cross feelings of her own]. . . . My Dad's OK [*again, a change of tone*], but he *did* go away and somehow leave all the rubbish with us . . . [*long pause*] . . . but Iago—no, I can't be Iago." The session ended with a comment about how hard Sarah found it to think about the fact that feelings that she so deeply repudiated *could* be part of herself. It seemed that it was these very parts that were now so insistently forcing their way into her consciousness.

The next session began with a long description of the emotional turmoil in which her boyfriend, David, had suddenly found himself—mainly over his fraught relationship with his father. This relationship had been alluded to before, but in rather idealized terms. Now it was represented as tormented and profoundly wanting. She, Sarah, had been feeling much better, but he, David, was in a terrible state. Sarah described him as weeping for the first time in their relationship. She had found herself feeling stronger in response, able to help him and be less pathetic herself. She also thought that she had been really selfish: "going on and on about my own problems all the time, when underneath David was so very unhappy. I do feel much better now. Probably I don't need to come here anymore." I suggested that today she was bringing David instead of herself. She nodded in recognition and reiterated her comment about feeling so selfish: how could she think that she had problems when others were so much worse off. I wondered whether the "problematic" side of herself seemed just too menacing to consider, and it was easier for her to think of someone else having the problems and not herself. Sarah said reflectively, "Well, I did have this dream."

> It was about being in a really dingy flat with several people, certainly David and his father. A plug had blown and I was terrified of a conflagration—no-one else seemed to be worried. I looked outside and there were, in fact, little fires. But somehow they seemed manageable. My terror was that the conflagration would be inside the flat. David was comforting me.

Here, in the third session, there seemed to be evidence of Sarah's need to retreat from an Iago-self into care and concern for David. The dream offered a clear suggestion as to why that should be: the breakdown of her infantile, splitting mechanisms (David is wonderful; Sarah is terrible) and of the associated axes (strong/weak; brilliant/mediocre; secure, loving family/fractured, non-functional family). The undermining of her good-girl persona threatened terrible conflagration—some catastrophic explosion, feared less from without than from within. When her difficulties in not being a good-girl were alluded to, Sarah became very tearful. There was a long silence. ". . . It's just that I've talked about some parts of myself that I have never known about or mentioned to anyone before—ones that it's very difficult to think about."

The process of this assessment, unusual in its quantity of dream material, was one of trying to establish both the general area of Sarah's difficulties and whether or not she could bear to acknowledge where the roots of those difficulties might lie. The cost to her could prove to be too high for the time being. Sarah feared a conflagration. Her defences now represented themselves as flimsy polystyrene boards, lacking strength or weight, liable to be blown hither and thither. Her exceptional capacity to "think", in the narrow sense of the term, had certainly provided her with an important bulwark against the turmoils and vicissitudes of her family life. But these defences had also offered a false security, one that cut her off from areas of her personality that were now beginning to assert themselves. Sarah was struggling. She felt that Iago was deeply disreputable. She could not bear to acknowledge that anything associated with him could also be part of herself.

An extended assessment had offered Sarah an opportunity to examine the relationship between the developmental possibilities of her burgeoning capacity to think in a different way and the risk posed to her peace of mind by the destructive parts of her personality, which were becoming evident. There remained a fourth session during which agreement would be reached about possible treatment. Whatever the decision, there was a sense that an important piece of work had already been done. It might not be followed through at this stage, in terms of further sessions, for the threat of conflagration might, indeed, be felt to be too great. But this brief experience of risking "thinking" could well be one to which Sarah might return in stronger—or perhaps in more desperate—times.

Conducting an assessment over a period of a few weeks offers some opportunity to test the strength of the impetus that first brings a young person to the clinic; to discover whether that impetus came from him/herself; to see whether it is possible to hold on to trains of thought and emotional links over periods of separation; to foster a relationship with a therapist which could be a thinking one and not merely a "dumping" one. How is it possible to judge, at this early stage, what the gains or losses may be? A crucial question that has to be determined, one only touched on in Sarah's case, is that of to whom does the pain really belong? Is it to the adolescent or to the parents? To a boyfriend, to a sibling? Does it perhaps reside in a complicated tangle of all of these?

A brief look at a second assessment may throw some light on this last issue of where the problems originate and where they reside. Anne had just taken her GCSEs. She arrived to her first session breathless and chatty. She was thin, somewhat leggy, attractive, and wore owl-like glasses. She filled the corridor with conversation: "Hi! What a massive place. I'd expected somewhere really small." As we entered the consulting-room, she looked suddenly shy, "Well now that I'm here, I don't know what to say." Fifty minutes later, Anne had barely paused for breath. This was the gist of her story: her many physical complaints had been exhaustively explored by the GP who had originally referred her. She had feared that her stomach pains were appendicitis. Or maybe she had M.E.? Or perhaps she really only had terrible digestion. She couldn't eat. She felt awfully ill a lot of the time. She thought that she felt a bit better when she was talking to Dr S, but every time she did so some other worry emerged. Possibly it wasn't physical at all? Maybe it was just stress? When asked what she might feel stressed about, Anne said, "The difficulty is that I feel guilty about everything . . . and yet I don't actually feel seriously guilty because there is nothing really to feel guilty about. That is, I'm not much of a worry to anyone. I've behaved reasonably ok, and yet, somehow, I can't cope with feeling bad and criticized about everything I do." Several anecdotes followed that did indeed indicate an exaggerated sense of guilt for comparatively minor offences. Anne described herself as falling into a "near frenzy of anxiety" at times, states that her parents didn't seem to understand. "They just criticize me for being so ratty and disagreeable. Well, not exactly criticize, but, well, you know."

In the course of the assessment it came to light that Anne's childhood had been extremely unhappy, dominated by her father's alcoholism and her parents' commitment to concealing the problem, even from the children, who, they believed, had not noticed. Many painful instances were described, culminating in her father's attempted suicide. One fairly accessible source of guilt seemed to lie in the double lie she had been living (colluding with the "not-knowing"), both within the family and among her friends. But a different and more complex picture began to emerge in the course of this first outpouring of family history. Some of the stories seemed to involve a feeling, on certain occasions, of betrayal of her father when Anne, driven to distraction by his drunken behaviour, could no longer pretend that it wasn't happening. Her father seemed to have relied on his daughter, rather than on his wife, to be a tacit source of support and understanding. Meanwhile, her mother's respect and affection was said to have been directed to a younger brother, Tom. Anne enviously described him as witty, intelligent, good-looking, and successful, by contrast with her own self-description as "thick, ugly, and bad". Anne was deeply pained by what she felt was her mother's withholding and critical attitude towards her, and she was confused by her father's dependency.

In puzzlement, she also described her passionate attachment to her father, despite his hurtful and destructive behaviour. She recounted numerous terrible occasions when, during marital rows, her father would invoke Anne's emotional and behavioural difficulties as ammunition against his wife. Anne was quite aware of feeling guilty about being implicated in these tangled family alliances and identifications. She consciously felt bad about her troubled behaviour seeming to be the cause of marital disharmony. But she was also beginning to touch on another source of guilt, of which she was less aware. Perhaps she also felt bad about the strength of her attachment to her father, at her mother's expense. Indeed, perhaps she herself was more withholding and critical towards her mother than she wished to realize. The first session was ending. "I never thought of anything like this before. I can't believe it," she said. "I've only just arrived and I thought that I had nothing to talk about. Phew—I really must start thinking."

In subsequent sessions these initial possibilities were confirmed, and Anne's inexplicably intense guilt and her somatic problems seemed, increasingly clearly, to be linked both to unresolved difficulties in the family as a whole and to Anne's own oedipal conflicts. She became very anxious at my idea that it might be helpful for her whole family to come and think about things together. It emerged that her father had, in fact, stopped drinking, and Anne felt that the family equilibrium was now maintained by her playing the part of the problematic member.

Anne was fascinated and disturbed by beginning to think about things in this way. Like Sarah, she feared conflagration, but for her the risk seemed to be an external one—that the family would blow up and fall apart—rather than an internal one. Her own sense of guilt and her stomach pains seemed preferable, at this point, to feeling responsible for the family structure giving way, which she felt would only compound her guilt. At the end of the assessment, Anne felt that once-weekly psychotherapy for herself would be the best way forward.

I have been describing, thus far, valiant efforts on the parts of two young women to "think" within the containing structure of the assessment process. By contrast, however, especially in work with adolescents, there are those frequent, less happy outcomes when assessments break down in the early stages. Ambivalence about, or even hostility to, exploring difficulties may be expressed by a variety of behaviours and attitudes, often characterized, in terms of the present frame of reference, by the "non-thinking" or "pseudo-thinking" mode.

What may lie behind a resistance to the kind of thinking that links up emotional states will be familiar to those working with this age group. In the case of the addictive pull for adolescents towards all manner of acting out, the lure towards perverse gratifications is often stronger than the distress consequent upon them, and also stronger than the underlying pain. But, more generally, there will usually be varying degrees of anxiety about disturbing the family equilibrium (as was the case with Anne), about change, separation, identity, intimacy, even madness.

As we have seen, integral to the assessment process and its outcome is the extent to which it may be possible to address these problems as part of the assessment itself, despite the fact that the form that such problems may take often runs counter to the means whereby they may be overcome, or at least mitigated. Apart from the intrinsic difficulty of facing the fact that something feels so wrong that professional help must be sought, there are a number of predisposing factors that will always have to be taken into account before the actual assessment begins: the degree of parental support for the treatment; the nature of the preparation, in terms of what the individual adolescent has been led to expect; whether there is a hidden agenda (for instance, an imminent court appearance, a threat of school expulsion); whether the referral is basically at another's behest rather than on the part of adolescents themselves; how long a wait there may be between the initial contact and the appointment sent—and so on. Rather than elaborating on these issues in the abstract, it may be more helpful briefly to characterize two cases that between them illustrate some of the foregoing considerations. In each case, the assessment did not extend beyond the first or second session.

Jonathan was 17 when one of his teachers wrote to our Department about her concerns. She described Jonathan as having become increasingly withdrawn, depressed and rather obsessional. She then outlined some background problems. Jonathan was an only child; his father had suddenly moved out of the family home four years earlier, leaving his son mainly responsible for his physically disabled mother and ailing grandmother.

When Jonathan arrived for his first assessment appointment, his opening remark was: "The past has come and gone. We are what we are now." He went on to describe his current interest in Eastern philosophy: "*I should be in full control of my present life, nothing else* should determine it. The past certainly doesn't." There was a pause. "Have you read *Zen and the Art of Motorcycle Maintenance*? I mean, do you understand what I'm trying to say?" His therapist suggested that Jonathan might be anxious about being in this strange setting and not feeling in control. "It's very important for me to be with someone who respects my intellectual interests", Jonathan replied. "I feel the need to go beyond the ordinary understanding of things. I have been thinking about this for about four years now." His therapist recalled that that must have been around the time his had father left home. She asked him to tell her a bit about what had happened. Jonathan began speaking, much less formally, but still rather dispassionately: "I suppose it was the usual sort of thing when parents don't have a loving relationship. There were constant arguments, an affair I think; worries about money—that kind of thing." It transpired that Jonathan's father had left his mother lying on the floor, unable to get up: he had "just gone". Jonathan said he felt sorry for his father. "He's ruined his own life really, but living at home for me is fine. Mum looks after herself and Granny now, so I don't have much responsibility." There was a long pause. "By the way, *I* didn't make the request for help here—it was Mrs T, my teacher." The first session ended.

The second session was not dissimilar. Jonathan was reading *Ulysses* in the waiting room. He questioned the therapist, as they walked up the corridor, about certain philosophical authors with whom she might be familiar. He began the session saying that since discovering his therapist was a psychiatrist, he'd been worrying that she might think about things differently from him. There was a pause: "Or even know best", he added. When it was suggested that he might be afraid of becoming hurt and confused if he let go of his own picture of things, Jonathan replied: "I see what you mean, but I'm not superstitious. I have total control over my emotions. I am capable of protecting myself." After a moment's silence, he said, rather shakily, "What I *am* a bit anxious about is whether what I am doing and thinking *is* right, because I am willing to consider changing my course if you persuade me that I am wrong." Then he added, questioningly, "Perhaps Eastern philosophy *is* rather superficial?"

This was a poignant and unsettling moment. Jonathan was admitting to himself his doubts about his mode of mental functioning, but only momentarily. He immediately closed up again, and, for each interpretive comment that was ventured, he found an intellectual basis for objection or distortion. "That's clever, but not fair." "I think you're turning questions around on me." "I can, of course, see what you're doing and why. . . ." After some time, his therapist drew attention to the way in which he was using his mind to protect himself from having any feelings. There was a pause, and then Jonathan said, uncertainly, "After we've had *loads* of sessions, you might know me better." The session ended, and he did not return to the clinic nor get in touch.

In these two sessions, Jonathan showed his therapist, very clearly, how he erected barriers of philosophy and logic, relying on his intellect to control any dangerous feelings or uncertainties that he might have. The possibility of engaging in any kind of intimate way was, at this point, too alarming a prospect for him, and he fled. The fragility of his intellectual constructs and the reality of his own pain were clear, even fleetingly to himself. But the anxiety was immediately attributed to his mother, or to his teacher. The need was there "after loads of sessions . . .", but the fear of imminent catastrophe if his defences were to be dismantled and genuine contact allowed was simply too much for him.

This brief and worrying sketch perhaps evokes some of the pain and frustration of beginning this kind of work with adolescents as well as the rewards described earlier. Jonathan was suffering and had been drawing on defensive measures against experiencing his pain— measures very typical of his age group. An earnest teenage isolate, he used his intellect and his philosophy to try to evade both what the sad experiences of his life really meant to him and his fear of not being known or understood. Yet he *had* risked coming to talk, and despite breaking off almost immediately, the encounters did turn out to be helpful for he re-referred himself to the clinic a year later, this time more resolute about the necessity of facing things that, previously, he had been unable to bear.

The second case involved 19-year-old Elizabeth, who came to the clinic as a result of a "very urgent" letter from her GP following a serious overdose—her second in two years. A handwritten letter from her mother arrived a few days later, reiterating the doctor's comments and describing her concern for her daughter's safety. Neither GP nor mother gave any information beyond the barest facts.

Elizabeth was brought to her appointment by her mother, whose palpable anxiety in the waiting room was in marked contrast to her daughter's look of somewhat blasé uninterest. Indeed, it was almost as if the mother, dressed with inappropriate youthfulness, was considerably more concerned to get into the therapy room herself than her cool, rather elegant and detached companion.

When she first entered the consulting room, Elizabeth said: "I only came today because she [indicating the waiting room] promised me a car if I did. She is the one who made the appointment." This was rather a startling beginning, and I wished that I had not departed from the usual practice, with a 19-year-old, of establishing willingness and motivation, independent of the referral, before setting up an assessment. The apparent urgency of the situation, in this case, however, led to an assumption that intervention would be both needed and appreciated. This assumption was swiftly confounded by Elizabeth's denial that she had any difficulties. I decided to ask her about the overdose. It had followed, I had been told, an argument with Elizabeth's mother . . . ? She confirmed this, adding that they were always rowing. Her mother was constantly worrying about her, about her friends, her drinking, her drugs, smoking, the hours she kept, and so on. She herself saw no reason for concern. When questioned about these habits she replied that she usually smoked several joints a day (15 or so, she thought) as well as, maybe, 40 cigarettes. "I drink quite a lot too—probably half a bottle of Vodka. . . . The hours I keep . . . well, I get up about four in the afternoon, I go out and get back about the same time next morning." She smiled slightly at this picture of herself and then added, rather mischievously, "I really *don't* know what she's so bothered about."

She then resumed her rather brittle and defiant tone, describing the kinds of things her mother objected to—none of which Elizabeth found "too serious". She said that she often obtained goods by forging her mother's signature, regularly using her credit cards, or rifling her stepfather's pockets when in need of "a bit of cash". Occasionally, she went shop-lifting. She said that she wanted to become a model and to marry a rich boyfriend and "spend all his money like my mother spends Charlie's" [her stepfather]. She laughed.

This account was given with an impenetrable, slightly amused, calm. Details of Elizabeth's background emerged. She knew nothing of her real father who had left the family home when she was a year old, and whom she had seen only once since then, "for a minute", when she was 12. Her mother refused to discuss him, "but that's fine, because I'm not in the least interested". Each of her present parents had had a daughter by previous relationships, neither of whom Elizabeth had ever met. Elizabeth's sense of isolation was, for a moment, palpable. She recovered instantly, though, and went on to describe how, when her mother married her stepfather, circumstances changed dramatically. They moved from a council flat to a luxury home, but there were periodic financial crises that threatened the stability of this new situation.

As she described this move from relative poverty, she conveyed scorn for her mother and found it hard to take in the link that I was suggesting between the way in which Elizabeth spoke of her mother, and the way in which she herself behaved—that is, insecurely clinging on to the importance of money, and a variety of indulgences, which she, in turn, viewed with contempt. Elizabeth did, however, acknowledge that despite not being entirely reliable, the money provided some sort of security and containment for the family relationships, which were, themselves, she indicated, measured purely in material terms.

It was not until I came back to the circumstances of the overdose that any further crack appeared in Elizabeth's carapace. She wept briefly and silently as she described her boyfriend meeting her at the hospital and asking her what had been so wrong, "as if he really wanted to know what *I* felt". A moment later she had returned to her complaints about her mother's incapacity to understand her, to let her have any "space", or to deal with her own childishness: "It's not me who has the problems, it's my mum."

Predictably perhaps, her mother telephoned a few days later to say that Elizabeth was now "much better" and did not want to come any more. Could she herself come to Elizabeth's appointment instead? With Elizabeth's permission, we offered Mrs M her own time the following week to help her think about her anxieties about her daughter and her own feelings as the parent of so troubled a young person.

Again, we can only speculate about what specific areas of pain lay beneath Elizabeth's alarmingly self-destructive behaviour. Mother and daughter seemed locked in a mutually projective relationship: most of Elizabeth's anxiety seeming to be split off into her mother, who may, in turn, have been locating some of her own hostile, damaged, and destructive parts in Elizabeth. Certainly, I had what felt like a rather "uncanny feeling" in the course of the assessment that it was somehow "proceeding by proxy". I felt that Elizabeth had reluctantly offered herself as a kind of template from which I might develop some understanding of her mother's enormous needs for meaningful fulfilment, contact, and gratification. But she could not go on. What had allowed her to come at all, bribe aside, was probably a fleeting hope that someone—like her boyfriend—might understand *her* feelings and the degree of desperation, uncontaminated by other considerations. When a transference interpretation along these lines had been offered, however, Elizabeth had ignored it and returned to her catalogue of grievances.

These last two brief accounts may evoke some of the pain and frustration of assessing adolescents, as well as the rewards described earlier. Each of these young people was suffering, and each had been drawing on defensive measures against experiencing their pain— measures very typical of their age group. Elizabeth adopted a very different way from Jonathan of dealing with things: as a frantic group member she drank, took drugs, laughed, and stole, engaging in all sorts of delinquent enterprises in order to escape the underlying misery, which was nonetheless ultimately expressed in her suicide attempts. From the brief contact with her in one assessment, I had a clear sense of how impoverished was her internal world and of how she had suffered from the absence of any secure parenting in her life. Elizabeth might well have collapsed into too painful a therapeutic dependency were she to feel that there was someone who *could* be relied on to listen and to care about her. Yet each of these adolescents had risked coming to talk, and, despite breaking off the assessment, it is possible that the encounters were nonetheless helpful. As we have seen, in Jonathan's case this turned out to be so.

These four accounts have described the notion of assessment as "process". The team have found this approach to be the most useful one in the difficult task of sorting out how we might best help the troubled youngsters to find their way, by whatever route, to our services. During the sessions, these young "novices" are introduced to a way of thinking about themselves that they may find too frightening or too disturbing to sustain, however sensitive the approach. But they may equally discover that there is available to them a safe and thoughtful place where they can begin to make sense of themselves and of their lives.

Notes

An earlier version of this chapter was published in M. Rustin & E. Quagliata (Eds.), *Assessment in Child Psychotherapy* (London: Karnac, 2004).

1. The Tavistock Clinic is now the Tavistock and Portman NHS Foundation Trust, and the Adolescent Department has become the Adolescent and Young Adult Service.

CHAPTER NINE

A mind of one's own:
the search for identity—a case history

Establishing an identity is a central and usually very troubling task for all adolescents: discovering who one is, finding a mind of one's own—an internal analogue to the room that Virginia Woolf (1929) designates as essential not only to the capacity to create, but to the possibility of "living in the presence of reality" (p. 109). How does a person's internal room become structured and furnished in its own unique and idiosyncratic way—not as a pre-fab, identikit, design-catalogue sort of room, but as a space of one's own? These are the sorts of quandaries that arose in my work with Tom, with whom I learnt so much about the challenges of the adolescent process.

Fortunately, having assessed 19-year-old Tom over a four-session period, I was able to continue to see him myself, three times a week. A mind of his own was what he—then a university college student in his first year—most needed and wanted. When he started treatment he was locked in an entrenched and protracted adolescent state of mind from which he seemed unable to emerge. Of medium stature and strongly built, with dark, prematurely receding hair, he could, at times, be strikingly good-looking. This was not a view he shared. Tremendously sensitive to his appearance, his loss of hair was a source of constant anguish; it was a narcissistic affront, fuelled by the relentlessly cruel jokes of his hard-drinking, "macho" friends.

His culture had been typically adolescent, in the pejorative sense. It was gang, rather than group, orientated, and predominantly mindless and aimless, though not without some mutually supportive qualities. His own life featured slavish attention to physical appearance: excessive drinking bouts in pubs (alcohol having succeeded the extensive drug-taking of his early teens); states of languid and mawkish self-pity, alternating with energetic and competitive sportiness; periods of, by turn, obsessive philosophical and political ruminations and manic excitability. Like his friends, he had become a chronic underachiever and had exiled himself from his professional middle-class upbringing and joined an "underclass" mentality, taking casual work on building sites. The only preoccupations that were not group-orientated were his erotic fantasies and, at times, activities. These were kept frantically secret, with enormous shame attached to the risk of discovery.

In the early months of his treatment, Tom described, scarcely coherently, his inability to think for himself or to concentrate. For his mind was continuously filled with perverse sexual fantasies—something that had not come up in the assessment sessions. With great difficulty, he told me how he would spend an inordinate amount of his time in a frenzied, masturbatory state of excitement, using sex-phone-lines and calls to prostitutes, with whom he continuously made and broke arrangements. He had only recently stopped exposing himself to women in parklands and open spaces. He told me that he was born out of wedlock and that his parents had never lived together. His father, a painter and writer of some repute, had maintained sporadic contact with him over the years. His mother had married an Englishman and left her country of origin to come to London with Tom when he was 4 years old.

This marriage seems to have constituted a major blow to Tom at the time, and, subsequently, he told me, it deteriorated into sado-masochistic misery. His stepfather was felt to be a tyrant and a bully. Alcoholic and morose, he would dictate rules to the household, and to Tom in particular, of peevish triviality, relating with a sort of dour imperviousness to any joyfulness or finer feeling. Tom hated him. Shortly after the birth of a second son, two years after the marriage, Tom's mother had a full puerperal breakdown, which initiated a chronic schizophrenic illness. Despite conscious idealization of his earliest years alone with his mother, it seemed more likely, in the light of his subsequent difficulties, that even this early "idyll" had been shadowed by maternal depression. From the transference could be inferred an experience, at least some of the time, of a brick-wall sort of maternal mind, unreceptive and unresponsive to Tom's projections and attempted communications. There would seem to have been an absence of vitality, thoughtfulness, interest, or hope of the kind that might have enabled him to feel understood, and from which he could have derived a sense of himself and internalized a capacity to think for himself. Indeed, his extreme difficulty in "thinking" at all, in the sense that I have been describing, suggests that he had experienced so little containment in infancy, particularly of his sadistic and aggressive impulses to excite and then frustrate, that a good object would almost have to be "constructed" *for* him—by way, initially, of thinking for him and then, only slowly, with him. He alternated between a fear of being merged with me or of being totally cut off. Either way, he was unable consciously to think.

In the literal sense, Tom did have a room of his own. I often heard about it—together with his attendant longing that I might actually see it. He believed that were I to do so, I would be thrilled by it and much better able to understand him. For, apparently, every square inch of wall and door was covered with memorabilia. The room was papered with fragments, relics, reminders of past events. The memorabilia offered recollections of experiences, relationships, and exchanges that dated back to the early days of primary school, through his teenage travels abroad, his chance encounters, and his important relationships, to the present day. There were photos, postcards, bus-tickets, labels, letters, matchboxes, concert-tickets, napkins, notes, stamps—every imaginable object that could be stuck to a surface. To know his room, he insisted, was to know him. In a sense, he was right, for what the room demonstrated was his belief that these multifarious, two-dimensional, stuck-on, images of himself amounted to an identity.

The room represented, rather, in my view, an agglomeration of disparate and discrete bits and pieces, many of them filched or stolen, odds-and-ends—a sort of potpourri of a life, wholly lacking coherence or integration. His mistaken conscious notion was that this accumulation of scraps, with its strong, quantitative, and scavenging emphasis, had something to do with an identity. Unconsciously, he knew better. Indeed, at times, he could reflect that his room felt, even to him, in his less excitable moments, like a "stolen identity". He could be described as taking refuge within an exoskeletal structure, made up of serial accretions, with adhesive and projective characteristics, in essence narcissistic. It sounded to me as if he had created a kind of self-protective carapace in order not to be in touch with the actual emptiness within. What he lacked was an introjective capacity that could have helped him to internalize that face, experience, or event, such that they might "exist in the mind" and form part of a vibrant and unique internal world. He had a physical room, then, but no mind/room of his own—no internal place where meaning might be generated, no secure inner relationship with constant and developing figures, as opposed to the shifting insignificance of concrete ephemera and the unreliably receptive nature of his mother's mind.

The capacity to construct, internally, a room of one's own is based in the experience of having had "room to think"—an experience located, from the beginning, in the matrix of relations between mother and infant. As we have seen, Bion describes thinking as a function that, initially, the mother's internal capacities perform for the baby—drawing on her being able to experience the nature of her infant's passions, storms, and terrors unconsciously as well as consciously. In good circumstances, she is able, in a state of rêverie, to take in communications that the infant, himself, is not yet able to think about or understand. In making emotional sense of them, she enables the baby slowly to acquire the internal resources to process experience himself and thereby to render it meaningful. This capacity to "hold" or "contain" the baby's states of mind is dependent, as we have seen, on the mother being able to be continent and cognisant of her own mental states, neither intruding them into her infant nor presenting an unreceptive surface to the infant's projections and need to communicate.

Central to Bion's contribution was the notion that the vicissitudes of embryonic thought lie at the heart of psychic development. The essential question, as we saw in chapter 5, becomes that of what kind of thinking is going on and how it links to emotional, by contrast with merely cognitive, processes. In *Learning from Experience*, building on Freud and Klein, Bion added to the more familiar conflict between Love and Hate that between Knowledge (or the desire to know and understand) and an aversion to knowing and understanding, as fundamental to the personality's capacity to grow. It is in the course of adolescence that the battle between L, H, and K on the one hand, and their converse—the negative grid of –L, –H, and –K—on the other are often violently, and, in terms of the ultimate outcome for the personality, crucially fought. For learning about oneself can, as we have seen, be a very painful process. It is the capacity to think about emotional experiences, to engage with them, suffer—and bear—them, that feeds the mind and promotes growth—a capacity constantly opposed by intolerance of fear, of frustration, and of the pain of emotions. At the root of the distinction is, crucially, the contrast between cleverness and wisdom. In Tom's case, this was a distinction that he seemed to recognize: he was "clever" enough to pass his A-levels at 17 but not, at this stage, he realized, wise enough to do a degree in English. Instead of applying to university, he had taken off, for two years, into a kind of London underworld of drink and motorbikes, financed by occasional labouring jobs.

In essence, the process of acquiring a mind of one's own involves the shedding of defensive, look-alike characteristics (abandoning adhesive modes)—moving away from projective identification would be a way of describing it—and engaging with one's own felt experience by way of more introjective capacities. He had realized that he had to take off the "mantle" of his "beetle-self", as Simon put it (chapter 6), and learn to live with the pain of his vulnerable self. Simon, as we saw, was all too aware of his tendency, when venturing out of his comfort zone, to draw back into his shell of cleverness. As Shakespeare so beautifully put it in *Venus and Adonis*:

> Or as the snail, whose tender horns being hit,
> Shrinks backward in his shelly cave with pain,
> And, there all smothered up, in shade doth sit,
> Long after fearing to creep forth again.
>
> (ll. 1033–1038)

Growing up at this stage of life needs immense courage, and many youngsters feel completely unhoused. Introjective identification is a process that, over time, enables the baby or patient to acquire the capacity to take in and then draw on supportive and loving figures and experiences that safeguard, protect, and encourage the growing personality.

It is important to dwell for a moment on the specificity of the kind of introjective process being described. The process drawn on here could be said to lie at the core of development, as recounted in Kleinian and post-Kleinian thinking. A difference has to be established between the all too readily made, indeed ready-made, identifications—on-the-spot ones (especially in adolescence)—with unhelpful internal or external figures and dubious parts of the self. This rather "snatched" sense of identity is in contrast to a much more positive kind, one with the qualities and functions of a helpful figure or figures, and particularly those with some sense of an internal, mature parental couple, whatever the external reality. Meltzer (1978) suggested that this latter kind of identification, on which the adult part of the personality is premised, is resourced by truth-telling as a mode and by sincerity as an emotional stance. He has called introjection "the most important and most mysterious concept in psychoanalysis" (p. 459). It is marked by a capacity to bear uncertainty and not knowing, by contrast with "irritable reaching after fact and reason"—as Keats describes it in what he called "Negative Capability" (letter, 21 December 1817, in Gittings, 1970, p. 43) and which Bion drew on extensively. It distinguishes what it means really to be grown up from the predominantly adhesive and projective states that tend to characterize adolescent struggles, in particular, and may, unconsciously, masquerade as "grown-up". It is the phenomenology of this mode of introjective identification that may help in thinking about Tom's coming-to-be himself, or coming-to-have a mind/room of his own.

Early on in his therapy, dream images of different houses and rooms in the process of being built or decorated permeated Tom's sessions in a fascinating way. During his mid-adolescent years, he had had many jobs, as a casual builder, painter, and labourer. His ever-changing dream experiences of these spaces charted his relationship to the therapy and to me: by turn, spoiling with shoddy work; trying to cut corners and get away with it; overcharging; undercharging; desperately trying to make progress yet finding himself delaying or malingering; blaming bad work on other workmen; taking responsibility for mistakes; discovering false walls with a succession of hidden rooms still to be worked on; spilling paint and destroying the carpet; staining; repairing, and so on.

A brief, early dream, already quoted in chapter 5, encapsulates his ongoing struggle in the transference to experience me in terms that Bion might regard as a "thinking breast", one that could offer the mental and emotional structure that Tom needed in order to begin developing.

> I was trying to play tennis on an indoor court of which one of the walls was missing. Every time I threw the ball up to serve, it hit an unnaturally low ceiling and bounced back at me prematurely, making it impossible to set the ball in play.

This dream, and others like it, would seem to describe a very early experience in which Tom's having a containing structure at home with his mother was felt to be alarmingly fragile. So too in the transference, I was felt either to be unwilling or unable to take in his communications. Yet were I to do so, he believed, I would be put in danger of being driven mad by them, in just the way that he feared his mother had been incapable of withstanding the toxicity or the supposed erotic excitement of his impulses and projections. We might conjecture that, as a baby, each time he attempted to project his feelings in the hope that, once received, the process of projection and introjection might be set in play, a blank-wall-eyed expression in his mother's face and mind (the unnaturally low ceiling) prematurely bounced his feelings back at him, leaving him confused both as to the meaning of his experience and as to the disjunction between what he thought his eyes could see in his mother's face (or did they?) and the ugly and empty feelings that he was left with. Put another way, perhaps the unnaturally low ceiling prevented Tom discovering that something fundamental *was* missing and that if he were to succeed in serving something up and actually getting it across the net and into the far court of his mother's awareness, that "something" would end up in outer space. How could he construe the meaning of the inside from the contours of the outside? One defensive manoeuvre was to become, literally, confused, so attached to this or that narcissistic identification that he was in a chronic muddle about the boundary between his mind and the figure to whom he was attached, between internal and external, self and other.

The adhesive qualities of the room/womb that he had constructed for himself externally seemed a very accurate representation of his internal state too. Lacking a psychic container, he had resorted to two-dimensionality—to the sort of skin-container described by Bion (1962a) and Esther Bick (1968) in the absence of a sense of three-dimensionality—an internal place where emotions might be put. His unsatisfactory early experiences seemed to have left him completely unhoused mentally and emotionally, wholly ill-equipped to take the necessary developmental steps towards the acquisition of his own identity. Instead, he had settled for someone who resembled a self, but who functioned more as "a cardboard cut-out figure" (his own term) than as a fully-dimensional person. Tom described himself as forever propping up such a figure in front of himself, changing the appearance according to which group he was with at the time, an ever-shifting appearance of an identity. A scavenger himself, he assumed that others were too. "I open the door of my personality and let everyone in to take what they find, different things for each of them. But really, whatever the outside looks like, the inside is empty." He spoke with uncharacteristic sadness, coherence, and insight at this moment. He felt himself to be but a series of surfaces with no substance at all.

By the end of the first year of therapy, Tom was starting to apprehend (with fear and trepidation) the meaning of beginning to think, both the nature of the process and the risk that it posed to him. Just before the summer break, he had the first of his train dreams:

> I was at an underground station where the line was about to take a sort of loop. I was not sure whether to get on the train there, or to catch it on the way back.

Tom started his journey to the clinic on the Piccadilly Line, and the "underground" comings and goings were recurrent features of his dreams, particularly in terms of expressing his orientation to me and the work. Tom's immediate thought about the dream was that it had something to do with his travelling to Heathrow Airport the following day to go abroad for a holiday. There is, indeed, a loop in the line between terminals. His dream-predicament seemed to be to do with the danger of maintaining a train of thought in my absence (i.e., without me to hold his mental states and think with him). If he kept me in mind as a continuation of his treatment, he would be having to keep his loopy-self in mind, with the danger of this driving him round the bend. Would it be better, perhaps, to cut off completely and simply to get back on the train again on the way home? Or did this dream represent the possibility of maintaining mental continuity in my absence? I rather suspected that "going on thinking" without a container present and available to hold the emotionality and render it bearable threatened him, at this point, with madness.

Some time before this, there had been a dream-image of bodies on a train track, with the implication, as we examined it, that "laying things on the line"—managing, honestly, to identify them, to "think" them, to know them and name them—was death-dealing: the kind of death that, in fact, is a necessary part of any psychological birth. This was the measure of risk involved in the inception of the thinking process. It was one that, at the time, he hardly dared take. Indeed for several months after that dream, Tom withdrew into obsessive sexual ruminations, feeling that he had thoughts about which he dared not think. The "train of thought" metaphor was ambiguous: it expressed the capacity to sustain a thinking process in a creative and developmental mode, and also a notion of being trammelled, linear, and therefore limited to a narrative, a "then, and then, and then", mode.

Tom's emergence, shortly before the summer break, from this rather mindless state was heralded by a dream of which the content, together with the nature of the responses to my comments, demonstrated both his struggle to be born as a "thinking being" and his aversion to it:

> *I was experiencing a kind of sickening pressure, a panic about having to make sense of something in a very short time. I was trying to write, but there was not enough time to get whatever it was down. I was unable to order things properly. I knew there were thoughts but I couldn't think them, could not give them shape or substance. Gradually it became clear that what I was trying to write about was the discovery of a man's body which had been confined in a wall and was being dug out. Astonishingly, the man was still alive. The facts seemed to indicate that there was a question of usurping—someone had taken the man's place in life, operating as some kind of peasant, revolutionary hero. The discovery that the man was still alive was going on in the very process of trying to think about it, and write about it—hence the confusion.*

I suggested that the struggle to write (i.e., to articulate the process symbolically and thus to give it meaning) might describe the struggle to think about the experience of being dug out of his walled-up mentality and emotionally fragile identity (just alive), one that had been usurped long ago by, in his case, look-alike "identities", grandiose fantasies, not unlike his early adolescent daydreams of undifferentiated heroics, whether as part of the SAS or of some far-flung revolutionary cause. Coming alive would mean not so much a fantasied revolution but a real one, signalled by catastrophic anxiety. Pressurized by the impending break, he felt panicked by not having enough time with me to think things out and make sense of his experience.

My talking in these terms first evoked doubt in him about whether his dream narrative was true—that is, as he had dreamed it or as he had described it. "Maybe it wasn't like that?" It then aroused a violent impulse to say something dismissive and spiteful to me and, following that, to reach back towards me with a violent, strangling hand. The final destructive impulse felt to him like the urge, at times enacted as a child, to break up and stamp on his precious toys before his mother's horrified eyes—wanting to cut off and strangle my speech (the helping hand that is being refused) and break my thoughts into meaningless fragments. It was the impulse to destroy something he deeply cared for, I suggested to him. Nodding tearfully, he said, "I *am* worried about the break." Though long walled-up, the "real" self was alive, but being in contact with that self, that identity, rather than usurping it with heroic imitations, threatened disintegration. The fear of dependency, separation, and loss simply felt too overwhelming. Hamlet-like, he attempted to disorder or dismantle his thoughts through a range of moves, from doubting the analysis, amounting to falsification of the original narrative (perhaps it wasn't true), to cynicism, and eventually to destructive enactment.

A further dream, around the same time, described a similar process, one that was often to be repeated in the sessions themselves. Tom would struggle towards an experience of a thinking container of meaning in his relationship with me, only to leave it immediately, unable to stay with the experience itself.

> *I reluctantly left behind a group of my mates* [male, pub-drinking, biker friends]. *I travelled up a mountain on a steep railway-track with a female companion. Quite high up it became colder and I noticed a beautiful house. I wondered how it could have been constructed, how building materials could have been carried up there. Briefly I seemed to be in the house itself, wandering around its spacious rooms, thinking about its structure and the fact that it seemed similar both to the house of my mother and stepfather, and also to that of my dad and his partner. I wished that the house was my own, or that I could have such a home. The next moment I found myself alone back in the train, descending now, and finding myself with one of my pub mates, who told me that I had won a $64,000 quiz prize. I got very excited and waved the cheque around. On closer inspection, however, I became unsure as to whether the cheque was or was not for $64,000, perhaps it was $600, or even $60, or maybe for nothing at all.*

The dream was typical of holiday-break dreams to come. It graphically described the central importance of the comings and goings to the sessions, by train. It also described a recognition of the extreme difficulty of staying in the house/session/mind itself—the construction of which had so captured his imagination. Having left behind his group-orientated, posturing, anti-developmental self, at the bottom of the hill, the journey towards the psychic container takes him up, in the company of a female companion, to a place that he expects to be colder but also, perhaps, brighter and clearer. He can appreciate the structural qualities of the analytic/house/mind and the evidence of its inner workings. Once in the house, however, he almost immediately finds himself going down again, this time alone, suggesting the danger of staying with a creative engagement with a different structure of thinking rather than succumbing to an impulse to possess that house/structure, to imitate it, or merely to envy it. This sets him back on a downhill track. Unable to bear the frustration of not daring to have it, he finds that he has already lost the good experience. He is back on the train, leaving the house behind. His state of mind degenerates further into the manic grandiosity of hitting the analytic jackpot: "winning" an answer to the $64,000 question, which would constitute a Eureka-type breakthrough experience (often quite consciously and explicitly longed for), without the hard work of sustaining the treatment and the pain of dependency and separation.

As soon as he had an inkling in the dream that there existed a house/mind that had an internal structure, one that had to be worked upon and was linked, somehow, with a parental function, and to me as therapist, he began to think about how to construct such a building himself. But without yet having understood or experienced much of a sense of external or internal parenting—of parents who could be allowed to work together for his welfare—he could not sustain it and gave way to envy and idealization. He certainly admires the house, internally supported, as it is, by paternal and maternal structures, but he is not able to respond to it or to stay with it. He is left with an impoverished conceptual framework. He enquires no further but moves back down the mountain where he attempts to master feelings triumphantly by winning a jackpot, only to be left with doubts as to whether he can trust his senses and thus, finally, with feelings of emptiness and meaninglessness. The delusion of being the "winner" puts him back in a state of confusion.

It will be noted that the extensive travelling to and from the house/mind, akin, perhaps, to a "room of one's own", still takes up most of his emotional energy. The time actually spent in the house is very brief and scarcely connected to the journey. Nonetheless, I think that the house on the mountain does, again, represent the "apprehension" of a thinking process, the beauty of which is inseparable from the anxiety and the hard work of constructing it in the inclement conditions of the mind's struggle to change. There may certainly be some idealization of the house too, but I rather think that the dream indicates something of the perception of the truth on the one hand, and the urge to distort it on the other; the step-by-step process of a striving towards truthfulness (K) and the forces that are mobilized to counteract that (–K), the forces that distort incipient thought—in this case, envy, idealization, omnipotence, and self-deception.

To illustrate how Tom approached a particular developmental hurdle, one that so frequently proves the site of adolescent torment and breakdown—taking his final university exams—we must move forward two years. He was understandably very anxious about these exams, for during mocks he had got into a manic and persecuted state in which he had been unable to work and had had to ask for a deferment. It had seemed as if his recently acquired capacity to think things out and to write essays was feared to be of a projective and imitative kind (mainly in relation to me and a much admired tutor), and not one based on stable internal resources. He had, at that point, been granted a time extension. Relieved of external pressure, the world had regained more ordinary proportions. But little light had been shed on the source of Tom's extreme panic. It felt as if issues had been shelved rather than resolved. Now, with finals looming, the same already familiar disturbances again alerted us to impending danger. Tom had become much more articulate and clear-thinking about his experiences. He described his increasingly persecutory state of mind very graphically: his sense of total isolation in a corrupt and destructive world—a world in which it was vouchsafed to very few to share his nihilistic visions, probably, he thought, only to Ken Kesey, Doris Lessing, and possibly Anthony Burgess. His ability to think or to concentrate again became minimal, and he lay locked in a panic of fragmentation and despair. He felt impelled to take on the mantle of a prophet of doom, planning to preach in the Underground that the end of the world was at hand; to harangue the Adam Smith Society; to stick up posters and make speeches. The dreams that week made it clear that Tom felt he had lost his way and needed me to lead him, only to find himself terrified that the boundary between his mind and mine had broken down, that he had induced me to be both mad like his mother and brutal and tyrannical like his stepfather. At times he was able to articulate this clearly: "I am afraid that I will persuade you of my picture of the world—that it will get into you and you won't be able to tell me about what my mind is doing"—a mental fusion that left him without resource.

At the end of that week and the beginning of the next, it became possible to make some links between his exam panic and a number of hitherto unconscious determinants of his fear of success and his courting of failure. Two events prompted me to think about the degree of wilfulness and rage that were involved in Tom's seeming inability to bear being tested in this way. A phone call from his mother enquiring when his graduation would take place, so that she could arrange her holiday accordingly, prompted a furious outburst from him: "Graduation, there won't be a graduation." His mother, thinking unusually coherently and thoughtfully on this occasion, had to be brutally punished.

He then described a dream in which:

I was in a desperate panic about being late for a therapy session. In order to get to it, I had to cross a park where I kept being waylaid, having to walk round, or through, various women's houses and gardens which stood in my path.

This was the very park where he used to expose himself before his therapy began. It was a world of other versions of me, whom he regularly sexualized in his erotic fantasies, and which tended to divert him from reaching the therapist/me. It emerged that his cruel wish to intrude on, and upset me, by threats to exhibit himself carried with them the perverse gratification of believing me to be aroused by such urges—filled, in other words, with his sexual desires and therefore unable to think about his predicament. At the end of this turbulent and distressing session, he brought a memory of having been told that, when he was very little in his country of origin, his mother had gone away and he had had to walk in deep snow because his father's back was bad and he was too weak to carry his son. Tom seemed to feel, at this moment, utterly bereft of any parental holding, mental or physical, internal or external. His father was experienced as not being there even when his mother was absent. There was, at this point, no parent at all, even residually.

The sessions were now almost too painful to bear. His articulate raving about impending destruction was unstoppable, punctuated only by his howling, gasping, writhing, and sobbing, in an agony of, by turn, terror, rage, and despair. Every experience confirmed his delusory picture of the world and compounded his panic. Like Doris Lessing with *The Golden Notebook* (1962), he said, he was the only one who could see what was happening to the world. The knowledge and the isolation felt intolerable: the economic system was crushing people to pieces, draining them of any hope or finer feeling. His attacks on his stepfather for similarly crushing and depriving him became ferocious, as did his threats of physically exposing himself to me, in part as a means of controlling and punishing me for not preventing his deteriorating state. He berated his stepfather for the sadistic negativism shown to him in the past, for his constant belittling and underestimation of Tom, for his imputed glee at Tom's failures, and for his general arrogance and superiority. He blamed him for his own sense of overwhelming failure.

At the same time, his erotic fantasies about me were scarcely containable. His thinking became increasingly concrete. I misguidedly, but all too accurately, described him as "stripping" me of my analytic self on one occasion. Tom gasped in recognition. For that was exactly what he was doing—"stripping" me in his mind. So powerful was the externalization of the sexualizing, hating, blaming self that the "I", in terms of the first-person pronoun, would disappear altogether. Different parts of the self seemed to be at play, with no ego to control or adjudicate:

> Feel ill; have to go into College; take library books back; overdue; keep thinking could ring them; fine would be bigger; feel compelled to go in; lecture stylistics; don't have to do it; must go, must go; unnecessary; got enough war poets; got twenty pages of notes; should be able to do it. Only two thousand words; have to read another book; can't read; have to do four essays; three would do . . . get very distracted.

Tom shouted, groaned, thumped the couch. He became terrified of putting his feet down in case, as he acknowledged, he actually messed me up and defiled me with his dirt. In the fantasy of exposing his penis he wanted to enact his aggressive sexuality and to triumph over me—his mind becoming the capitalist machine grinding me into sexual shape at the expense of my being allowed to be my therapeutic self. Yet there were calmer moments. On one occasion, in response to a noise outside the consulting room, he moaned that he couldn't bear to think that anybody else in the world might have a claim on me. He wept as I spoke of the pain of separation and his jealousy of anyone else in my life. He was briefly in touch with more ordinary, painful oedipal feelings that hurt him so much. But his state of mind shifted again almost immediately, and he described how talk of loss and separation itself aroused his sexual feelings, "as if I want to be able to hold on to something and keep it".

To deny loss, I suggested, he fed the fantasy that by keeping me alive sexually he could retain the illusion of keeping control over me. In response, he said after a pause that the word "porridge" had come to mind—he didn't know why. Puzzled, I waited. After a few moments, he recalled a very early memory, before he was 4 years old, he thought. He wouldn't eat his porridge. His mother said he could not have chocolate from the van unless he ate his porridge all up (the arrival of the chocolate-van was a very special event in his life since, at that time, they lived in a remote part of the country, and the van came round only once a fortnight). "I shrieked and shrieked, I couldn't believe that she could do that. . . . It seems such a vivid memory, maybe an emotional state more than anything else", he said. I suggested that it felt so cruel of me to offer the nourishing porridge/sessions and deprive him of the sweets he wanted—the eroticized moments that gave him power to deny separation. "You don't want porridge", I said. He nodded tearfully.

This recognition/acknowledgement of the extent to which he sought, or courted, mental poison (eroticized chocolate), rather than the truth of nourishing mental food, initiated an important shift that had a deep impact on Tom. Despite the pain, he slowly began to turn away from evasion, denial, and sexualization and towards truthfulness. He had, as in the previous year, requested a letter from the clinic to his college tutor, asking for a deferment of his exams, in mitigation, as he was attending the clinic for intensive therapy and was under stress. In the context of wanting a second letter, the issue now posed itself as follows: perhaps it was not so much a question of whether or not the college would believe him but, rather, one of whether he could believe himself. Was it really true that he could not sit the exams, or was he trying to enlist the clinic, and me, in a collusive manoeuvre to divert attention from other possible motives for not sitting them with his contemporaries and for being a special case instead? Was he trying to get the clinic, and me, to combine as a parental couple who were prepared to turn a blind eye and become complicit in a lie? If he succeeded in a deferment, he would manage not only to deny his mother the gratification of a graduation day, but also to spite my efforts to support his struggling, thinking self.

It became clear that, if Tom couldn't achieve a brilliant pass, he would have dramatically to incapacitate himself by doing badly. He could thus get the better of me as representing the malign internal couple either by being a success or by being a failure. The latter was a surer bet, rendered more attractive by the fear of losing me should he succeed. For what became increasingly apparent was that an aspect of his panic was lodged in an anxiety that I would mistake prowess in exam-passing for mental health, so that in doing well he would be hastening the end of his treatment. That thought was literally unthinkable. Even a whiff of it would stimulate an explosion of anxiety, expressed through sexualized fantasy and acting out elsewhere.

Taking exams represented deep-seated terrors about the nature of his internal relationships, involving blame, hatred, triumph, spite, and denial. Tom was faced with a crisis of unconscious indecision, one in which his thinking capacities became co-opted by a manic and massive externalization of his internal states, which then took over not only the world but also, in fantasy, the mind—my mind, that which had more recently enabled him to hold the boundary between inside and outside reasonably intact. My insistence on the spite and vengefulness that lay behind the apparent incapacity (for which he felt he deserved sympathy and support) was experienced as "running him to ground"—a painful but necessary process leading to a position from which he felt there was no escape. He could then make contact with the possibility of a more benign parental holding that was experienced as having his interests genuinely at heart. He began to calm down, to put aside his twenty pages of notes and settle for two ordinary, rather than brilliant, essays.

He brought the following dream to the next session (unusually, he had been ten minutes late the previous day):

> I was supposed to be meet a friend, Nick. I was meant to be doing a painting-and-decorating job with him on a house some distance away. Nick had a van and was going to drive us both to the house. I was late and was anxious, and worried about letting Nick down. I then realized that not only was I late, but I had left my tools behind, so there was a further delay while Nick drove me home to collect them. Contrary to my fears, Nick was tolerant and understanding of the delays and the extra time needed before we could get on with restoring the house.

The dream seemed to represent a figure who loans his supportive capacities to help decorate/restore the damaged internal structure, thus allowing Tom to fetch or to use his own "tools" for the task. A few weeks later, as his panic lessened still further and his capacity for study increased, a further "house" dream confirmed the changes that I felt were taking place. In this dream already cited in chapter 5, the house was no longer in the distance up a cold mountain, but present and reachable:

> I was in a house that was solid, well-built, and rather beautiful. I seemed to be staying with a group of friends, not my old drinking companions but college friends whom I did not yet know very well but whom I liked and who

seemed serious about what they were doing. Among them was a particular woman who had a name similar to yours, Margaret [someone who had often, in terms of looks, attitude, and qualities been associated with me]. The atmosphere was relaxed. I found that I was unusually unstressed, able to talk, to be myself. At one point I was riding a motorcycle. I stopped to fix an unsafe chain with one of my friends.

He realized, he interjected, that this was very different from his early motorbike dreams and, indeed, experiences, which had tended to be reckless and often rather out of control. His bikes were constantly in need of repair, and he had a tendency to put his own life, and that of others, at risk. By contrast, he thought that in this dream he felt he had control—"I don't mean in a bad way but I'm somehow able to pursue my own endeavours. It was a good feeling, sort of hopeful. I think maybe I'll come through all this." He then completed his account of the dream:

I spent the night in the house alone, my companions seemed to have gone elsewhere. In the morning, I discovered that the young woman had also spent the night in the house, but without my knowledge. I wished that I had known that she had stayed, but I also felt very good that she was somehow there with me, there whether I knew it or not.

He acknowledged that this containing-house felt much more solid than those of earlier dreams and that he felt at ease with the figures inside. He had a sense that he was building a stronger relationship with them, but also that they were themselves developing and changing. The motorbike-riding had more the feel of self-expression and individual spontaneity than of self-destruction and gang activity. But perhaps most important and illuminating of all was the description of the Margaret/me figure, somehow there with him, whether he was aware of her or not, present internally as a companion and resource "in the mind".

The dream impressed me by the clarity with which it conveyed a particular aspect of the mysterious process of introjection and introjective identification. Having recounted it, Tom said he wanted to thank me, to express gratitude. His saying this immediately put him in mind of his attempts to make his mother happy in the past—both her laughter at his antics but also, and he spoke with sudden, anguished tears, her indifference: when depressed she was unable to respond to him. "My sense of life just drained away", he sobbed. The impact of his despair at ever being able to repair that external mother was very powerful in the room.

This glimpse of a capacity to give and receive happiness seemed inseparable from his mourning over, and slow resignation to, a damaged external mother whom he could not repair, however deeply, or at times omnipotently, he wished so to do. Perhaps his greed and guilt were more bearable because of a strengthened sense of an internal resource, present irrespective of actual reflection or conscious attention. This recognition of aspiration and humility seemed linked to a mode of identification that was much more introjective than projective and was a fine testament to his therapeutic efforts genuinely and successfully to "grow".

Tom's long struggle to find, and establish, a mind of his own, a properly "housed" mind, was impressive. The increasing solidity of his internal structure was confirmed, both in his dreams and in his relationship with me, with friends, and with his fellow students. Early on he could hardly have been said to have a mind of his own at all, not one that could be described as carrying any consistent sense of identity. Rather, he had got through life by adopting a series of off-the-peg, look-alike selves of a very two-dimensional kind and so typical of the adolescent predicament. The tennis-court area where he had been trying to play out his life had had no fourth wall at all and had left him prey to psychotic anxieties and terrors of total impotence, emptiness, and exposure. As his sense of having been walled-up and walled-in all his life increased, and with it the recognition of his need for a protective and containing external and internal space, he began to recognize the existence of the kind of structure that he had so much wanted. It had hitherto seemed very far away and unavailable, perhaps hardly there at all—the house on the mountain.

His perverse fantasies and activities and his manic omnipotence, though themselves addictive and utterly unsatisfying, had functioned as defences against his experiences of loss and abandonment and of the hatred, desolation, and manic triumph that those absences stirred in him. The perversity militated against the capacity to think for himself (or, indeed, often at all), to be small, dependent, to own his feelings. He found staying on the track of the regular sessions very difficult, and repeatedly he slipped over the borderline.

Being "run to ground" by me, again and again, felt like a relief to Tom, despite his resistance to the "porridge". Furious, frustrated, and often desperate that his efforts to seduce me, mentally or physically, seemed always doomed to fail, he nonetheless slowly appreciated the protective nature of the various boundaries—of the clinic, the session times, the consulting room, and my mind itself and its capacity to bear both his attacks and his boundarylessness. Although still wildly jealous, he also, occasionally, felt reassured by thoughts of my having a partner and children—having a life from parts of which he was necessarily excluded. He even felt that, at times, the fantasized partnership helped me to help him. By this time, we could see that not only did he not have to restore the house all by himself—but that there was a solid structure that he could be inside because of a kind of confidence that there was also such a structure now present inside himself, whether or not he was always aware of it, and however much work still needed to be done on it.

It would be gratifying to end this chapter on a "happy-ever-after" note, but a characteristic of beginning to establish an identity is that it is beset by all the fiends and demons that lurk in the shadows of potential change, or of progression out of well-tried, albeit painful, anti-developmental modes: the nooks and crannies, in Tom's case, of dissimulation, perversion, and addiction to mindless states.

It is also a characteristic of working with adolescents that any hopeful notion, on the part of the therapist, of a "happy-ever-after" state must be resisted. For when the becoming-established identity is so recent and so fragile, extra stress can, at any moment, precipitate the emergence, or, rather, resurgence, of states of mind that we might wish, or have believed, to belong to the past. To work with this age group is often to work on the border: one learns the importance of eschewing notions that we might ever be "in the clear".

The convergence of a number of factors presented renewed threats to the stability of Tom's sense of being contained internally. As the Easter break from analysis approached, so did his final exams, heralding the end of the structure of the university course. All this also coincided with having to leave his actual "room" (the house was being sold), as well as the breaking-up of a friendship with a college student that he had hoped might deepen. He had been seeking to care for this young woman, to support and protect her from her own neurotic difficulties, and to rescue himself from the dangers of his eroticization and sexual perversion.

The chapter, therefore, concludes on this more uncertain note because such a note encapsulates something of the experience of working with this age group—the difficulty of bearing the fact that there is no certainty, that mental states are always in flux, but that, nonetheless, the carrying of hope is something that the therapist may have to sustain, at times alone and despite the negative odds. Tom dreamt that:

> I was standing on a platform waiting for a train that would take me to a station where I was going to meet Nick who would help me to move house. As before, I felt irritated and worried that Nick would be upset with me for being late. Then suddenly on the far line, a succession, almost a procession, of strange trains passed by—old Underground trains, bizarrely-decorated old steam engines, all sorts of extraordinary and exotic locomotives. People on the platform began to clap. I joined in, clapping too, as if for a liberating army. Eventually my train arrived. I later found Nick and his young daughter waiting for me at the designated station. I immediately became struck by the beauty of the landscape that I had been passing through—not at all as I had remembered it, but cradled in lovely hills, with vague mists, as in a Chinese painting, and, most important of all, in sight of the sea. To my astonishment and perplexity, I found myself in a wonderful seascape. I had remembered a lake in the area but not the sea.

Tom's immediate thought was that the bizarre trains were on the line that was normally the route towards the clinic—one where the direct trains rushed through on the far platform—that is, the line leading towards me. He would, he thought, join one such train further up the line. (It is perhaps, significant that he had been uncharacteristically late for a number of sessions prior to this dream.)

The dream seemed to me to describe a state of mind in which a very particular kind of delay occurred, a delay in getting to me, as with the Nick figure of the previous dream, to help him to move and settle into a different mind/room/house. It becomes clear that Tom is still, at times, too attached to the old trains of thought, bizarre ones (which would seem to have not been entirely superseded by the more direct line). In the dream these "trains" still command his attention, and he finds himself applauding them. He is worried about being late, but cannot quite admit that it is those very trains that, far from liberating the warring parts of himself, are in fact delaying his capacity to move on. It looks as though there is a situation in which he delays the process of separation and change, because that process involves the oedipal struggle of working with the reality of me as part of a parental couple, perhaps with a child

(Nick and his daughter) standing by to help him. Possibly, he hangs on to his old trains of thought as a way of putting off this separation. As a consequence, when he does find something good, he idealizes it—"a wonderful seascape". That is where the danger lies, and will surely do so for some time—in slipping back to a mode of functioning in which the pain of loss is denied in favour of elevating the "special" status of his old ways. This defensive mode holds up the move from that early adhesive room to a room of his own. Under the stress of his actual, external containing structures having to give way and of multiple losses he was having to sustain, understandably Tom shifts back, probably only temporarily, into more familiar, painful, yet fleetingly gratifying states.

Despite these final words of caution, one cannot but feel hopeful for Tom. Virginia Woolf would have been gratified, but not surprised, that with "a mind of one's own", indeed come renewed creative capacities. Tom had begun to write—plays and short stories, ones that he felt proud of and were admired by his fellow students and tutors. He passed his finals and was accepted for the first job he applied for as a social worker with a speciality in working with children.

Slowly, he started to experience the possibility of intimacy and to distinguish between the excitement of his omnipotent, masturbatory experiences on the one hand, and genuine emotion on the other—emotion that put him in touch with his dependency, his littleness, guilt, remorse, and fears of loss. Lacking the sense of an internal parental couple who might have been creatively concerned with his welfare, he had hitherto sought to elide the differentiation between excitement and feeling—attacking and destroying the latter with his perverse states of mind and activities. My conjecture was that Tom's developing a mind of his own was based in his increasing dependence on the capacity to recognize, in the analytic process, proper parental functions with his needs at heart; able to know the difference between a true struggle towards intense and honest links of relatedness and the distortion and perversion of those links. The struggle to sort out the distinction between, on the one hand, a genuinely reparative attitude to the various dream-rooms and houses, and a papering-over-the-cracks mentality, on the other, provided a leitmotif throughout the therapeutic work.

Tom's own writing would seem to represent a capacity to begin to set aside life-long grievances against a tyrannical stepfather, in favour of the introjection of a creative paternal figure linked, surely, to his natural artist/writer father. Tom's support and concern for the fragilities of a new-found girlfriend also suggest a burgeoning capacity to care for his damaged internal mother, rather than to berate, blame, or manically to entertain her.

What Virginia Woolf (1929) tells us she derived from reading *King Lear* or *Emma* or Proust's *À la Recherche du Temps Perdu* is part of the aesthetic experience that embeds psychoanalysis in the artistic tradition. Towards the end of *A Room of One's Own*, she writes:

> . . . one sees more intensely afterwards; the world seems bared of its covering and given an intenser life. Those are the enviable people who live at enmity with unreality; and those are the pitiable who are knocked on the head by the thing done without knowing or caring. So that when I ask you to earn money and have a room of your own, I am asking you to live in the presence of reality, an invigorating life, it would appear, whether one can impart it or not. [1929, pp. 108–109]

Note

An earlier version of this chapter was published in D. Anastasopoulos, E. Laylou-Lignos, & M. Waddell (Eds.), *Psychoanalytic Psychotherapy of the Severely Disturbed Adolescent* (London: Karnac, 1999).

CHAPTER TEN

Narcissism—an adolescent disorder?

No book on adolescence would be complete without a chapter on narcissism. Indeed, that chapter should perhaps be at the heart of such a book. For the phenomenon is one that is invoked especially often in relation to this age group. Yet, as we shall see, the essential fluidity of the adolescent organization, its culture of experiment and self-exploration, its rootedness in transition, and, despite all the usually glaring and obvious signs to the contrary, its developmental potential, tell a different story.

As we saw in chapter 1, Freud, in his *Three Essays on the Theory of Sexuality* (1905d), nominates adolescence as one of the crucial developmental phases in the human life cycle. Yet, fifty-two years later his daughter Anna was to refer to it as a "neglected period", "a step-child where analytical thinking is concerned" (A. Freud, 1958, p. 255). Her own suggestion as to why this should be so was that after her father's "discovery" of infantile sexuality, adolescence was, in a sense, demoted. In the *Three Essays* it is described as the time when changes set in that give infantile sexual life its final, normal shape. The tripartite achievement of this final shape was, as already stated, the crystallization of sexual identity; the finding of a sexual object; and the bringing together of the two main stems of sexuality—the sensual and the tender. There was nothing of the contemporary sense of adolescence as performing a major developmental task: that of providing a crucial period for the restructuring and final organization of the personality. My own sense is that, despite the impact of the developmentally orientated thinking of, in particular, those working with children since the 1920s, adolescence is, even now, seldom focused on as a source of interest or enlightenment about the nature of human development. Nowhere is this more definitively so than in the complex and theoretically contentious area of narcissism.

Prima facie, the multifarious presentations of the characteristically self-orientated and self-preoccupied adolescent attitude and behaviour could hardly be more "narcissistic" in flavour and tone, nor, indeed, in the flagrancy of exhibitionistic and selfish activities and affect, whether manic, destructive, depressed, obsessive, perfectionist, and so forth. In less superficial ways, it could also be argued that the classic manifestations of adolescent angst and disturbance correspond, in quite detailed and specific terms, as we shall see, to some of the unconscious mechanisms and modes of defence that are, with respect to narcissism, central to the classic psychoanalytic descriptive canon. And yet, in what I shall be describing as the specificity of adolescent states of mind, we have to be asking whether these mechanisms and modes of defence really are so pathological. Could it be that, where the adolescent process is concerned, we may need to focus, perhaps surprisingly, on characteristics that could, at a stretch, be regarded as developmental and not anti-developmental—the line between the two always being extremely hard to draw with any confidence.

The place of narcissism in adolescence can be better understood precisely by examining not just its presentation, but its purpose and function in the adolescent mind—a mind that, as we have seen, is at once fluctuating, concrete, self-deceiving, and, above all, turbulent in ways that, at other stages of life, would be straightforwardly recognizable as clinically disturbed. To some extent, they *are* recognizable and describable as so being, and yet the similarities are also, in some quite elusive sense, virtual. We have also explored how the "agitation of inexperience" of this age group inevitably locates its inhabitants somewhere between their infantile past and the possibility of a mature adult future. More specifically, they are caught, uncomfortably, "betwixt the unsettling of their latency period and their settling into adult life" (Meltzer, 1973a, p. 51). Being caught in this way leaves most of them, in one way or another, temporarily stranded, as if perched on some kind of raft in the tempestuous waters of unfulfilled need, unfamiliar sexual desire, unwarranted aggression, and felt deprivation; in a sea of what seem like unrealizable aspirations and, most significantly, all too real relinquishments and losses—losses, for example, of the known childhood-self with its known family structures. Yet in most, too, underneath all this there remains a striving towards independence, growth, and development, towards intimacy and the potential satisfactions of maturity. As Irma Brenman Pick so rightly puts it, "The powerful forces and pervasive defences of adolescence may disturb or interfere with further growth; [but] they are also forces which make for the charm, vitality, enthusiasm and development of adolescents" (Brenman Pick, 1988, p. 146).

It is thus an age group, especially where narcissism is concerned, that needs to be accorded its own particularity of reference and detail in order properly to trace and understand how the "classic" narcissistic mechanisms, whether thought to be primary or defensive, may, in any one case, be being deployed and exhibited to the detriment of the personality, and where, by contrast, what looks like the pure culture of narcissistic splitting and projection is actually a form of exploration, of temporizing, and of discovery—and thus much more in the service of development than it may appear to be.

In significant ways, the predicament of the adolescent state perfectly accords with post-Kleinian theory of what constitutes narcissistic pathology. It has all the characteristics of the adult "narcissistic" or pathological organizations described by Rosenfeld (1971), Steiner (1987), O'Shaughnessy (1979), Sohn (1985), Rey (1979), and others. Yet its essential fluidity, its culture of experiment and self-exploration, its rootedness in transition, and—despite all the usually glaring and obvious signs to the contrary—its developmental potential tell a different story. For these characteristics mark it out as a period that can eventuate, as Freud suggested, in the emergence of a sense of sexual identity and the bringing together of the sensual and the tender in a hard-won relationship that can bear the otherness of the other.

The point is that that emergence is predicated on the capacity for separateness and individuation, which is, in turn, dependent on the necessary and successful working through of narcissistically structured relationships, both within the self and in relation to the outside world. When this fundamental developmental shift cannot, for whatever reason, be made, the potential richness and creativity of the personality will be arrested, leaving it a prey to the more established pathology we encounter in adult clinical practice. Few have stated this shift more evocatively than George Eliot in *Middlemarch*. She described the painful recognition on the part of one of the central characters, Dorothea, of the contrast between those who take "the world as an udder to feed their supreme selves" and those who can recognize that others have "an equivalent centre of self, whence the lights and shadows must always fall with a certain difference" (1872, p. 243). When the adolescent process runs reasonably smoothly and a degree of maturity is achieved, there is usually a shift from the first outlook to the second, from selfishness and self-regard to generosity, responsibility, and the capacity to think for oneself and to be aware of the needs of others, genuinely as others. The world is taken as an "udder" to feed the supreme and overvalued self because this illusion is less intrinsically painful than suffering the necessary relinquishments and manifold losses that attend these years; than having to recognize the implicit loneliness and pain of struggling with the otherness of the other; than bearing separateness and the fear of feeling alone, despite being apparently surrounded by friends.

The ability to make such a shift and the failure to do so are highly contingent on the kinds of internal and external factors that I am about to describe. But perhaps I should qualify the notion of failure here, because one very recognizable characteristic of the adolescent organization, which was certainly so in the case of Susan whom I shall be discussing, is the swiftness with which what *seem* to be deeply entrenched narcissistic structures may be modified or modulated in response to even quite small internal or external changes. So, too, what may seem like quite small external changes, minor illnesses, losses, disappointments, or failures may swiftly propel an adolescent into narcissistic states that are near psychotic in their intensity (see chapter 11).

Why this should be so for some and not for others carries no ready explanation, although, as so often, the roots in infancy can make for a likely foundation. While in obvious ways the mental mechanisms characterizing the paranoid-schizoid position—those of splitting, projection, omnipotence, and denial—could be said to be intrinsic to the adolescent organization, yet its very fluidity suggests that if such internally or externally generated forces are engageable with, and even assimilable into, the personality, they can be the prelude to insight, self-knowledge, and the capacity to bear the daily humiliations and sensed inadequacies that shadow these difficult years, and to bear them without excessive denial, retreat, flight, or defensive manoeuvre. What looks like a narcissistic disorder may be nearer to a defensive/self-protective, two-stage process of the projection of unfamiliar, unwanted, or unmanageable parts of the self, or, indeed, cherished and loving parts, to be followed, in time, and perhaps with help, by a painful re-owning of those projections—an intrinsic aspect of a personality-in-the-making.

This kind of developmental picture moves us a long way from the traditional economic concept of narcissism as a libidinal investment in the self and towards a position, especially important during adolescence, that is more to do with understanding the role, or purpose, of the narcissistic mechanisms and presentations and what has made them necessary (Lichtenstein, 1964, pp. 25–26). "Selfish, self-engrossed, and self-indulgent" may be a superficially accurate descriptive set of terms for many adolescents, but its judgementalism may miss the point, or certainly a point. Just as the Narcissus story can represent a young male figure, having rejected Echo, as pining away for love of his own reflection, we might also construe it, as have others, as Narcissus needing to bolster his self-esteem by seeking a relationship with someone who looks like himself. Could this not be with a mirror image that might restore a fragile self-conception, a kind of intensely experienced twinning relationship, serving as a defence against feelings of isolation, and possibly of smallness and humiliation?

Just such vulnerability clearly plays a central role in, for example, the characteristic adolescent dress code. Similarity is all important, difference can pose a serious threat. Freud's notion of the "narcissism of small differences" is relevant here. Nowhere is the clannish, or tribal, imperative to establish a sense of cohering identity in the face of intolerable uncertainties and fears of being left out more evident than in the rivalry, even enmity, that can be stirred up among and between adolescent groupings. Here the small differences of, for example, the lacing of trainers or the cut of hair or jeans can become emblems of allegiance, or the basis for fundamental hostilities, determining inclusion or exclusion and even, at its most extreme, life and death.

Pausanias actually did give an account of Narcissus as having lost his twin and as refinding her in his own reflection in the pool. As Maria Rhode (2004) puts it:

> Narcissus pined away and died when his reflection did not respond to him; he declared his love to it as if it were another person, and as though he were a child who could not yet recognise his own reflection in the mirror. From this perspective, it is not so much that self-love made him turn away from other people, as that his sense of identity was inadequately developed, leaving him without the necessary emotional equipment to sustain reciprocal relationships. [quoted in McGinley & Varchevker, 2010, p. 26]

How true this is of adolescents generally, and how clearly stated in Shakespeare's extraordinary poem *Venus and Adonis*. In the face of Venus's intense erotic longing and protracted attempts at impassioned seduction, the beautiful youth Adonis protests his unreadiness to enter upon a mature sexual relationship. He wants to be hunting with the lads; he is still a group boy, running with the pack. He defends his lack of responsiveness as follows:

> "Fair Queen", quoth he "if any love you owe me,
> Measure my strangeness with my unripe years;
> Before I know myself seek not to know me;
> No fisher but the ungrown fry forbears;
> The mellow plum doth fall, the green sticks fast,
> Or being early pluck'd is sour to taste."

[ll. 523–528]

The capacity to tolerate two of the central tasks of adolescence—those of separating and of managing difference without flight into narcissistic states of delusional sameness—is rooted in, though by no means determined by, the earliest possible exchanges between the baby and the primary caretaker, usually the mother. Disturbances, of whatever kind, in early object relationships—whether because of inconsistency of care on the mother's part or, as Bion (1962a) stresses, because of intolerance of frustration on the baby's part—almost inevitably lead to emotional disturbance, especially to fears about separateness, and a tendency for those fears to be defended against through various psychic mechanisms. Thus a narcissistic object choice—that is, one based on maintaining, through projective identifications, a link with those aspects of the self that have been lodged in the other—can function as a means of controlling that other, in order not to feel cut off from or abandoned by it, nor to feel excessively envious of it. Not only does such an object choice affect relationships in the external world, it also links with internal structures, in that the reinternalization of the projectively possessed object has an impact on the structure of the ego and superego (Segal, 1964).

The following brief example may clarify some of the foregoing. Susan, aged 18, was originally referred for three-times-weekly therapy because of her generally oppositional behaviour, towards her parents and teachers in particular; for her extreme envy of and hostility towards her younger sister; and for her feelings of intense self-hatred and her "black" moods, alternating anger with despair. She was not only a trouble to others, she had become deeply troubled about herself.

These emotional difficulties manifested themselves in a "wilful" refusal to study and in bouts of self-harm—mainly superficial cutting and scratching on her arms and thighs—and also, latterly, in her increasing obsession with the spots on her face. These so-called spots were imperceptible to all but herself. Yet her intense suffering over how disgusting she looked kept her at times housebound for many days. She was described as being "hell bent" on failing her exams—a characteristic that drew little sympathy and was regarded, rather, as but another example of her generally self-destructive behaviour. She described herself as feeling miserable, constantly aggrieved, envious, and furious with everyone: the world was against her, full of critical people who despised her, and so on. She feared and resented what she took to be her parents' judgemental attitude and unfairness—while, according to them, behaving in ways exquisitely honed to provoke them.

It could well have been, as so often, that in Susan's family—second-generation immigrants from a persecutory regime—there was indeed an especially strong commitment to the children's academic and social success. The family culture was one in which the father was necessarily absent for work and the mother tended to invest her own disappointed aspirations in her daughters, leaving them confused as to whose ambitions belonged to whom. I cite these details as possible factors in the situation, not as explanations.

A year into her treatment, Susan recounted the following dream, one that seemed to describe the internal predicament very precisely:

I found myself in a forest near a little wooden house. I was feeling sick and lying on the ground. Three revolting-looking, green-eyed witches appeared and I was convinced that they were going to hurt me. I lay very still, hoping that they wouldn't see me. They came right up to me. I was terrified, but, instead of doing something cruel, they seemed sympathetic to my being so ill and weak. They carried me inside the little house and put me to bed. They tucked me up and gently looked after me. I was amazed. They were so kind, more like fairy godmothers really. Witches aren't supposed to be like that. At one point I started to feel too warm and threw back the covers, partly to cool myself but mainly, to be honest, because I wanted to have the experience of the witches covering me up again. This happened many times.

Reflecting on the dream, Susan at first associated the witches with her three close friends, with whom she felt, by turn, competitive, excluded, and often both envious and jealous. She was constantly (and usually groundlessly) worried that they would leave her out, make her feel inadequate, or humiliate her. It would seem that her envious attacks on the three friends' caring capacities (standing, perhaps, both for her mother's care and for her three sessions every week) constantly turned her good figures into bad ones. She then re-internalized persecutory versions of these figures who became components of the sort of ego-destructive superego described by Bion (1962a), Britton (2003), and O'Shaughnessy (1999). As a consequence, she felt not only threatened by the bad part of her self, afraid that it, or they, would attack her in return, but also left with very little sense of the support and internal resources of a more hopeful, valued, and aspiring part. (It is not unusual for the representation of goodness to be broken up into pieces in a patient's mind, that is, into more than one aspect—often signifying the hostile tearing up, or breaking up, that has been going on in infantile unconscious phantasy.) Her therapist, whether as "witch" or "friend", suffered repeated attacks on any emergent links or potential understanding between them. So, too, her relatively coherent and well-intentioned group of friends were, at times, subjected to the virulence of Susan's verbal—sometimes physical—assaults. Such assaults had been playing an increasingly destructive and regressive role in her life, the more so, it appeared, as actual separation from school and family increasingly shadowed her horizon. As so often, a fear of being outside and on her own had instituted a lurch backwards at the point when leaving suddenly felt all too imminent.

In Susan's dream, we also find an explicit allusion to the witches of myths and fairy tales, suggesting that something primitively evil is afoot, and, quite specifically, in this case, to the three witches in *Macbeth* and their associations with murder and guilt. Susan made this association herself, commenting that she was studying *Macbeth* at school for A-level. It may be remembered that the witches' cauldron contains a ghastly recipe of an especially nasty kind, epitomizing the killing off of infantile possibility rather than the fostering of it:

> Pour in sow's blood that has eaten
> Her nine farrow; grease that's sweaten
> From the murderer's gibbet . . .
>
> [IV.1:64–66]

and

> Finger of birth-strangled babe
> Ditch-delivered by a drab.
>
> [IV.1: 30–11]

Although, consciously, Susan felt almost continuously persecuted by the outside world, the dream suggests that, unconsciously, she was beginning to be able to render in symbolic form some insight into her predicament: that the problem was not so much that she was being attacked by hostile figures of mean intent, but that those she cared about became transformed into something bad by her own persecutory anxiety and her own destructive impulses and took up residence in her internal world, where they maintained an ego-destructive hold over her. The witches in the dream, however, were much less malign than she had feared. On the contrary, they had actually had her good at heart, to the point that, in Susan's mind, they became idealized "fairy godmothers", whose good offices she wanted repeated over and over again. This last is an interesting detail, for it suggests something of the emotional bankruptcy of the idealized, as opposed to the good, object. Such an object offers less the kind of strength that can be introjected and identified with internally (thus modifying the "frightful fiend" within) than a more superficial form of reassurance, one constantly having to be repeated and renewed. As long as this is the case, the internal structure remains unmodified and little genuine development can take place.

Moreover, the fairy-tale/mythic setting suggests how basic and polarized, all good or all bad, are the feelings to be found there. They belong to primitive psychic processes of splitting and projection in which, under the sway of "green-eyed" destructive envy, a perverse transformation takes place in which fair becomes foul and foul fair (to pick up the witches' deadly chant). The baby self is then left bereft of friendly internal figures and in thrall to persecutory ones.

In her own view, Susan's difficulties were compounded by the fact that, at age 18, she had begun to develop some slight traces of acne on her face and her back, about which she was desperately self-conscious. She took aggressive medication to cure what was, in fact, a simple outbreak of scarcely perceptible, age-appropriate spots. The medication, however, dried up the moisture and mucus in her system. Her skin became parched, cracked, and ultra-sensitive to light. She had to wear intensive, factor 40 sun-block, of the kind more appropriate to babies and young children, before she could even leave the house, let alone go into the sunshine. Her mother was enlisted in the application of the various emoluments. Susan could thus reclaim her position as the baby of the family, her infantile needs being attended to with the soothing, creaming, protective measures appropriate to an actual baby rather than to an actual adolescent.

The aggrieved and rejecting fireball who would dismiss her mother in contemptuous and denigrating terms—"you know nothing", "you haven't the faintest idea what you are talking about"—would, all too easily, herself collapse into an infantile state, needing physically to be calmed and contained. As with the repeated coverings-up in the dream, the mother's regular application of cream to her daughter's skin, "over and over again", would seem to offer reassurance to Susan that her destructiveness had not definitively turned things bad. The external repetition would go on being required until, internally, the ferocity of her superego could be modified and yield to objects that were less harsh and more containing.

It is hard to know, with any precision, the source of this fairly characteristic picture of adolescent narcissistic difficulties. They may, in part, for 18-year-olds, relate to an intensification of anxiety about the oncoming necessity for actual separation and individuation, academic failure betokening an unreadiness to move into the external world. In some of the extreme narcissistic pictures one encounters—in eating disorders, for example, and in the kinds of body dysmorphic disorder suffered by Susan—one becomes especially aware of the developmental stage that is being struggled through at the time. In Susan's case, this is the threat of having to leave the relative safety, turbulence notwithstanding, of the family and to emerge into the external world where she would have to be "seen" as some version of "herself", and not simply as the daughter of her parents. As John Steiner (2006) points out:

> Seeing and being seen are important aspects of narcissism, where self-consciousness is always a feature and one which becomes acute when a patient begins to tolerate a degree of separateness and becomes sensitive to being observed. [p. 1]

With adolescence, it seems to be more the fear of imminent separateness that propels many back into a strengthening of narcissistic structures that, although part of an adolescent's ordinary development, can become seriously destructive at points of external transition. This often precipitates breakdown in the face of apparent success, quite as often as that of failure. Susan did not break down. As her therapy progressed, the more hopeful elements indicated in the dream consolidated into a greater capacity to tolerate envy, frustration, and separation. What had looked like a particularly worrying adolescent organization loosened its hold on her. Her gratitude to her therapist increased, and two years later she managed to leave home and go to university. Had she been 28 and not 18, I suspect there might have been a very different picture and outcome.

Susan's adolescent predicament made clear the immediacy of infantile states in the adolescent and the recapitulation, by Ernest Jones (1922), "in the second decennium of life [of] the development he passed through in the first five years" (pp. 39–40). In the literature on narcissism, it is this link between narcissistic disorders and the nature and quality of early infant and young child experience, especially in the area of containment and of the development of the superego that has been particularly emphasized in some psychoanalytic thinking (e.g., Britton, 2003). This relationship between the containing function and resilience of the parent, and later of the family, and the manner and intensity of the baby's projections, continues to be important throughout life—but at no time more significantly than during the teenage years. For the particular stresses of puberty and the revival of oedipal conflicts test anew the emotional gains and losses of the early years as never before, trauma or deprivation often stirring teenage angst, thus strengthening the narcissistic defences.

By contrast, those who have experienced their parents as able to be continent and cognisant of their own infantile needs, and to relate to their children as "other" rather than as narcissistic versions of themselves, will be likely to fare much better. A passage from A. S. Byatt's novel *Still Life*, quoted by Gregorio Kohon (2005) in *Love and Its Vicissitudes*, beautifully evokes a mother's capacity to engage with her newborn son, not as an extension of herself, weighed down with preconceptions and expectations but, rather, as a separate human being whom she must slowly find a way to get to know:

> She had not expected ecstasy. She noted that he was both much more solid, and, in the feebleness of his fluttering movements of lip and cheek muscle, the dangerous lolling of his uncontrolled head, more fragile, than she had expected. . . . She put out a finger and touched [his] fist; he obeyed a primitive instinct and curled the tiny fingers round her own, where they clutched, loosened, tightened again. "There", she said to him, and he looked, and the light poured through the window, brighter and brighter, and his eyes saw it, and hers, and she was aware of bliss, a word she didn't like, but the only one. There was her body, quiet, used, resting; there was her mind, free, clear, shining; there was the boy and his eyes, seeing what? And ecstasy. Things would hurt when this light dimmed. The boy would change. But now in the sun she recog- nised him, and recognised that she did not know, and had never

seen him, and loved him, in the bright new air with a simplicity she had never expected to know. "You," she said to him, skin for the first time on skin in the outside air, which was warm and shining, "you". [Byatt, 1985, pp. 100–101]

This whole passage is touchingly suffused with a mother's capacity to allow her infant to emerge as his own personality, not to project onto him her own hopes and fears, but simply to be ready to engage in the reciprocal emotional complexities of their mutual development. As Kohon says, "It is these words, *there*, *you*, as we imagine them being spoken with love by the mother, which makes the subjectivity of the baby possible. *You*, she says, the giver of meaning, provider of goodness, source of contentment." "How does the baby", Kohon goes on, "interpret this declaration of love? The word of the mother [and, we might add, the look or gaze of the mother], if spoken [or offered] with pleasure, will create pleasure. If uttered with love, it will . . . generate love. But if the word [or loving look] is not there, or the voice [or glance] is hateful, uncertain or troubled by too much ambivalence, if [either] is misleading or deceitful, then the baby responds with confusion, insecurity and a sense of loss." And there is likely to be the concomitant difficulty of managing to retain some secure emotional hold on the object even in its absence. "Pleasure will be replaced", as Kohon suggests, "by uncertainty; love, substituted by fear" (pp. 66–67). Whatever the baby's natural disposition, it will always be trying to interact with these potentially traumatic impositions from the outside, in terms of the state of the mother's mind and of her internal objects, which have so profound an effect on an infant and young child and, in these terms, on the adolescent's capacity to manage the fundamental polarities of love and loss.

Steiner's (2006) work on gaze, and seeing and being seen, seems especially relevant to adolescent narcissistic structures, as with Susan. How different might be the development of a baby whose experience of word and look had the quality of the foregoing description. Britton (2003) draws attention to a lack of containment in infancy and early childhood as characteristic in cases of narcissistic personality disorder and, inseparably related to that, to evidence of an "ego-destructive superego" that powerfully works against the development of the personality and, along with envy, is defended against by narcissistic character traits in particular. As has also been well documented, clinically one frequently detects the operation of this kind of internal juggernaut, especially at moments of the emergence of insight or meaning between patient and therapist. Burgeoning possibilities of mutual understanding are immediately crushed by the force and weight of a superego that disarticulates any links of relatedness and relegates the individual back to the defensive locations in which he has been seeking uneasy retreat or refuge.

For adolescents, one such refuge is, as we have seen, the characteristic flight into an intense involvement in group life. This kind of passionate grouping may represent a form, effectively, of a ganging-up of the more perverse and destructive parts of the personality, whether located in actual external figures or in the kind of internal gang/group of witches revealed in Susan's dream. Or it may represent a denial of aspects of the self, thus diminishing the ego and draining it of its vitality. But it may, equally, indicate a healthy capacity to deal with a sense of internal fragility, even fragmentation, thus providing a constructive function, albeit narcissistic in essence.

By splitting off aspects of the self and locating them, variously, in different members of the group, it becomes possible to remain in touch with these parts without having to suffer them with too much immediacy. In this kind of group organization, as David Armstrong (2005) points out, the projected parts of the personality can be reassembled in a way that simulates the function of a containing object (p. 55).

Such seemed to be the case for young Andrew, who suffered a major breakdown at 14. Andrew described how little he could remember of his childhood, except the family house, the loss of which he had felt very keenly when his father sold it a few years after his wife had left him for another man. Andrew had no recollection of his parents being in any sense together in that house, only that the house itself provided what little feeling of "home" he had.

One particularly vivid recollection he did have, however, was of his own realization, at the same time as the house sale, that he was not "the same" as his older brother. He revealed that he had always felt identical to his brother, to the point that he was convinced that the two of them even shared each other's thoughts. He had, in other words, taken shelter from a sense of emptiness, loss, and abandonment in this close identification, oblivious of the brother's otherwise distinctive characteristics. This realization left him feeling very little and humiliated. He began to throw himself into group life, thereby constructing for himself an alternative container. It was as if he adopted group life as a way of "tiding him over" until he hit puberty. But with the added stresses of pubertal change and the dispersal of the friendship group into other school classes, he felt wholly alone and he completely broke down. In the face of what seemed a comparatively minor problem as to who was in which class, the narcissistic bonding that had, for a time, maintained an uneasy psychic equilibrium for Andrew unravelled and left him with no internal resource.

This kind of grouping can be thought of as a form of safety-net measure, which, developmentally, could support or obstruct, depending on the resilience of the internal structuring and on the nature of the external circumstances. As clinicians, we tend to encounter situations where things have gone wrong. Seeking an example of the adolescent organization as temporizing—that is, holding things together while internal growth continues—I have found myself turning to literature. For here, especially in the great nineteenth-century novels, one can appreciate the broad developmental sweep that embraces the minutiae of internal and external experience, often describing what we would think of in terms of narcissistic mechanisms as providing a kind of in-between phase that allows things to develop. Two outstanding examples of this are the characterizations, respectively, of Jane Austen's Emma Woodhouse in *Emma* (discussed further in chapter 14), and of George Eliot's Dorothea Brooke in *Middlemarch*.

Two of the central protagonists in *Middlemarch*, Rosamond and Dorothea, offer utterly contrasting studies of different kinds of narcissism that are, in a sense, the pure culture of the kinds of distinction I have been making. I shall describe only one of these young women in any detail, and that is Dorothea. But Rosamond must be looked at, briefly, as a brilliant delineation of a pretty, vain, and self-regarding adolescent—a nymph caught young and educated at Mrs Lemon's, as George Eliot puts it, whose ceaseless quest for admiration and social betterment brings disaster, or near disaster, on her marriage, herself, and those around her. She was, we are told, "little used to imagining other people's states of mind except as a material cut into shape by her own wishes" (p. 834). The anti-developmental picture is exquisitely drawn.

In Dorothea's case, the internal odyssey looks quite different: she grows up in the course of the novel, moving away from her metaphorically and literally short-sighted view of the world, one rooted in the projection into others of her own ideals, to a much more mature position. *Middlemarch* begins and ends with her marriages—the contrast between the two measuring her development over time. The first marriage is to the desiccated pedant, Casaubon. At this point, Dorothea is described as wholly caught up in her own youthful ideals. She is imbued with a soul hunger to escape from her girlish subjection to her own ignorance and "the intolerable narrowness and purblind conscience of the society around her" (p. 60). This is a wonderful evocation of the adolescent's omnipotent wish to by-pass the pains of ignorance and inadequacy and the defensive intolerance, superiority, and slightly prudish judgementalism that so often characterize an attitude to the rest of the world—to a society that is felt to be so woefully wanting.

Dorothea's response to Casaubon's proposal, we learn, is that of one "whose whole soul was possessed by the fact that a fuller life was opening before her: she was a neophyte, about to enter on a higher grade of initiation" (p. 67). Infused with adolescent idealistic fervour, Dorothea seeks to render her life complete by union with one whose mind, as she subsequently discovers, reflects "in vague labyrinthine extension every quality she herself brought" (p. 46)—a vivid description of projective identification. She had learnt from him and had been impressed "by the scope of his great work, also of attractively labyrinthine extension" (p. 46). She has, in other words, fallen victim to her own projections, to the idealization of a much older and, she believes, wiser man. She was "altogether captivated" by one whose work, to her mind, "would reconcile complete knowledge with devoted piety; here was a modern Augustine who united the glories of doctor and saint" (p. 47).

Early on, Dorothea, like Casaubon, suffers from the delusion that to know *about* things, to accumulate sufficient "learning" or information, would provide "the Key to all Mythologies"—a key that would bring about a solution to life (again expressing the adolescent delusion that there could be such a thing)—a flight, in other words, into certainty at the expense of a sense of reality. As Bion put it, she "could not see the wisdom for the knowledge" (2005, p. 42). Dorothea's slow and painful disillusionment challenges to the uttermost her capacity to learn from experience. It initiates in her a state of mind in which, as admiration for erudition yields to appreciation of wisdom, and as narcissistic relations yield to those of self-and-other, she can begin to envisage a very different kind of relationship, one that also brings together "the sensual and the tender".

In the course of the novel, Dorothea loses those infantile dreams, relinquishes her projective fantasies, and, in the ghastly loneliness of her honeymoon in Rome, discovers the difference, noted earlier, between a narcissistic orientation to the world—as "an udder to feed our supreme selves", and an attitude of mind which can recognize "an equivalent centre of self whence the lights and shadows must always fall with a certain difference" (p. 243).

The working through of the adolescent's narcissistic orientation to the world is intrinsic to being able to tolerate the loss of a sense of one's own centrality in it. During her first marriage, Dorothea suffers the loneliness of disillusionment and separation, but she also begins to recognize the significance of separateness. With Casaubon's sudden death, she lets go of her omnipotent adolescent ideals for the more painful reality of frustration, disappointment, and a circumscribed life, her husband's will forbidding further marriage. During that first marriage, Dorothea discovers the emptiness and mistakenness of her choice:

> . . . that real, new future which was replacing the imaginary drew its material from the endless minutiae by which her view of Mr. Casaubon and her wifely relation to him . . . was gradually changing, with the secret motion of a watch-hand, from what it had been in her maiden dream. [p. 226]

When she believes (wrongly) that her new love, Will Ladislaw, has betrayed her in favour of Rosamond, she is wracked with utter anguish as "the limit of her existence was reached". Yet, unlike her former self, she is now able to draw on capacities that she has "acquired" over time, as she begins to learn from her own real experience, relinquishing the "learning-about" side of her and the "unselfish", "under-labourer", or "too good-to-be-true" versions of herself.

The inner reality and meaning of this momentous expression of the thrust towards development is beautifully described in external terms—a kind of "objective correlative" for internal processes.

> She opened her curtains and looked out towards the bit of road that lay in view, with fields beyond, outside the entrance-gates. On the road there was a man with a bundle on his back and a woman carrying her baby; in the field she could see figures moving—perhaps the shepherd with his dog. Far off in the bending sky was the pearly light; and she felt the largeness of the world and the manifold wakings of men to labour and endurance. She was a part of that involuntary, palpitating life, and could neither look out on it from her luxurious shelter as a mere spectator, nor hide her eyes in selfish complaining. [p. 846]

This is not only a movingly understated description of the generosity of a mature mind, it is also a marvellous evocation of introjective identification having been taking place over time. In the face of Dorothea's conviction that the external object has been lost, the internal object holds. It does not vanish or collapse because the external representation has gone. Unlike Rosamond, Dorothea is able to look outside the "entrance-gates" of her own mind to the existence of others' lives, "whence [she is learning] the lights and shadows must always fall with a certain difference".

In conclusion, the term "adolescent organization" designates not just narcissistic states of mind and behaviour which are actively anti-developmental, but also ones that can have a developmental function too. In other words, narcissism *can* be designated an "adolescent disor-der", but that would be to oversimplify the situation. For, as we have seen, the pathological impasse of 18-year-old Susan was already, at 19, yielding to a capacity to make more helpful internal alliances of a kind that permitted a degree of growth and change. The dream described is suggestive of an emergent self that is distinctly different from that of her early years. Andrew, too, began to recognize the dearth of any early experience to which he could attach any meaning and the catastrophic impact on him of the collapse of his substitute containing structures or devices. Yet in families where periods of emotional drought have not been as extensive as in Susan or Andrew's, or where the underlying foundations are strong, the positive function of the narcissistic *modus operandi* can be more evident, as seems to be the case with Dorothea. One might even say that the adolescent organization can offer a sort of *sine qua non* for those kinds of exploration and experimentation that promote a sense of identity that is both internally reliant upon, and allied with, good-enough relationships with a good-enough internal parent or parents. Yet it needs to be one that, by turn, is also distinct from these parents, to the point that the individual can feel confident in something called his own self, confident in a capacity to come into one's own. During adolescence, drawing any clear distinction between what might be called mental "order" and mental "disorder" is always a challenging and subtle business, defying ready categories or formulations. This is why living or working with this age group presents, to repeat, such alarming, and at the same time such reward-ing, challenges.

Note

An earlier version of this chapter was published in 2006 in the *Journal of Child Psychotherapy*, Vol. 32, No. 1, pp. 21–34.

CHAPTER ELEVEN

The difficulty of diagnosis
in the liminal world of adolescence

Where diagnosis is concerned, the adolescent age group really does need to be accorded its own specificity of reference and detail. The traditional wisdom of the Tavistock Clinic's Adolescent Department has always been that of the central importance of observing the realities of this state of liminality—that is, the frame space between two states: of being no longer a child, but not yet an adult either; a state in which previous identities are dissolved before new ones are formed (Brawer, 2017).

The types of developmental problems that can typify adolescence are familiar: self-hatred, anxiety, depression, manic enactment, internet addiction, self-harm, suicidal ideation, gender confusion—among so many others. Each of these may be manifestations of the tip of some kind of iceberg of mental illness. But they may equally be a particularly troubling phase, possibly drug or alcohol related, that, with appropriate support, often passes with time. The approach in the Department was always to avoid, for as long as possible, an adult-type diagnosis and the associated medication, which can tend to lock youngsters into a particular developmental picture. Adult categories of diagnosis are being increasingly drawn upon, and at younger and younger ages, in the context of the relative paucity of ongoing long-term psychodynamic treatment. Bitter experience has led clinicians, including many psychiatrists, to resist

thinking in terms of depressive "illness" and the resultant pre-
scriptions of antidepressants or a range of antipsychotic medicines,
which, as many have learned to their cost, can result in serious
manic episodes. As Jill Vites, a long-term colleague in the Department, confirmed to me, clear diagnoses of a manic-depressive illness
used only to be made after one or more adolescent breakdowns. I
was struck by her adding that the now increasingly popular diagnosis of Attention Deficit Hyperactivity Disorder (ADHD) for adolescents tends to fade out soon after the college years have passed.

The significance, here, is to emphasize the respect that has to be
paid to the particularity of this period of ambiguity and disorientation
and to the significance of approaching psychological problems accordingly. Chapter 10 ended with a statement of the extreme difficulty of
determining where the line between adolescent order and disorder
should be drawn. That predicament takes us into a whole range
of important diagnostic questions about the complex relationship
between troubling development, on the one hand, and what is often
referred to, during these uncertain years, as "emerging borderline
personality disorder". As Jill Vites said to me recently: "The problem
is that adolescence itself is a borderline state."

I shall begin by clarifying, now at greater length, what D. H.
Lawrence meant by the term "hour of the stranger". In his 1923 essay
already quoted, *Fantasia of the Unconscious*, he writes at length about
the impact of puberty:

> A strange creative change in being has taken place. The child before
> puberty is quite another thing from the child after puberty. Strange
> indeed is this new birth, this rising from the sea of childhood into a
> new being. It is a resurrection which we fear.
>
> And now, a new world, a new heaven and a new earth. Now new
> relationships are formed, the old ones retire from their prominence.
> Now mother and father inevitably give way before masters and
> mistresses, brothers and sisters yield to friends. This is the period
> of *Schwärmerei*, of young adoration and of real initial friendships.
> A child before puberty has playmates. After puberty he has friends
> and enemies.
>
> A whole new field of passionate relationship. And the old bonds
> relaxing, the old love retreating. The father and mother bonds now
> relax, though they never break. The family love wanes, though it
> never dies.
>
> It is the hour of the stranger. Let the stranger now enter the soul.
>
> And it is the first hour of true individuality, the first hour of genu-
> ine, responsible solitariness. A child knows the abyss of forlornness.

But an adolescent alone knows the strange pain of growing into his own isolation of individuality.

All this change is an agony and a bliss. It is cataclysm and a new world. It is our most serious hour, perhaps. And yet we cannot be responsible for it.

Now sex comes into active being. Until puberty, sex is submerged, nascent, incipient only. After puberty, it is a tremendous factor. [pp. 102–103]

What Lawrence is so passionately and eloquently writing about is far from being a new idea—for example, the prerequisite for, and the nature of, the transition from parental authority to sexual, coupled maturity lies, as we shall see (chapter 15), at the heart of many of Shakespeare's plays, engaging, as they so often do, with the perennial dramas of the tragedy and fulfilment that occupy, or track the move towards, adulthood. One has only to think of *As You Like It*, *Twelfth Night*, the History plays, *The Merchant of Venice*, *A Midsummer Night's Dream*. These plays are about capacities and incapacities to get to know oneself and others and the difficulties of so doing; about the differentiation between kinds of knowledge: the genuinely exploratory and developmental purpose of the acquisition of knowledge on the one hand, and the questionable use to which it might be put on the other. For the adolescent, in particular, the factors that can determine the predominance of the one mode of mental functioning over the other are rooted in the inextricable relationship between the internal emotional and psychological experiences of early development and the external realities of culture and circumstance during these transitional years.

The adolescent years tend to epitomise contradictory pulls between polarized states of mind, between the adult and the infantile, especially that between the tender and the aggressive, between acquisitive greed and generosity; between elation and depression; between the lures of dishonesty and the desire for truth; between hate and love; between a sense of confusion and a conviction of certainty.

We have seen how, during the years that Lawrence so vividly describes, the boundaries of the hitherto "known" personality often become very blurred, confused, challenging, frightening, or perhaps even excessively rigidified. In the hormonally fuelled, febrile, and fragile states that so often characterize their daily lives, these youngsters can become very self-preoccupied, apparently selfish and uncaring of others. One could describe such states, sometimes protracted, as a kind of narcissistic defence against pain, although, as we have seen, it is seldom as simple as that.

With these generalities in mind, I shall describe two mid-adoles-cents, both boys, and both of whose plights bring to mind so many for whom, all of a sudden, "things" fall apart, for whom, as Yeats put it in "The Second Coming", "the centre cannot hold" (in Yeats, 1933). In the light of what happened, it became clear that, in each case, the boys' respective achievements in early adolescence—one as a very talented cellist, the other a brilliant rugby player—had functioned, in part, as a carapace of the kind that can, temporarily, hold together, and disguise, what turn out to be extreme emotional fragilities, ones, in these cases, stemming from early traumatic and destabilizing experiences. For these boys, their very different forms of focused prowess had, for the time being, seemed to have protected them from more turbulent states.

The cellist, Theo, had suffered not only his parents' stormy divorce but also the death of a little sister when he himself was 6 years old. His school had tried to encourage his musical talent by entering him for all kinds of competitions, ones that he had always won. Then one day, for the first time, he came not first but third. It was as if the bubble into which he had retreated even before puberty had been burst. Theo was shattered. He felt scarcely able to play at all. His cello practice dwindled and then stopped completely. He spent increasing amounts of time in his room, playing online computer war games, first nation-ally and then internationally. This meant that the varying time-zones disturbed his sleep patterns so that it became increasingly hard to get up in the morning in any regular way. He started to miss more and more school, to get behind with his work, to be cut off from his school friends. He became not so much linked up as "wired up" to other people, whom he had never met. Before long, he found himself to be what could be regarded as a teenage isolate. Previously academically enthusiastic and able to balance the demands of cello playing with the run-up to GCSEs, he began to direct all his attention to winning in other ways, now as accomplished in the cyber world as he had been in the concert hall. Depressed, friendless, obsessed, he became a boy of unrecognizable pallor of personality—cold, withdrawn, aggressive, superior, miserable, yet utterly recalcitrant. He was failing at every-thing except computer games. His distraught mother was furious and arranged for him to see a psychiatrist—she wanted a diagnosis. And she got one: "emerging borderline personality disorder".

The rugby player, Adam, had also in his earliest years lived alone with his mother, but in this case his circumstances during infancy were terribly sad. His father had committed suicide while his mother was pregnant with Adam, her first child. Traumatized, bereft, and scarcely able to cope, she had sent him, at an early age, to boarding school. Here, at least, he found a supportive structure, of sorts, and had managed friendships and academic work quite adequately. He had also become a startlingly talented fly-half. He loved rugby; he loved the team life, the intensity of the relationships with the other boys, and the sense of competitiveness and achievement. Though physically well-built and very strong, he was, in fact, the youngest in the team by two years. Then, one day, he suffered a sports injury, which, after several operations, meant that he would never be able to play competitively again. As with Theo, with this catastrophic set-back Adam's life fell apart. He refused to go back to school but got a job as a runner on film sets and suffered a number of further injuries in the many minor accidents (quite possibly self-inflicted) that he sustained.

Then, one day his mother found him in the bathroom cutting his legs quite deeply with a razor blade. The wounds were sutured, and he was referred to a psychiatrist who, looking at the overall picture, diagnosed "emerging borderline personality disorder". A week later he was hospitalized after a serious suicide attempt—he had been discovered trying to hang himself. On discharge, he was offered ongoing therapy in the local services. He attended very sporadically, finding fault with successive therapists, before dropping out completely. The last that was heard of him, from his bewildered and desperate mother, was that he was refusing all treatment, was remaining in his room at home, completely withdrawn from all familial or social life for long periods, although at other times taking lowly jobs from which he was repeatedly sacked for bouts of unprovoked aggression or "peculiar", irrational behaviour.

Theo was also referred for ongoing therapy. Like Adam, he had a profoundly negative and contemptuous reaction to the treatment, also insisting on changing from one "inadequate" therapist to another and eventually dropping out. Some years later Theo's father wrote to the clinic and described how, following a re-engagement with music through a rather inspired and unconventional teacher, and also through an impressively self-motivated and equally unconventional route through university (without A-levels!), Theo went, as his father put it, "from strength to strength". He successfully graduated, gained a peripatetic job teaching music, and, at the same time, began, informally, counselling online computer-addicted young people. He moved in with a girlfriend and started performing publicly again, though now with contemporary bands rather than as a solo player.

Theo's immensely relieved father generously wrote to the Department about how helpful, in retrospect, it had been for him, himself, to be told at the time that it might very well be that Theo was suffering, as not uncommonly, and to paraphrase, from a "particularly extreme case of adolescence" and that Theo might, with time, quite possibly emerge from those dark years and get back into a world of work and relationships and even, perhaps, music. This had apparently somewhat allayed the father's own agitation about his son's state and enabled him to offer ongoing support to him without excessive interference. He noted that therapy, though helpful to many, was "irritating" to those, like Theo, who "need knowledge of the world rather than of themselves".

I found this a very instructive and helpful comment about the enormous difficulty of assessing disturbed adolescents' needs, in terms of finding the most appropriate treatment modality. The diagnostic picture is so very difficult to establish at this transitional time when the ways of defending against characteristically intense confusion are so varied and often so very extreme. Development runs unevenly, and everyone goes through adolescence in their own way and at their own speed. Each of these boys, as Lawrence put it, was coming to know "the strange pain of growing into his own isolation of individuality".

Adverse early events, as in both Theo's and Adam's cases, can have perhaps unexpectedly extreme, destabilizing effects, and the developmental picture really does always need to be kept in mind. External achievement may mask internal uncertainties, making it all the more difficult to manage the ordinary—as well as the less usual—conflicts that attend this testing period. For Theo and Adam, with their early, adverse experiences and the bulwarks that they had each had to erect to protect themselves from the force of the winds of pain, the stage was set. Once those bulwarks were breached, all hell was let loose.

How, psychologically, does one understand all this? Just for the historical record, "Emerging Personality Disorder" has been a recognized diagnosis since 1980 as part of *DSM–III* (APA, 1980). But it had been described by psychoanalysts, of different persuasions, for over forty years before this. For example, for Stern (1938) borderline patients showed symptoms that seemed to belong somewhere between neurosis and psychosis. Deutsch (1942) formulated a picture of the "as-if personality", suggesting fluctuations in identity, adapting to a different role in any specific situation. Schmideberg (1947) suggested "disorder of character" for both psychopathic and borderline patients and of emotional lability, leading to "stable instability". Knight (1953) used the term "borderline states" for those admitted with psychiatric features but who were not schizophrenic. In the 1960s, the concept was extended to include cognitive disturbance and an impaired sense of self.

Much has happened in the last forty years, during which the great contribution of disposition, the role of infantile anxiety, environmental failure, and their respective meanings began to take precedence, by significant contrast with the view in the earlier psychoanalytic days—one that had tended to be based on the quantitative intensity of biologically driven forces. More recent psychoanalytic theory is inclined to view borderline states as a way of describing people who, as Henry Rey put it (1979), have "achieved a kind of stability of personality organization in which they live a most limited and abnormal emotional life which is neither neurotic nor psychotic but a sort of frontier state" (p. 203). John Steiner (1987), who has done extensive work on what have become known as "pathological organizations", describes such an organization as "a set of defences not only against the fragmentation and confusion of the paranoid-schizoid position, but also against the mental pain of the depressive" (p. 328). Again, as Spillius (1988) paraphrases: in borderline and narcissistic states there is some sort of "unhealthy liaison" between the more paranoid-schizoid side of the self and a person's capacity to contain or neutralize such destructive parts within the more healthy side of the personality (p. 201).

I would like to include here a further term, one that I drew on in chapter 10: the "adolescent organization". In the case of adults, the prognosis for the stuck or restrictive characteristics of the classic borderline, pathological, narcissistic organizations tends to be rather bleak in terms of psychoanalytic outcome or future development. The adolescent age group, on the other hand, as I know it, needs to be accorded its own particularity of reference and detail. Disturbed states in adolescence, such as those of Theo and Adam, so often have many of the characteristics of the adult organization referred to above (and described in detail by, for example, Rosenfeld, Steiner, O'Shaughnessy, Sohn, Rey, and others). But what has to be borne in mind is the specificity of the developmental stage under discussion: primarily its fluidity, as Lawrence describes it; its confusion around encountering as yet uncharted territory; the unrecognizable in the self, because hitherto unseen and unknown. Where do they find a foothold? So many describe themselves as "stranded", beset, perhaps, by unrealistic aspirations and, most significantly, all too real relinquishments and losses—losses, as Lawrence put it, of the known childhood self, with its known family structures and relationships.

Both Theo and Adam would have been significantly affected by their traumatic experiences and by an unstable and uncontaining early infancy and childhood: Theo was contending with a toxic parental relationship, in the context of the trauma of his sibling's infantile death; Adam's mother was confounded by her husband's death and scarcely able to care for her baby once born. We might fairly speculate that puberty and adolescence would be especially difficult for these two and that defensive measures against engaging with the resurgence of infantile states would need to be taken.

The apparently different, yet also quite similar, defences adopted by each precluded at the time the needed exploration and experimentation involved in the ways of bearing the daily humiliations and sensed inadequacies that so often shadow these difficult years—bearing them without excessive denial, retreat, flight, or evasive manoeuvre. Each developed very different displays of excellence, in part, at least, to protect themselves from what must have been deeply unwanted or unmanageable feelings. These were displays that, to start with, and because so successful, did not draw attention to the underlying tumult—not, at least, until a time when, the protective function having been shattered by what each regarded as "failure", the infantile pathology and inability to cope with the outside world became so terribly evident. Theo's father was right, in a way: Theo really did need to know how to cope with the world, but he, like Adam, also needed to understand why doing so felt so impossible at the time, as did the task of knowing, or managing, the as yet undeveloped parts of himself.

It seems probable that Theo's musical talent had, in the early days, functioned rather on a kind of –K scale of achievement—that is, simply for the sake of it. For the time being, it held him together. He needed not so much to "break down", as he effectively did, but to "break through". This he was eventually able to do, "through" to a state of mind where his talent could be harnessed to a way of playing that was more social, not so much competitive as more spontaneous and more authentic. His recovery took a deeply reparative form: it was linked to helping others to play, and his own familiarity with mental pain and computer addiction was drawn on, in turn, to counsel others. What had looked like a serious borderline retreat from life could be left behind so that he was, very impressively, step by step, able to start to live again.

Adam's development, however, seems likely to have been more deeply fractured. As long as he could exert his physical prowess and, importantly, to do that within the containing structure of the school rugby team and its culture, he could hold together the underlying unintegrated parts of his personality. But his injury exploded his attempts to manage his disorientated self by joining in and winning plaudits and status. His underlying emotional reserves proved wholly inadequate. Although diagnoses, in themselves, may often not be of great service, sometimes they can be the reverse: it could be that, for example, in the aftermath of this second massive trauma, Adam would long be struggling with the manifest states of borderline pathology that could have been setting in. Yet, with time, and with the slow move beyond the "hour of the stranger", it is by no means impossible that, with Adam too, there might develop a greater capacity to tolerate what he regarded as his impossibly diminished self, and that his very worrying adolescent organization might, albeit belatedly, loosen its hold on him.

In concluding, I shall draw on some dream material of a 16-year old girl, Vanessa, whom I saw for assessment many years ago. This detailed fragment of a clinical account revealed significant aspects of Vanessa's internal world and may complement my more anecdotal material about the plights of Theo and Adam. Vanessa had presented herself to the clinic in a seriously distressed state. She had already, repeatedly, pleaded with her GP to refer her for a psychiatric assessment. Her GP had resisted but, during a summer break, Vanessa had, astonishingly, managed to set up a brain-scan for herself and to have a consultation with one of the duty psychiatrists at the clinic who had told her that the scan was clear. In his medical report he had apparently described her as "rather borderline". The presenting problem was a dramatic, seemingly hypochondriacal symptom: Vanessa was convinced that she had a brain disorder. Possibly, she thought, she had a tumour, or was it mad cow's disease? Or was it, simply, that her brain was disintegrating and her mind simply "draining away"? In the course of the assessment many very important issues had emerged—in particular, just as in the case of Adam, the impact of the death of a younger sister from a heart condition when Vanessa herself was 6 years old and her sister about 4. It was striking to me that some of Vanessa's descriptions of the behavioural characteristics of this little girl shortly before she died were very similar to Vanessa's own erratic behaviour, in terms of her panic-stricken certainty that she was suffering from a terminal illness, related to her brain. Vanessa's family, and in particular her devastated mother, had, so understandably, been unable fully yet to mourn the death of this dead child, nor to provide their older daughter with the succour that she so needed. Vanessa had sought her own support, as so often, in musical and academic prowess. But now, perhaps with the added pressure of exams and the prospect of leaving school, her defensive strategy was crumbling. In effect, she was breaking down.

Vanessa brought a dream towards the end of her very last assessment session, only a few minutes before she and I were going to part (I was referring her on to a colleague for intensive therapy). The dream touches upon many aspects of fantasy and behaviour that characterize the adolescent psychic organization, with, as we have seen, its simultaneous drives towards integration and fragmentation and its constellation of drastic defences against the turmoil involved.

> I was at school, standing near the vending machines with my friends. My philosophy tutor was saying to my year group that in these very troubled times [post-September 11th] the responsibility for the future of the world rested on us, "on the intelligent and capable shoulders of you bright young women". ("This idea disturbed me a lot.") Then, in the next part of the dream, I was floating somewhere high up above London, looking down on life and myself there, but also, somehow, at the same time, I was on quite a different planet, one from which I could observe the daily events of the world. I was both part and also not part of that world. Then I was on a hill, sort of responsible for the behaviour of a number of baby tomatoes which were rolling away from me and which I knew, in some sense, were my friends. ("Oh God, this does sound really weird.") I had a bit of control over the baby tomatoes—for example, it was up to me to say where they rested and where they kept going. But then there was another bit—a sort of extraordinary, bizarre contraption thing, with bits and pieces jutting out of it. It was going to rise vertically into the sky, as if from a rocket launcher, and there was a cat, somehow reclining and displaying its [at this point Vanessa became covered with confusion and embarrassment at what word she should use. Eventually, she settled on] "Well, its sex."

When I commented that sexuality was an area that she would probably be exploring once she was settled with her therapist, Vanessa melodramatically clutched her head in her hands and exclaimed, with anguish, and yet almost with a touch of humour, "Oh—sex—oh no, not that." Sexuality had not come up as an explicit issue in the course of the unusually long, six-session assessment. She had not mentioned it, and, although noting its absence, I had not raised it. Now, at the eleventh hour, she had delivered a set of unforgettable dream images, with little opportunity to examine or interpret them. (During the assessment I had had many experiences of this "projective" tendency, at the end of sessions, to expel anxiety and concerns into me, which is so characteristic of the adolescent *modus operandi*.)

The central issues of this dream were clear and could be said to typify the preoccupations and defences of a 16-year-old young woman. Vanessa was anxious about the expectation that she, as a high-achiev- ing, idealistic, well-educated *"girl"* (for so she seemed) would have to shoulder the responsibilities of an unstable and threatening *adult* world, which was, in the Autumn of 2003, in such a frightful mess. She would rather stay near the "vending machine", safely, that is, within her school peer-group structure and, one might infer, close to an ever- present source of hot chocolate—that is, having unlimited access to creature comforts. Perhaps, too, this wish expressed Vanessa's anxiety about leaving the familiar "hot chocolate" of the assessment period and having to embark on what she felt was the dangerous and respon- sible process of the therapy to come, thus mirroring the frightening transition from adolescence to the expectations of taking up a place in the adult world.

The next part of the dream seemed to represent the kind of split response, so typical of the adolescent, to the anxieties of adult life. It described a vivid experience of separation between mind and body, of being physically part of the maelstrom of hurrying existence, and yet also, mentally and emotionally, of being able to view that threatening world from afar—perhaps from the safety of Vanessa's own version of mother-earth, anchored to a no-change, as opposed to a changing, world of the kind that involved the "sex, drugs 'n 'rock 'n roll" culture of ordinary teenage existence. In adolescence, such dreams of "floating above" so often reveal the psychic necessity to split the self by being "above it all". The mind can be doing one thing while the body does quite another.

The next "scenario" had that same air. The infantile parts of her- self—the little tomatoes bizarrely rolling in all directions, apparently recalcitrant and unbiddable—were not as random and fragmentary as they at first appeared. Again there seemed to be a separation between Vanessa's mind and the rest of her body—expressed here in concrete, "baby" terms. But she did have a sense that these "parts" were, none- theless, still under her control, just as I felt that, however weird and alarming were the behaviour and mental states described in the course of the assessment, Vanessa did not completely inhabit that mad self and was never wholly out of control. But the rocket-pad/spaceship, with jutting "bits and pieces" and ambiguously sexed cat within—that was just too much for her. Like the "baby tomatoes", there was something too sexually suggestive about this final image.

As this assessment progressed, a number of serious concerns had been raised, fears about madness, unresolved grief at the loss of a sibling, extreme hypochondria, panic attacks, and especially anxieties about becoming like, or even being, her mother, at the very time when she needed to be separating from her. These symptoms were severe in themselves, but they may also have served, in part, as a defence against a recognizably adolescent crisis: the failure to resolve ordinary teenage problems of identity, sexuality, and separation. Sexuality, at least at this point, was a kind of no-go area—one that was now surfacing, despite resistance and would have to be addressed with extreme delicacy. It seemed likely that unresolved oedipal problems underlay this resistance, for the expected reappearance of oedipal passions during adolescence was fully evident in Vanessa's idealization of her father and denigration of her mother.

For Vanessa, hypochondriacal terror, dreadful as that was, was preferable to being able to bear to think about the necessary rite of passage from childhood to adulthood. It did feel to her as though the structure of her previously known personality was dissolving—madness threatened. Her unconscious was launching an attack on her physical, mental, and emotional capacities as a form of flight from her predicament.

At root, my sense was that a great deal of Vanessa's hatred of herself or of her body related to her difficulties in separating from her mother, the infantile longing for the mother, the fear of fusion with her. This fear of excessive dependency may well take the form of hostile attacks not only on the mother, but also on the self—whether directly on the body, or, in a more indirect way, through hypochondria, as we have just seen, or through focused dismorphophobia or body dysmorphic disorder, or indeed, a generalized hatred of appearance and an accompanying lack of self-esteem. In each case, there may be very fine lines between ordinary adolescent processes and perplexing issues that go deeper—those of gender identity, for example. Finding a way to discriminate between the two is a perennial problem as much for the adolescent as for parents.

From the foregoing, it must be clear that more than at any other developmental stage, during adolescence a person is stirred by the concatenation of internal forces in the personality, physical changes in the body, and specific pressures from the outside world. The way in which all this is negotiated is rooted in early developmental processes, and they, in turn, importantly depend on the extent to which states of anxiety have been variously modulated, modified (by way of the containing functions that I have alluded to earlier), or, alternatively, evaded from the first. Subsequent experiences will have a significant bearing on this picture of things, but much depends on the extent to which frustration can be borne, thinking can occur, and mental pain can be tolerated—all of which capacities are beginning to be established in the course of the internal structuring of character in the very early days. Theo, Adam, and Vanessa had each had deeply troubled early experiences. During childhood they had found ways of holding out, but with the pressures of adolescence and a range of narcissistic blows, they had each "fled" into pathological states. Such states may be temporary. They may take new forms. They may, equally, contribute to an overall capacity to develop, and to develop all the better and stronger for having weathered the set-backs and to have "grown up" as a consequence.

CHAPTER TWELVE

Self-destructive states of mind

Dying
Is an art, like everything else
I do it exceptionally well. I do it so it feels like hell.
I do it so it feels real.
I guess you could say I've a call.

Sylvia Plath, "Lady Lazarus" (1962)

Mind led body
to the edge of the precipice.
They stared in desire
at the naked abyss.
If you love me, said mind,
take that step into silence.
If you love me, said body,
turn and exist.

Anne Stevenson, "Vertigo" (2000)

I shall begin by quoting from an unforgettable self-referral letter received many years ago, from an 18-year-old who was in a suicidally depressed state and seeking help from our Department. This young man includes in his letter what he describes as "a summary of the factors that have severely restricted my progress and contributed to my depression":

"1. Feeling excluded, isolated, ostracized.

2. Intrinsic loneliness.

3. Awareness of being distinctly different, an "oddball".

4. Intense shyness.

5. Inability to maintain conversation, being intimidated by silences when talking or being alone with someone.

6. Inability to form close friendships especially with those on the same emotional or intellectual level.

7. Precarious financial position.

8. Inability to find employment, meaningful or otherwise.

9. Self-doubt, which persists even when others reassure me of my talents, especially in music and literature.

10. The sensation that I have achieved nothing in my life and never will.

11. The fear that others perceive me as being aloof, diffident, inaccessible and threatening. Worst of all they may consider me to be boring.

12. Shame and anger at having to leave school with insufficiently good results.

13. A sense of directionless drift which permeates my life, exacerbated by idleness and self-pity.

14. Despair and distaste at other people's conformity and emotional coldness.

15. Frustration at my own failure to derive something profitable from my non-conformity.

16. Hypochondria—in particular a conviction my intelligence is continually diminishing.

17. The paradox of being both lethargic and restless simultaneously. Relaxation eludes me.

18. Morbid obsession with death and the passage of time. Belief that my peers have overtaken me and that I am destined to remain solitary and unfulfilled.

19. The realization that I have plenty to contribute artistically and personally, but this is countered by a sense of desperation in creating something which will have an impact on others before my death. This tentative confidence in my gifts is also eroded by fear of rejection, critical ridicule or worst of all indifference.

20. Inability to form lasting relationships with a woman.

21. Unfeasibly high standards.

Ultimately I am troubled that I will degenerate into a bitter, cynical, anti-social reject instead of a loving, sensitive, successful young man. I feel old before my time. I hope that I have not exaggerated my condition or overstated my case, or that my litany of woe is too self-pitying and tedious, but I think the list is a pretty accurate representation of my problems. I also apologise if the writing is illegible or impenetrable. I would be extremely grateful if you would give my case careful consideration."

Seldom can there have been a more eloquent and poignant expression of psychic pain and desperation to find some relief than this tormented itemization of scarcely bearable states of mind.

For those working clinically with adolescents, the title "Self-Destructive States of Mind" may well cover most of our practice. The term designates not just behaviour that is actively destructive— whether to the self or to others (for example, eating disorders, drug abuse, antisocial acts, cutting, suicidal gestures or attempts)—but also those aspects in the personality which can test and combat any creative impulses that might generally be described as being on the side of life and in the service of growth and development. In the history of psychoanalytic theory these destructive impulses have been gathered under various umbrellas—in Freud, the death instinct, in Klein, primary envy, and in Bion, the minus linkages of –L, –H, –K (see chapter 6). In other words, a historical shift has occurred roughly from the opposition of life and death instincts in Freud, to the opposition of love and hate in Klein, to the opposition, in Bion, between the capacity for feeling, for emotion, and for a getting to know and understand, and an aversion to these resources. For example, while not being overtly a problem to the self or the wider community, an adolescent may, nonetheless, use his mental and emotional capacities to destroy any possibility of intimacy—to attack, dismantle, obstruct, confuse, negate, pervert, or distort relationships, whether in the therapeutic setting or more generally. In straightforward terms, we are thinking about the angry, aggressive, sadistic, and frightened feelings common, on some level, to us all.

This chapter focuses on the troubling areas of self-harm and suicidal impulses and acts among adolescents in the context of the alarming statistics of a rapid rise in the instances of each—what is referred to in Vaspe (2017) as "the mute depression of an adolescent who habitually manages any painful feelings by cutting off from their mental awareness and cutting into their skin" (p. 44). There is an age-related specificity to these disturbing self-destructive acts, one that belongs to a developmental stage during which, where suicide itself is concerned, there is often an unbearable degree of difficulty in sorting out precisely what is happening in any particular instance. Is someone, for example, convinced that he is killing just the body—with the delusion that the self will somehow continue to exist, now relieved of the hated somatic encumbrance (Laufer, 1995)? Or is he killing the whole body/self—total annihilation? Or is there a killing of the self that is identified or merged with the other, usually a parent? Or, as an ultimate punishment for that self/other? Or is it an act of pure hatred towards someone who is felt totally to have let down or betrayed trust? Or is it someone killing off the body of what is felt, unconsciously, to be an unwanted-baby-self? And so on.

On the whole, suicide and self-harm are post-pubertal phenomena. There are tragic examples of younger children hurting, even killing, themselves, but, by and large, increasingly widespread suicidal presentation belongs to the conflict and angst of adolescents and to 20– to 30-year-old young people who are struggling amidst the multiple challenges and confusions of their lives. I think of this group as being, essentially, Janus-faced—that is, looking both from the present to the unknown and therefore unsafe future, and also from the present back to the past. The Roman God Janus was, in fact, known as the god of Transition—hence January. The libidinal and aggressive feelings triggered by the massive, though very varying, hormonal changes occurring at puberty usher in, as we have seen, bodily preoccupations of all sorts (see chapter 4).

The common agonies of this pubertal state are beautifully captured by Donna Tartt in *The Little Friend*:

> And all this was bad enough. But Harriet was going to be in the eighth grade next year; and what she had not expected was the horrifying new indignity of being classed—for the first time ever— a "Teen Girl": a creature without mind, wholly protuberance and excretion, to judge from the literature she was given. She had not expected the chipper, humiliating filmstrips filled with demeaning medical information; she had not expected mandatory "rap sessions" where the girls were not only urged to ask personal questions—some of them, to Harriet's mind, frankly pornographic—but to answer them as well.
>
> During these discussions, Harriet burned radiant with hatred and shame. She felt degraded by Nursie's blithe assumption that she—Harriet—was no different from these stupid Tupelo girls: preoccupied with under-arm odor, the reproductive system, and

dating. The haze of deodorant and "hygiene" sprays in the changing rooms; the stubbly leg hair, the greasy lip gloss: everything
was tainted with a slick oil of "puberty," of obscenity, right down
to the sweat on the hot dogs. Worse: Harriet felt as though one
of the gruesome transparencies of "Your Developing Body"—all
womb, and tubes and mammaries—had been projected over her
poor dumb body; as if all anybody saw when they looked at her—
even with her clothes on—were organs and genitalia and hair in
unseemly places. Knowing that it was inevitable ("just a *natural
part of growing up!*") was no better than knowing that someday she
would die. Death, at least, was dignified: an end to dishonor and
sorrow. [2002, p. 364]

Like Harriet, the tribulations of the "developing body" constitute a
central plank in many adolescents' troubled experiences of these years.
Such tribulations have recently become all the more agonising by the
door that technology has opened to compulsive image sharing and
numerous websites and chat rooms offering "advice" on "ways to do
it". Many young people suffer such somatic versions of the "who am
I?" identity crisis. Who is this looking in the mirror, and who is staring
back from it? Is it the same person? What do other people see? Such is
the present–future axis. But there is simultaneously, and inextricably,
the present–past axis: the traumatic re-evocation of infantile dependency; the childlike loves and hates; the possessiveness and murderousness associated with oedipal feelings; and the fear and pain of the
process of extrication from entangled family bonds.

How can one tune in, as a clinician, or a parent, to the situations
in which one is encountering the stirring of new, and the re-stirring
of old, feelings that can exert so unbearable a force on the young person, to the point at which the only solution is felt to be attacking, or
doing away with, that body/self altogether? And when, by contrast,
may the pain be acute but nonetheless be felt to be bearable, sharable,
manageable, within sustaining social, familial, or therapeutic relationships? How does the clinician assess the risks? Many would rightly
say that the tick-box risk-assessment process is painfully imprecise in
the context of often-profound professional worries. For the emphasis
also needs to be on a psychodynamic assessment in a clinical context
where deeply despairing and destructive feelings can be sensed and
emotionally held, held without necessarily offering recommendations
to the young patient to, for example, contact a GP or emergency
services if the suicidal urges are felt to be unmanageable. The recommendation to "go home" or to contact local services if feeling suicidal
is, in so many cases, entirely irrelevant (despite the tick) because

although the young person may have fantasied about, or even specifically planned, suicide before this, the actual act is so often characterized by an insistently, or impulsively mindless and unthinking state. A troubled 14-year-old comes to mind who had recently told a member of her school staff that she was frightened about how she was feeling. She was told that she could go home if it got worse. She hung herself that day in the school grounds. "Home" may well offer neither solace nor protection.

Seventeen-year-old Laura told me that she had had another quarrel with her mum and had had a bit of a headache as a result.

> So I took a few pills, ones a bit stronger than paracetamol, and then I just went on and on. I think I took about forty or maybe it was sixty, and then I decided I'd better cut my wrists as well, in case I was found too soon. So I went upstairs to get a blade but was afraid of waking my mum so I took the blade downstairs. I was getting drowsy and trying very hard to cut as deep as I could when my mum unexpectedly heard a sound and came down. She got me to hospital "in time".

As far as Laura was concerned, she really, *really* did not want or expect to wake up: "I would have had to deal with the 'awful consequences'", she said, as if rationally. What she meant by this was that she would have to face the pain and distress that she had actually overwhelmingly caused to her single mother, whom she also believed that she hated. The mode of Laura's narrative was wholly chilling in the degree to which she was cut off from the content of her account, and in the ambiguity of her phrase "in time".

There follow two further and not dissimilar examples. Fifteen-year-old Sam was a teenage isolate. His GP referred him, unwillingly, to the Department. He had, he said, jumped off London Bridge late at night. He didn't know why, but he thought he might just kill himself. He had, he said, felt troubled and sleepless and was wandering around London very late by himself (seriously risk-taking behaviour in itself, one might think). He had got from Tufnell Park to the bridge randomly, or so he thought, though he had subsequently remembered having been told earlier that day that his uncle (his absent father's brother) had committed suicide on that very bridge when Sam was 4 years old. He thought that this fact was irrelevant: "I can't remember that", he said, "it was too long ago. Anyway, after a bit of reflection about my unhappy life, I found myself just jumping off the bridge." It seemed that the impact of his head hitting the water so hard jolted him back into his normally depressive, though usually clear-thinking self. He thought that he had better swim hard or he might die of hypothermia.

Eighteen-year-old Jack dropped out of boarding school after warnings about his bullying behaviour. His GP referred him for therapy. Though deeply depressed, drug-taking, and oppositional, Jack had insisted that he would never kill himself because his mother (whom he persecuted continuously) would be too upset. One evening, after his third assessment session when his therapist, though concerned, felt that she had mentally ticked all the "suicide-risk" boxes, he went home, had a physical fight with his older brother, turned a knife on himself, and ended up in a mental health inpatient unit. He was discharged back into the care of our clinic, and it later emerged that when he was a baby, his mother had been severely traumatized by his father's violent death by suicide.

Multiple identifications with loss, betrayal, abandonment, and murderousness would seem to have a part in all these stories. Jack's mother was especially vulnerable in that, in addition to the traumatic death of her husband, she had had three miscarriages with her subsequent partner. The very air that this family breathed seemed to be one of trauma and death. So, too, though to a lesser extent, was this the case with Laura and with Sam.

For all three of them, there was an early traumatic death in the family. I later learned from Laura that the morning before her suicide attempt she had been sitting sobbing on the gravestone of her baby sister who had died when Laura was but 2 years of age. A further significant characteristic common to all these cases was that the mother–child relationship was exceptionally enmeshed and that the father–child links were either non-existent or markedly distant. In each case, there seemed to be elements of hurt and guilt in a deeply entrenched projective system between parent and child, whether characterized by love, by hate, or by general confusion.

In Jack's case, could this suicide attempt, if so it was, have been detected in the here and now of the consulting room? It may be that, to a large extent, it would have been very difficult for a clinician to have done so with any confidence, although, with rigorous hindsight, in any one case there are likely to be some significant clues. A clue in this instance was, perhaps, that the crisis took place in the course of an assessment after which Jack knew he was going to be referred to a different clinician, if he were to see anyone at all—which, at this point, he, like Sam, was firmly resisting. With the sorts of losses just described in the background, one might suspect that Jack would be especially affected by separations of any kind, however seemingly minor. Another significant clue could be the likely, although usually utterly denied and rejected, possibility that any change at all—of the setting, the time, the professional availability, of the sessions themselves (as in an imminent break)—may have had a much greater impact than the therapist had realized, or guessed, at the time.

In relation to this last point, I shall touch on another case seen in our Department. The therapist had been worried for some weeks as to whether the impulsive, self-harming behaviour of her rather inarticulate and concretely thinking 15-year-old patient Anna might escalate into something more serious. Impulsive slashing or scratching at her abdomen (because hidden) tended to occur when this young woman felt intensely distressed by, in particular, not being "heard by her parents", who, assiduous as they were in their attention to her physical needs (at puberty she had had mysterious blackouts and occasional fits), nonetheless were not really experienced as "hearing" her. This had felt to be acutely the case in the context of a couple of recent funerals that Anna had been forbidden to attend, despite her affection for the two people concerned. They had both died totally unexpectedly—one having hanged himself, the other from a heart attack. The trainee clinician involved had missed a couple of her supervisions with me (it turned out that she had been away on holiday but, uncharacteristically, had not mentioned the plan to me ahead of time). When she returned, she learned from Anna that, after a row with her father, she had tried to hang herself with her dressing-gown cord, having previously felt tempted to jump out of a third-floor window. The apparent precipitating factor (the row) was, we later learned, comparatively minor. Less minor, perhaps, was the fact that the clinician had given her patient very little notice of her impending absence. The therapist had felt so inadequate, it emerged, so unimportant and generally unhelpful to Anna, that she had not registered the impact that the cancelled sessions might have on her patient. Even after the near devastation to which she had returned, it had not struck her, shocked as she was, that her unusually timed holiday could have meant anything significant to her patient. This was unsurprising in the light of Anna's "style" of draining her communications of any apparent meaning. It was also unsurprising that, when the psychiatric services and parents had properly been put in the picture and Anna was asked what *she* felt, she answered in mysteriously dismissive and unemotional terms: "I didn't want to harm myself".

In two very worrying cases that I heard about at the beginning of one December run-up to the Christmas two-week break, a similar situation was described. My own sense was that the dynamics were clear and were a familiar indication of the projective power of these youngsters, rather than any particular weakness or failing on the part of the therapists themselves. I was struck that the therapists described themselves as almost "embarrassed" to suggest that the sessions, albeit ones during which they were regularly denigrated as completely useless, could have anything to do with anything, beyond the fact that they felt they really *were* unable to offer any helpful insight or understanding.

It should be clear that all these cases give powerful evidence of just how challenging and disturbing working with this age group can be. One of these young women, Emma, was explicitly suicidal (she, like Laura, had taken large quantities of paracetamol after a row with her mother). The other, Sally, was as near to a suicide attempt as might be: "I have come to the end, what shall I do?" "I am afraid of giving in and giving up entirely. . . ." There were other marked similarities in the two cases. I think it likely that both these two girls were identified with internal figures who had either abandoned them or "died on them" (the self-destructive, abandoning yet idealized-in-their-absence fathers that each of them had). The identification could, alternatively, have been with an internal figure who was simply incapable of keeping them properly in mind in a way that we would regard as sufficiently containing, despite endless well-meaning attempts to manage the pain. Such attempts were variously expressed, on the whole, in external ministrations—as with Anna. The impact of an impending break was clear in each of these cases—an impact the likely force of which the clinicians had not expected but that certainly needed team support from within the Department.

I felt that a recent dream of 22-year-old Lizzie also described such a predicament very clearly. How could this young woman keep herself safe if the mother/therapist on whom she so depended was "happy" to go away for a Christmas break with her "happy family", in which Lizzie so longed to be included? Such a longing was particularly extreme in this case. (During an especially silent session in that last pre-break session, she was asked what she was thinking. "That you must have a very big Christmas tree", she replied.)

When Lizzie was referred by her GP, she had just come back from two years in Berlin, having brushed off A-levels to join a group who were dedicated to an extensive variety of self-harming behaviour, whether individually or collectively. Drugs, alcohol, and self-harm (cutting and burning, mainly) formed the background to minor pedestrian accidents, but also car crashes and hospitalizations. The group seemed addictively drawn to dangerous, risk-taking behaviour, and there were many near misses that would have invited a verdict of "accidental death". There were, in fact, two fatal casualties, and the general unconscious motivations were not difficult to discern. It was becoming pregnant, with what turned out to be twin girls, that prompted Lizzie to return to England, to an unpleasant hostel that was riven with drugs and varieties of self-harm, whether casual or death-dealing. Nevertheless, it could be said that the birth of the twins may have saved Lizzie's own life. It was as if being able to care for them could function as a belated mode of care and repair for herself, though the stresses of being a lone parent of twins were certainly immense and often fed into her deeply self-destructive impulses.

When the twins were about 4 years old, Lizzie had the following dream:

> I am looking after my young daughters and some other children in a house somewhere. Maybe it's my parents'. I am aware of something falling and check that all the children are alright. Then I realize that my own head is pouring with blood. I ask one of my daughters to go upstairs and get my mother. My mother eventually comes down, unfussed and in no hurry. There is blood everywhere. We set off to A&E but mother insists on stopping at McDonald's on the way. I am very anxious and try to see in the mirror in the Ladies what the wound looks like. Despite the blood, nothing is apparent because the cut is not obviously on my forehead. Despite my previous certainty, I start thinking that maybe what I "knew" to be a wound wasn't one, in fact, and that perhaps I didn't need to go to hospital after all.

Lizzie had associations to many situations when, as a child, her actual physical cuts and bruises or illnesses tended to be overlooked by her parents. She had, at the time, explained this away to herself as being because her older brother was autistic and needed a lot of attention. Whatever the reasons, the toll on Lizzie was a high one. In many sessions she spoke about passionately ambivalent feelings towards these parents, hateful and murderous ones of biting and scratching, especially of stabbing her mother's—and sometimes her therapist's—eyes out. These were very powerful and dangerous impulses that seemed to have resulted from her intense identification with a neglectful, unloving figure and the desire to kill it off by killing herself.

The dream suggests the emotional uselessness, indeed bankruptcy, of the defensive manoeuvre that Lizzie had unconsciously adopted some years ago—that of looking to her own undoubted capacity, despite everything, to keep herself alive through making sure that she became pregnant at a very young age and giving birth to her girls when she was herself still a teenager. The unconscious phantasy was very likely to have been that from her beloved babies she would get the care that her financially successful but self-preoccupied parents had never managed to offer, despite all too obvious signs of extreme childhood disturbance on Lizzie's part. Significantly, in the dream, it is not the children who are damaged but Lizzie herself. She sends her daughter as an emissary to try to engage some kind of belated care and capacity in her mother that might save the situation. The eventual defensive procedure that the patient has to mobilize in the dream is the scotomization of the actual experience of damage done to her hurt-self (no visible actual wound, only blood) and the felt necessity to carry on as if nothing had happened. Was she really expected to survive the break—at Christmas of all times—unscathed? Was this mother/therapist (off to McDonald's) really taking in the seriousness of the impact that this particular festival would have upon her? Was this what the dream conveyed?

It seems as though Lizzie's defensive self-protection had been to try to look after herself in the closeness of the caring relationship with her children. Yet her capacity to be appropriately worried about herself at the beginning of the dream evaporates in the face of the McDonald's-holiday-break-mother, to the point of not being able to worry about herself at all. The receptive therapist rightly took heed of this despairing abdication of responsibility.

In the case of the two other patients, Emma and Sally, I felt especially concerned about risk. This holiday break was occurring relatively early on in the treatment of each, before the transference had really been established sufficiently for the therapists, let alone the patients, to have confidence in their own therapeutic capacities. I did not feel that it was enough to suggest that these young women should be told to contact their GPs if they felt at risk. When under stress each would very likely become too mindless and impulse-driven to be capable of that. They, like several of the other young people I have been describing, tended, at times, to suffer what Anthony Bateman called an "affect-storm" (Bateman & Fonagy, 2003, p. 203), rendering them incapable of thinking in any rational way at all. With Lizzie, by contrast, I felt that there were two important safeguards: one that the actual survival of her daughters was also some measure of guarantee of Lizzie's own life; second, that, in the dream, she had quite reliably communicated what her therapist's absence meant. Beyond a certain point, she could not be sure of being able to get herself to safety and she needed to know that her therapist knew that too, and that the latter would genuinely maintain a thinking mind and not lose track of Lizzie as she disappeared into her own happy family Christmas.

Of course, after all the listening and interpreting, in the end we can never be sure about a patient's safety, and holiday breaks are bound to remain very precarious times for some. In Lizzie's case, as some kind of safeguard, I *had* recommended a psychiatric consultation in the Department to check what had recently become worryingly insistent, debilitating, and more than usually pervasive depressive anxieties and panic symptoms. This is always a fraught move for it may indicate a possible source of refuge during the break, but it could equally flag up the therapist's anxiety that her patient really *is* at risk, thus undermining the patient's own capacity to feel that she can cope. But there was nothing further that could have been done beyond registering, taking in, and mentally and emotionally holding, for Lizzie, the anxiety about these head/mind wounds now opening up and bleeding anew. Working with adolescents, while often rewarding, is frequently also a fraught and challenging task.

If one reads a checklist of risk factors to look out for, Lizzie had always chronically exhibited pretty well every one of them. Robin Anderson (2013) helpfully itemizes such a list of the sorts of factor that need to be borne in mind in his article, "Assessing the Risk of Self-Harm in Adolescence".

» Preoccupation with themes of death expressed in talking or writing.

» Expressing suicidal thoughts or threats.

» Actual suicidal threats or gestures, even in the distant past.

» Prolonged periods of depression, with attitudes of hopelessness or despair.

» Physical symptoms of depression such as change in sleeping patterns, too much or too little sleep, or sudden extreme changes in weight and eating habits.

» Withdrawal and isolation from family and friends.

» History of prolonged family conflict and instability.

» Deteriorating academic performance reflected in lower grades, dropping lectures and tutorials, dropping out of school or college activities.

» A history of severe or prolonged bullying.

» A history of family suicides.

» Persistent abuse of drugs or alcohol.

» Major personality and behavioural changes indicated by excessive anxiety or nervousness, angry outbursts, apathy, or lack of interest in personal appearance or the opposite sex.

» Recent loss of close relationship through death or suicide, or a suicide within school or college.

» Making final arrangements, leaving a "goodbye note", drawing up a will, or giving away prized possessions.

» Telling someone of their intentions.

» Previous suicide attempts.

» Sudden unexplained euphoria or heightened activity after a long period of depression. The decision to commit suicide may be felt as an abandonment of a painful conflict and, in consequence, can actually lift depression.

» The development of a psychotic illness—schizophrenia is associated with a markedly increased risk of suicide.

» Anxiety about sexual orientation in young people, often connected with bullying.

» Asian girls in conflict with parents. This group shows a higher than average risk of suicide.

» Disturbing internet activity.

You might think that the items on this list pretty well characterize, at some point or other, many, if not all, of the adolescents seen in a clinical situation. The criteria for determining how serious any one of these states of mind may be in relation to risk are obviously very subtle ones and are precisely those that most preoccupy clinicians and that emphasize the importance of the group support offered, if need be, within a department's structure.

Jill Vites suggested to me in a discussion that an important early question during a consultation could helpfully be: "At the time, what stops you killing yourself?" A response along the lines of, "Because it would upset my parents", would be taken as a good sign. She continued: "*Never* don't take it seriously", adding that she always finds that psychotic elements are present at the time of the action— that is, that there is a distortion of reality, including the delusion that the person concerned does not matter to anyone.

In Sally's case, the therapist had actually picked up the intense sadness. Sally described herself as feeling like crying—"If my skin were torn, tears would simply pour and pour out and that's why I can never cry." What her therapist was not, at first, aware of was Sally's anger. In relation to one particular exchange in this same pre-break session, Sally unexpectedly said that she had suddenly remembered being alone as a child and savagely biting her nails. The explanation she gave for this was that she always felt that when she was doing this she was "punishing the others". It is interesting here to see how the concreteness of apparently very minor self-harm nonetheless, in fantasy, for *her* meant that she was expressing her true feelings of anger and hostility. Here we have momentary insight into the extent of her long-standing, underlying anger and destructiveness. Sally was brought up in an extremely guilt-inducing family ("my mother was never satisfied"). Such additional clues (and there were many others) to murderousness and punitiveness should start ringing alarm bells somewhere along the line. This same mother had, reportedly, herself been quite depressed, and her daughter complained that her mother would constantly, and worryingly, say, "I don't want to live like this". There were similar details in Laura's background. She had impulsively taken sixty paracetamol (her mother's!), again following a row. Significantly, Laura's lethal dose of painkillers also seemed closely related to her passionately ambivalent feelings towards her mother. This young girl and her mother appeared to be completely mixed up with one another, just as, it emerged, her mother had been with *her* mother. There was even a confusion about their first names and which name each would use. Laura had recently changed hers by deed-poll, as if in a concrete, legal attempt to extricate herself from the enmeshment.

It is not hard to imagine that the follow-on from the legal procedure might well be a suicide attempt. What became apparent was a tremendously powerful narcissistic identification and idealization of her daughter on the mother's part, and extreme contempt and hatred for her mother on her daughter's. Another alarm bell would be raised by this mother's account of her daughter's interest in death. Laura would listen, her mother recounted, almost admiringly, over and over again to Mozart's *Requiem*. She would read Sylvia Plath's poems and would sit for hours on her beloved grandfather's gravestone writing poetry. This grandfather was referred to by Laura as "daddy"—her own father having moved from the grandparents' home before Laura was born. Laura was to be the "only one", and mother and daughter were to a share a father.

Moses and Eglé Laufer did a great deal of pioneering work in the 1960s and 1970s on the plight of adolescents. In his book on suicide, Moses Laufer writes about how often, as in some of the cases described here, everyone is taken by surprise, but, how, in talking with the suicidal adolescent himself, a quite different picture often emerges.

> What we hear, and know to be true, is that thoughts of his own death, or of doing something that would result in his death, have been silently present in the adolescent's mind well before the time of the more organized and determined ideas of doing something that would result in his death. [Laufer, 1995, p. 71]

In the case of Laura, the poet, her assurances "because of the consequences" rather than "because I don't want to die" are definitely cause for concern. As Laufer put it, "it is essential to help the adolescent to create a continuity in his life and acknowledge that he remains vulnerable to further attempts unless or until the reason for the first attempt is understood and made part of the adolescent's mental life" (p. 80). The promise not to do it again "leaves the adolescent feeling abandoned, frightened, alone, and very much at risk. . . . The adolescent is not lying when he says that he has given up his earlier idea of killing himself, but we must be aware that he is not in touch with his reasons for wanting or needing to die" (p. 80).

Such a position on these issues is very helpful. The fact is that we, as therapists, are looking not only for the obvious signs of danger and suicidal intent but the unobvious, unconscious motivation. The question is, how does that unconscious motivation get assessed and how does it sit with conscious intention? For example, the extreme stunt-biking activities and many accidents of one young 17-year-old seen in the Department are clearly not intentionally self-harming, but a case could be made, taking into account other risk-taking behaviour on his part, that there is an unconsciously perverse satisfaction in self-harm—a release from pent-up feelings, *perhaps*, yet the scars, cuts, and bruises so often displayed to his therapist would seem to offer evidence of pride, even satisfaction, perhaps, in what were felt to be the insignia of manhood.

Underlying the specificity of self-harm and suicide among adolescents and young people is a wider picture, only implicitly touched on in the foregoing, and that is the relationship between practice based on rules and guidelines, in contrast to that based on intuition and experience. Of course the two are not mutually exclusive, but adolescent mental health can, perhaps fruitfully, draw on medical research into the relationship between the two (see, for example, the 2017 work of Trisha Greenhalgh). Suicide risk among young people draws such external and internal factors remorselessly close together, in both patient and clinician. Standing back, one can make some helpful generalizations, but faced with that deeply suffering, riven, and conflictual other, how is it that we can determine what it is that best enables one part of the personality eventually to be able to say to the other, "Turn and exist"?

I shall conclude with a quotation from James Baldwin (1955), which powerfully states a very significant factor that so often underlies destructive acts:

> I imagine that one of the reasons people cling to their hates so stubbornly is because they sense, once hate is gone, that they will be forced to deal with pain.
>
> [quoted in Naomi Klein, 2017, p. 61]

PART **IV**

FICTIONAL WORLDS

CHAPTER THIRTEEN

Adolescent fiction:
the eerie and the upside down

In examining, in this chapter, the fictional worlds to which adolescents are themselves drawn, further light will be thrown on what Eglé Laufer described as:

> . . . a kind of capsize of the personality, rather like the way massive icebergs turn upside down when the warmer seas melt the lower part. . . . This means that all the more disturbed parts of the personality have to be helped into the new situation. In those vulnerable adolescents, the violent murderous version of human relations which exists in all of us breaks out from its place of residence in the mind and can be played out in reality. . . . [quoted in Anderson, 2008, p. 71]

The best-selling fictional works for and about adolescent states of mind often depict worlds in which the protagonists seem to be both fully involved in the everyday preoccupations of adolescent life and yet *also* live in an ongoing reality that offers a quite different set of strange, eerie, and often violent experiences.[1] The elision that occurs here between simultaneous yet distinct internal and external worlds, though not wholly unfamiliar, has rarely been more dramatically and disturbingly presented than in these contemporary works. I shall be focusing, now, on what is known as Young Adult literature—reading being less a relic from the past than parents often fear.

A reason that these "young adult" books are selling in such large numbers lies, perhaps, in the fact that they speak to the "uncensored"

mental and physical spaces and settings that adolescents feel themselves actually to be struggling with, in contrast to the worlds that to
others, especially adults, they *seem* to inhabit. These fictional narratives
so often depict at least two layers of reality simultaneously. They tend
to be infused with alarming and incomprehensible forces of weirdness
and confusion, with other-world destructiveness and perversity, that
the characters are having to manage in concert with their day-to-day
preoccupations, themselves ones often fraught with the real-life challenges already described. In this literature, such other worlds, even
universes, are brought powerfully and vividly to the fore amid the
ordinary experiences. The characters are often portrayed in terms of
occupying what seem like parallel universes, ones that may or may
not always be evident, visibly or audibly, to others.

During the teenage years, as we have seen, things take a rather
different turn. The regression to infantile states of mind, typical of
adolescence and characterized by Klein's paranoid-schizoid position
(i.e., by extremities of splitting, projection, and denial), is also typified
by a powerful attraction to evocations of the primitive nature of these
other worlds: worlds where states of impulsiveness, omnipotence,
elation, despair, frustration, rage so often prevail; where situations
of persecution and mystery hold sway, and death so often threatens.

The curious and disturbing settings that we encounter in teenage
fiction are often destructive and perverse in the extreme. The external
settings may range from war zones to space invasions; to interactions
with vampires (*Cirque du Freak*; Shan, 2000); to fights to the death
with bizarre, primitive, and malevolent forces (*Chaos Walking*; Ness,
2008–2010). Many such forces seem to belong to quite other systems of
being and to function with varieties of indeterminate extraterrestrial
threat and retributive rancour. The question is often one of the survival, or not, of the hitherto known self, indeed of the hitherto known
civilization, in terms of a character's assumptive world of family and
school structure, of the self's very sense of having something called a
"self". The question is often also one of whether it is still possible for
any of the young characters to find and sustain a trusting and intimate
relationship with loyalty and love, despite what seems to be going on
in the world as they experience it.

In other words, the question at the heart of many of these works
is that of the survival of the protagonists' known worlds in relation to
life as it has been lived hitherto, before the great "capsizing" or "up-
ending" of the personality during this alarming period. They do, in
fact, have to suffer the pains of total uncertainty, of dread, loss, often

guilt, need, persecution, sexual and destructive urges, and so much more. They occupy a kind of "edge-city"—a term originally used to describe a type of American novel that addressed itself to evocations of life lived at the limit, whether that "limiting" was a demarcation between life and death, sanity and madness, thinking and mindlessness, depression and mania, intimacy and perversity, fantasy and reality, or accommodation and "rebellion" (Tanner, 1971). All of these are usually somewhere in the mix. To varying degrees and extremity, they also characterize the profoundly disturbing mix to be found in many of the stories that so engross this age of reader.

I shall be drawing, initially, upon a novel by Patrick Ness to focus attention on some of these similarities in the broad spectrum of young adult fiction and the grip that they have on their readership. *The Rest of Us Just Live Here* (2015) departs, in some significant ways, from Ness's earlier *magnum opus*—*Chaos Walking* (2008–2010)—a brilliant trilogy that I shall be considering in due course. I choose *The Rest of Us Just Live Here* because it is centrally and specifically about transitions, both in terms of developmental stages and also between different states of mind. It artfully positions the lives of ordinary, middle-class American teenagers within a context of extraterrestrial phenomena that the friendship group is fully aware of from the first pages of the book. What goes on in these extraterrestrial settings are, in their detail, confined for the most part to the extensive headings of each chapter, which almost constitute a separate "plot", rather than being expressed in the text itself. It is here, in the headings, that the epic gods-and-monsters-with-pillars-of-light plot belongs, despite the bizarre periodic appearances of these characters throughout in the main events of the youngsters' day-to-day activities. These other-world forces and creatures intrude, especially at times of momentous change, into the lives of the basic friendship group and, seemingly, have overall control, as suggested in the title, "the rest of us just live here". In other words, the narrative structure of the book presents a further device to convey parallel realities.

The youngsters are negotiating a particularly significant adolescent rite of passage: from the final days of school and home-life (marked by the celebratory school prom) and away into the various college worlds of the "outside" (and beyond). Indeed, here it is almost as if adolescence constitutes a world of its own, self-enclosed, all absorbing, fragile yet also curiously robust. Leaving that familiar world is as if the whole thing simply explodes and disappears, which is marked in the story by the school—literally and utterly mysteriously—blowing up on prom night. From the very first, the ordinariness of the youngsters' transition from school and family to college and the outside world is shot through with the weird, apparently cyclical (as generation succeeds generation) impact of incomprehensible, destructive forces that belong to alternative universes. The external events mark just how internally terrifying such transitions may be. There is a stupefying sense of the loss of any sense of internal gravitational pull. Here, the transition is that of leaving the carapace of the world of school settings and friendship groups and to facing the horrors of "not knowing", of having to start again, now as a big, sensible boy or girl. It is also that of recognizing and engaging in acts of exploration and intimacy—a sort of "pairing off" from the group as hitherto constituted.

In this novel, much of the young people's chat is to do with trying to understand things: their own feelings, fears, and attractions, those of their friends, their parents, and of the "others". But each has his or her own unique, starkly realistic story: Mikey, for example, the main protagonist and the first-person narrator (as so often in this literature), is plagued by eczema and OCD rituals that drive him mad, *actually* mad, he fears—"going crazy" always threatens him. He has, moreover, recently almost "lost" his older, severely anorexic sister who has been brought back from the heart-attack of technical death by crisis medical intervention. All these young people "have their stories". Patrick Ness perfectly captures the lingo, humour, sadness, loyalty, fragility of adolescent siblings and friendships and effortlessly weaves together the thin-skinned touchiness that pervades the groupings of this age— their anxiety to understand, or make as-if to understand, sexuality, homosexuality, faith, parents. There is a whole gamut of uncertainty about the vulnerable selfness of the self and the "otherness" of, in this case, the "indie kids". These "beings" exist as some kind of alternative version of themselves—both a part of, and yet utterly apart from, their daily lives. Each character is very distinctively bound up with his or her own particular problems of identity, of difference, of intimacy, of belonging. They are bound up with their respective parental legacies, their sibling crises; with the huge challenges of simply sorting out who on earth they are. The "sorting" has to occur in relation both to this world in which they find themselves and also to the "outside" world towards which they are, of necessity, heading.

In Mikey, it would seem, there is a fundamental split between the struggles of ordinary, social everyday life and the realities of having to contend with all kinds of disturbing and extraterrestrial phenomena—as, for example, battles with vampires and, indeed, with the "undead"; with "soul-eating ghosts"; with waves of spooky deaths and explosions, by which, fascinatingly, the adult world seems to be either oblivious or not especially bothered. "Honestly. Adults. How do they live in the world?" (p. 39). For the adolescent, this is the question: "the world?"—which world and where? And how can the adults possibly be so blind and cut off? The felt chasm between the experience of the youngsters and that of the adults (in Mikey's case, an alcoholic father and a politically ambitious and remote mother) is excruciatingly immediate. Mikey is very aware that his family's social existence in the community rests, in fact, on lies and embezzlement, a cover-up in this particular family that becomes the basis for the children—as for many others in such teenage novels (and in life)—to experience themselves as bringing themselves up, without parents, or struggling with the supposed secrets of a lying, or self-deluding, parental world.

The coterminous reality of dual registers in which the young people are trying to live their lives has never been more apparent than in this literature. Put a different way, it is as if the stories are the narratives of the characters' internal worlds, and the external facts of the lives they live simply provide the settings. Here, internal reality and external reality are one, explicitly rather than, as in psychodynamic accounts, implicitly. While the professional clinical "work" would be to untangle the relationship between the two, in this fiction the coexistence is assumed. For example, instances of telepathy, of the uncanny, and of preternatural insight are quite common in many of the stories. Some characters can "literally" hear what other characters are thinking: "Watch what you think when he's around", says one young friend about Edmond, a main protagonist in Meg Rosoff's *How I Live Now* (2004). In Patrick Ness's work, such phenomena can take the form, as in his trilogy, of the significantly varying functions of a character's "Noise" (i.e., the availability of their unique inner thoughts and feelings both heard and unheard by others; known and unknown by, and to, themselves). A character's Noise constitutes a selective channel for understanding the thought processes and inner feelings of self, located, it seems, somewhere between the unconscious and the conscious and definitely a barometer for awareness of the self. We encounter the varying abilities of the characters themselves to have more or less selective access to their own Noise. We also encounter (Ness, 2008) the depiction of a whole traumatized and humiliated people, the Spackles, punished by the crippling impact of being rendered without any Noise at all. The presence or absence, strength or weakness, of peoples' Noise is a significant indication of the nature of their authentic contact with different parts of themselves, or the lack of such contact.

These sorts of phenomena vividly express the adolescent experience of there, indeed, being no safe boundary between internal and external experiences: the fear that, for example, their faces, even thoughts, can be read "like a book", or the sense of power, as well as dread, that they omnisciently know what other people are *really* thinking. Common, too, to many of the plots are the overwhelming persecutory feelings of helplessness in the face of monstrously powerful forces of control, submission, and domination. Yet, so often, the stories also involve the sorts of scenario that have long been at the heart of myth and adventure literature: the giants, ogres, and dragons of old, stretching back to Homeric times, themselves in age-old bardic traditions. More recently, they tend to feature the evil enemies against which the young hero, and possibly heroine, have to pit themselves to save the planet, or to save civilization itself. We may also think back to the *War of the Worlds* type of scenario, at the birth of the cosmic battles depicted in H. G. Wells's finely crafted science fiction at the turn of the nineteenth to twentieth centuries. In the fiction under discussion, however, the degrees of savagery, betrayal, and destructiveness can be quite shocking to the adult reader, especially, perhaps, in Suzanne Collins's (2008–2010) *The Hunger Games,* where the television game-show is constructed around children actually killing each other. Here we are taken to areas beyond the ordinary levels of merciless aggression and into extremely primitive mental states that really are the stuff of nightmares and of infantile worlds of persecution and aggression—yet quite familiar to those who work, as did Melanie Klein, with very young children. As long as these states prevail, dog-eat-dog mentalities supervene.

Yet, so often, there is a different register of experience also being tracked, again reminiscent of age-old stories in which hero and heroine combat the forces of evil and exhibit, in so doing, capacities for loyalty and love, for honour and truth-telling, which, in some way, seem to belong almost to a chivalric era, one quite apart from contemporary reality. This, too, is a powerful element in the fascination of *The Hunger Games.* Moreover, what prevails beneath the action-packed dramas of world, or "other-world", domination tends to be scenarios in which parents are, for one reason or another, physically or emotionally absent—sometimes dead, sometimes cut off by mysterious wars or obscure persecutory events. Part of the attraction must be the cliff-edge variety of who will reveal themselves or be revealed, and when, as clever saboteurs; also, if, and where, there can be any sense of confidence in the triumph of good, of courage and sacrifice, of love and redemption.

In these young characters' worlds, individuals tend to be on their own, in relation to any sense of positive parental awareness. They are having to work out for themselves the perennial difficulties of whom to trust, including themselves, of how to hold fast to their values despite doubts, and of how to digest the extraordinary complexities of individual life or existence in these vast terrestrial and extraterrestrial universes. The infantile states that engulf so many are ones that are primarily self-interested—riven, persecuted, especially by absence, by loss, by frustration, or by the threat of the bizarre or unknown. In effect, in these texts, the characters are at constant risk of psychic disintegration, states akin to those of very early infancy described so vividly by Klein (see *Melanie Klein Revisited*: Sherwin-White, 2017). In Klein's work with young children, she stresses, in this early phase of mental development, oral sadistic and destructive scenarios and the fundamental roles of phantasy, unconscious persecution, anxiety, fear, and desire. So too, we find, in this "young adult" literature.

What Patrick Ness, Meg Rosoff, Frances Hardinge, John Green, Anne Cassidy, John Lucas, Hilary Freeman, and many others among these writers for adolescents have in common is not just the immediacy of a certain literary brilliance in relation to their varied evocations of the age group generally, but a considerable depth of insight into the inside story of adolescent states of mind, so closely expressing the more primitive and infantile internal states already described.

Central to so many of the fictional scenarios of this literature is dis-illusionment with the parental generation and the, as yet unresolved, relationship between the rejecting and the dependent urges that tend to plague these years. Pre-puberty, parents have, for good or ill, been a kind of "base-camp" for the personality. The transitional period of adolescence takes place when a different base for security and identity is not yet formed, nor to be found. It is as if each individual carries within himself the great dilemmas of social and political change, so powerfully expressed by the commentators on, for example, the Victorian age of transition and so pertinent to the confusion and loneliness, the desolation and despondency of these youngsters, as they feel their way towards different forms of understanding and enlightenment in a world that seems to offer them less and less—for some, little or none. This is beautifully expressed in Hardinge's *The Lie Tree*, a powerful rendition of, among so many child and adolescent preoccupations, the impact on the young personality of parental distraction, deception, evasion, and falsity. The youngster who finds out the truth is, as so often, in grave danger. Meltzer (1973b) locates this assault in an adolescent's sense of disillusionment, which so often sets in after puberty, as the discovery that "while the small child thinks his god-like parents know secrets, the adolescent knows that his clay-footed parents have not found them" (p. 159).

Contemporary fiction for this age group can, at its best, convey enormous insight into adolescent crises of transformation, about the degree to which many suffer incomprehensible extremes of weird, not-me feelings—often of lust and violence—resulting in uncharacteristic enactments. The literature vividly brings alive the shock and misery of the discovery of life as it is. Such experiences, both mental and emotional, run counter to the standards and values of what might be described as a normal range, as hitherto known, of moods and behaviour. Yet these young people are actually undergoing shocking new feelings and impulses that can seem quite mad to those who thought they knew who these children, even their own children, really were.

Many parents describe how swiftly their child has become scarcely recognizable, almost overnight. Indeed, the youngsters are also, often, scarcely recognizable to themselves, a state powerfully depicted by Hilary Freeman (2015) in her fascinating novel, *When I Was Me*: "Yesterday, when I was me, I had a life. It wasn't a particularly great life, but it wasn't a terrible one either, and at least it was mine" (p. 19), says 17-year-old Ella, in the opening lines of the book. And a few pages later:

> . . . but that was yesterday, when I was me, fully me. Today, everything is different. And now I'm wondering if yesterday actually happened, if yesterday really was yesterday, or if yesterday and all the yesterdays that came before it were a dream. Memories are fallible, aren't they? It's what you can sense around you that is supposed to be true: what you can see, hear, touch and taste. That's the first rule of science. So if my memories seem more real, more tangible, than the world I find myself in, what does that mean?
>
> Either I have lost my memory.
>
> Or I have lost my mind.
>
> And if I am not me, fully me, then who am I? [pp. 21–22]

Ella struggles to make sense of things; she tries to rationalize to herself what is happening to her:

> The truth is, I have already lived many lives in my lifetime; there have already existed more versions of me than I can count. I have been constantly changing, little by little, cell by cell, pore by pore. These other transformations were so slow that I simply didn't notice them happening. This one is different only because it was so violent and sudden, because it happened overnight. [p. 69]

It is unusual that so drastic a transformation should not take place until age 17, as opposed to the more usual 13 or 14, as puberty first breaks in upon individuals who thought they knew who they were. But the suggestion, in this novel, as in many others, is that it is sexuality that arouses very particular fears as well as pleasures and introduces the sense that one's body is no longer one's own, nor, in this novel, is the previously "known world", both within and outside the home. At one point, Ella's mother comes downstairs eager to hear about her daughter's first date. Ella resists: "Who gives their mother a blow by blow account of a date? If this is something the other Ella would do, she must have been a lot closer to her mum than I am" (p. 153). This is a good example of the dramatic change in parent–child relationships that not only does, but should and must, to some degree happen during these tumultuous years.

A little later there is an, again wholly typical, episode with a counsellor whom Ella finds intensely annoying and patronising: "I look at her, so full of herself, thinking she knows everything and I have the urge to shock her . . ." (pp. 157–158)

Needless to say, there follows, during this reflection, Ella's determined decision never to go back again. But towards the end of the book, things become much more worrying, in the sense that other universes actually obtrude and seem to have a decisive influence on the action. For compelling reasons, Ella feels that she must jump from what is known in North London as "Suicide Bridge", over Archway Road. Once up there, she discovers that she is "too chicken", as she thinks, and goes down the steps again only to find herself in hospital having, quite unbeknownst to herself, had a car crash while being taught to drive by "one of the boys". Ella seems to be having some kind of experience of living in parallel realities, a phenomenon not so unfamiliar to Hilary Freeman's readers, nor to many others.

* * *

Here, the question of what *is* reality extends into the final pages of this disquieting tale, essentially about being able to "jump universes". There are three versions to the final chapter: "Afterwards" (a), (b), and (c). The last version returns Ella to "normality":

> And, it turns out, I've got a phobia of heights.
> It's not a particularly exciting life, but it's my life.
> And I'm bloody well going to try my best to live it. [p. 262]

It must be clear from the foregoing that there is, in the fiction that I have been touching on, much happening in the situations described—they tend to be swift-moving and action-packed. The emotional experience of many of the plots can best be described in terms of the uncanny, the weird, or the eerie. Freud (1919h) begins his well-known paper "The 'Uncanny'" by describing his own feeling of being "impelled" to investigate the subject of aesthetics, by which he means not only the theory of beauty, but the "theory of qualities of feeling" (p. 219). This, he says, is rare for a psychoanalyst. His musings on his chosen subject, one that he had clearly been pondering for a number of years, begin with, for our purposes, a very helpful examination of the varieties of meaning and nuance that are evoked by his title word, "*Unheimlich*", inadequately translated into English as "uncanny". Freud's word is much more suggestive in its penumbra of associative possibilities—primarily that of implying something like "unhomely". He quotes the philosopher Friedrich Schelling: "Unheimlich *is the name for everything that should have remained . . . secret and hidden but has come to light*" (p. 224). Freud also traces the various meanings of *heimlich* in relation to *unheimlich* before going on, in the main body of the paper, to cite a range of stories and interpretations of *unheimlich*, as, for example, in E. T. A. Hoffman's, the "Sand-Man".

> Thus *heimlich* is a word the meaning of which develops in the direction of ambivalence, until it finally coincides with its opposite, *unheimlich*. *Unheimlich* is, in some way or other, a sub-species of *heimlich*. Let us bear this discovery in mind though we cannot yet rightly understand it, alongside of Schelling's definition of the *Unheimlich*. If we go on to examine individual instances of uncanniness, these hints will become intelligible to us. [p. 226]

Drawing on Freud and the work of the cultural critic, Mark Fisher (2016), we find much that is pertinent to the present discussion. What, says Fisher, the weird and the eerie have in common,

. . . is a preoccupation with the strange. The strange—not the horrific. The allure that the weird and the eerie possess is not captured by the idea that we "enjoy what scares us". It has, rather, to do with a fascination for the outside, for that which lies beyond standard perception, cognition and experience. [p. 8]

There is something in this genre of fiction, for and about adolescence and young adults, that arouses two rather distinct ways of thinking. First, that the inner turmoil of the adolescent is often so extreme that a preoccupation with the undoubtedly "strange" is, perhaps, less an expression, or projection of, the internal states themselves (in terms of symbolic representation) than a refuge from them. Such a refuge can be thought of as constituting rather compelling "psychic retreats" (Steiner, 1993) of a kind that express something strange and spooky but are, in fact, less weird and eerie than the youngsters' own actual internal fears and phantasies. There is, in other words, a defensive dimension that can hold things, somewhat, until these testing years pass, as a protection, a relief, and form of escape from the real horrors within.

There is another possibility, however. One that relates more closely to what Freud seems to have meant by "*Unheimlich*"—that what in particular characterizes this stage of development is precisely that the whole concept of there being a genuine "home", either externally or internally, is very much in doubt. The individual adolescent often feels entirely cut adrift from the *lares* and *penates* of what had been felt as an internal hearth. The emphasis is now on moving away from base, or, rather, reconstruing what had, hitherto, felt like base. It is this state of metaphorical homelessness that often underlies the 14- or 15-year-old's retreat into the bedroom and the internet world of gaming and relationships conducted online, either with friends or with persons unknown. Here a temporary home can be found, one apart from the nominal home that no longer feels in the least bit "homely".

Many of Mark Fisher's descriptions of what he designates as weird or eerie can be seen closely to evoke characteristics of the fictional plots that I have been discussing. In relation to the eerie, especially in Patrick Ness's work, we find issues of time and causality that are quite alien to ordinary perception, "but it is also eerie in that it raises questions about agency: who or what is the entity that has woven fate" (Fisher, 2016, p. 12). And it is precisely this kind of release "from the confines of what is ordinarily taken for reality, which goes some way to account for the peculiar appeal that the eerie possesses" (p. 13). "The sensation of the eerie occurs either when there is something present where there should be nothing, or there is nothing present when there should be something" (p. 61).

The eerie, suggests Fisher, has to do with absence. The weird, by contrast, is the fact that, as we see with especial clarity in Ness's fiction, the "outside" "can make an irruption through time and space into an objectively familiar locale. Worlds may be entirely foreign to us, both in terms of location and even in terms of the physical laws which govern them, without being weird. It is the irruption into this world of something from outside which is the marker of the weird" (p. 20). What clearer description could possibly be needed of the world of the "indie kids"? Or the setting of *Chaos Walking*?

Interestingly, as Fisher comments:

> The perspective of the eerie can give us access to the forces which govern mundane reality but which are ordinarily obscured, just as it can give us access to spaces beyond mundane reality altogether. It is this release from the mundane, this escape from the confines of what is ordinarily taken for reality, which goes some way to account for the peculiar appeal that the eerie possesses. [p. 13]

Moreover, this escape is also from any sense of the old clarity about moral categories, about the loss of childhood certainties about right and wrong or about goodies and baddies. This is all extremely troubling during these adolescent years. Notions of the weird, the eerie, the uncanny introduce all manner of questions and nuances to these erstwhile clear categories. In the adolescent world, the distinctions between the good and the bad are now ever-shifting, often leaving the reader as puzzled as the participants. In Ness's work, as in that of so many others writing for this age group, we find vividly brought to life the ongoing, weird, and eerie complexities of the youngster's lives while they are, ostensibly, in the course of the ordinary, albeit momentous, transition from one stage of life to the next—for them, literally, from one world to the next.

The young adult literature, in general, depicts so powerfully the sense of the "capsizing" of the personality, with no rescuing buoy in reach, or even in sight. It brings into focus the weirdness and the fragility of experience, the eerie confusion of the whole enterprise. Yet the books do, most of them, represent a kind of fictional "working through", in the sense that the endings feel neither hopeless nor tragic, but somewhat determined and realistic—expressed by Ella.

The last stanza of Emily Dickinson's (1862) poem, "We Grow Accustomed to the Dark", expresses it beautifully:

. . . as they learn to see—
Either the Darkness alters—
Or something in the sight
Adjusts itself to Midnight—
And life steps almost straight.

Note

1.   These themes are also frequently explored in film and TV. Of particular note is the 2016 Netflix hit series *Stranger Things*, in which "The Upside Down" is an "alternate dimension existing in parallel to the human world. It contains the same locations and infrastructure as the human world, but it is much darker, colder and obscured by an omnipresent fog" [http://strangerthings.wikia.com/wiki/The_Upside_Down].

CHAPTER FOURTEEN

Late-adolescent fictional lives

"... certain books, like certain works of art, rouse powerful feelings and stimulate growth willy-nilly."

Wilfred Bion, "Commentary" (1967, p. 156)

During the adolescent years there is a likelihood that, as we have seen, to both good and bad ends the projective tendencies will predominate over the introjective. The anxiety involved in a young person's attempts to discover who he is and to define more clearly his sense-of-himself-in-the-world often arouses extremes of defensive splitting and projection. But in the course of this quest for self-definition, other more moderate and exploratory ways of establishing a better understanding of himself are also in play. These other ways involve less intense and extreme degrees of projection and include the capacity to value and to take in the kinds of mental and emotional qualities that can help to support a young person's developing self. More detailed emphasis now needs to be given to the nature of introjective processes—those that were, as we have seen in earlier chapters, so integral to Simon, Tom, and others being able to change.

Intrinsic to the introjective process is the capacity to relinquish external figures of dependence and attachment and to install a version of them within, as resources that inspire and encourage the independent development of the personality. Such processes, as already described, involve the capacity to mourn what is being let go, or what is felt to have been lost. Strengthened by such an undertaking, it may be felt to be possible to move on. The process occurs over time. The changes may be akin to those internal shifts in Dorothea already noted and so subtly described by George Eliot in *Middlemarch*:

> That new real future which was replacing the imaginary drew its material from the endless minutiae by which her view of Mr. Casaubon and her wifely relation, now that she was married to him, was gradually changing with the secret motion of a watch-hand from what it had been in her maiden dream. [p. 226]

We are familiar with Freud's view that central to the achievement of adolescence is the satisfactory fulfilment of the task of crystallizing sexual identity, of finding a sexual partner, and of bringing together the two main stems of sexuality, the sensual and the tender (chapter 10). The struggle towards an internal capacity for intimacy is what, in important ways, adolescence has been working towards all along. Developing such a capacity may, for some, take many more years and possibly several different attempts. And, indeed, the pairing-off that does occur at this stage of young adulthood may, despite appearances, have little to do with a genuine transition from adolescent to adult states of mind. It may have little relation, of any real kind, to the internal capacity that is now being described. Indeed, such couplings can constitute precisely the opposite—that is, a defensive bonding in the face of anxiety about what stepping into adulthood might really entail.

As we have seen, one of the main undertakings of adolescence is that of establishing a mind of one's own (chapter 9), a mind that is rooted in, and yet also at least partially distinct from, the sources and models of identification that are visible within one's family or in the wider school and community setting. In late adolescence, the struggle for separation, one that is fundamental to this capacity to be one's own person, tends to take on certain characteristics that differ from the early teenage years. Usually the young person will, by this time, be emerging from the often addictive complexities of group-life and of the multifold and shifting relationships that have hitherto been part of the process of separating from parents and family. He will be facing a different and more extreme separation: that of leaving school or college, often also home, of having to be independent as never before. It is a time of hope and expectation, but, for many, also of extreme sadness, distress, confusion, and even, for the few who find themselves unequal to the task, of breakdown.

The success or failure of this challenge will importantly depend on how experiences of love and loss have been negotiated in the past— indeed, from the very beginning. The nature of the negotiation, as repeatedly stated, is deeply affected by the extent to which the parent, or parents, can bear to relinquish their children and to help them on their way. The pain of so doing often carries with it an intensity and a poignancy that tests the bravest of hearts. Intrinsic to this stage in the separation process is the seeking of an intimate partnership outside the family. The capacity to establish a deep and lasting relationship is dependent on the outcome of a number of complex internal processes that will, almost always, have been problematic as well as rewarding during the adolescent years. At the heart of the matter lies the degree of a person's capacity to experience loss, a loss especially stark as childhood is definitively left behind and engagement with the adult world becomes a necessity.

The task of becoming oneself, now and always, thus involves relinquishing the denigrated and idealized versions of the self, and of other people and relationships, in favour of the real. It involves renegotiating dreams, choices, and hopes, whether self-generated or imposed from without. It involves tolerating opportunities lost, roads not taken. Painful conflicts are aroused as the young person has to set forth and, simultaneously, to let go. Such difficulties confront them at every stage of life, but they are perhaps most demanding and intransigent at major points of transition, whether it be first going to school or finally retiring from work, or, as in this case, embarking on the rest of one's life. These sorts of losses test the capacity to mourn, to feel remorse, to take responsibility, to experience guilt and also gratitude. All such capacities are fundamentally involved in a person's being able to love, and all are intimately linked to the nature of the balance between the projective and introjective processes that have been established from the very first.

It would take a whole book about a patient's life to describe the introjective processes taking place in the course of an analysis. In fact, it is the book-length accounts of a character's development that *do* encompass the extensive chronology of the capacity to grow, or failure to do so. The scale of the nineteenth-century novel particularly lends itself to such an enterprise, for, in the course of the narrative, what is so often established is precisely the late-adolescent process under discussion: the gradual development of a character's internal capacity for intimacy. The external event of "marriage" functions as a symbolic representation of the point of emergence into adulthood, of the culmination of late-adolescent struggles towards establishing a place of his or her own, by contrast with that which is conventionally assigned to them. Thus "marriage", emblematic of lasting commitment, marks the realization of internal capacities that have been developing in the course of the narrative, promoted by the impact on one or other of the characters concerned. In many nineteenth-century novels, a shift can be described as having taken place from an initial *idea* of marriage, often culturally and contractually framed, to a final *capacity* for marriage. The shift is effected by the gradual yielding of the temptation towards splitting and projection in favour of a deeper sense of the value of internal figures in the introjective mode, perhaps by a gradual rebalancing of the two tendencies, with all the problems that that rebalancing entails.

Drawing on *Inside Lives* (Waddell, 1998), the nature of these inner developments is explored here in Jane Austen's *Emma* (1816) and, very briefly, in Charlotte Brontë's *Jane Eyre* (1847). The developments are characteristic of, but by no means exclusive to, late adolescence. In these novels the institution of marriage is naturally, in terms of social and cultural setting, very differently underpinned from marriage today. But there is a shared developmental thrust, one that still informs the process of late adolescence, albeit often in much less obviously conventional form. This thrust is towards encountering, or recognizing, a true partner and developing the capacities to sustain a committed relationship.

The capacity for marriage must not be confused with the contractual relationship of marriage. In nineteenth-century novels, as in life, people continue to get married to each other. But they do not all do so on the basis of what is being described here as an "internal capacity for marriage"; nor, indeed, do they have the capacity not to be married. For contractual marriage, as already suggested, often functions either as a defence against separation, loss, and intimacy or as a perpetuation of an unresolved oedipal problem. Jane Austen's novels, in particular, both wittily and painfully depict any number of bad marriages. These unions are wholly distinct from the kind of central progression in which development proceeds as the protagonists engage ever more deeply with their lives and loves.

A compelling aspect of each book is the nature of the internal odyssey that is embarked upon. The central characters suffer, endure, weather self-deception and, perhaps most importantly, face and survive the experience of loss. At one point Emma exclaims: "I seem to have been doomed to blindness" (Austen, 1816, p. 398). Whence does

Emma derive the capacity to learn from her mistakes and her errone-
ous perceptions? How is it that one person embraces and another
evades the possibility of growth, settling instead for a less disturbing
conformity, or a reinforcing of the defensive fastnesses? These narratives are explorations of how a young woman joins the adult world,
not only the constricted world of the writer's youth, but the contemporary world of any young person's struggle towards maturity. This
is rather literally demonstrated by the 1995 "teen movie" *Clueless*, a
hugely popular—if somewhat loose—adaptation of *Emma*. Whether or
not the original texts are familiar, the psychic predicaments described
"speak" for themselves.

Emma Woodhouse was, as the opening paragraph of the book
establishes,

> handsome, clever and rich, with a comfortable home and happy
> disposition [she] seemed to unite some of the best blessings of exist-
> ence; and had lived nearly twenty-one years in the world with very
> little to distress or vex her. [p. 8]

In the few, densely packed pages of the first chapter, the subject of
marriage is immediately introduced. Indeed, the beginning, middle,
and end of the book are marked by marriages. Emma's part in these
different unions charts the shift in her from child-like omnipotence,
through defensive manipulation (typical of the projective mode), to
some degree of self-knowledge and that more mature sense of dependence, gratitude, and unworthiness that is characteristic of the introjective mode. The key factor in this shift is the changing relationship
between Emma and Mr Knightley—a figure in whom, as Tanner
(1986) suggests, Emma, the arch-matchmaker, finally "meets her match
and, in a sense, her 'maker': the conflated words have to be properly
separated (and morally monitored) so that Emma can become most
properly—Emma" (p. 176). It is the oscillating progress of a capacity to
recognize Mr Knightley as her "match", as the embodiment of qualities that were becoming internal to herself, that provides a sustaining
source of fascination and instruction in the course of the book from
the beginning. The reader is left with no doubt but that Mr Knightley
(a local landowner and the most gentlemanly and eligible figure in
the community) is the man for Emma. But Emma turns a blind eye,
only slowly, and with great difficulty, relinquishing her projective and
narcissistic defences against "seeing" what to others has long been so
clear.

On the first page of the book, the marriage takes place between
Mr Weston and Miss Taylor, Emma's governess since her mother's

death sixteen years previously. "It was Miss Taylor's loss which first brought grief. It was on the wedding-day of this beloved friend that Emma first sat in mournful thought of any continuance" (p. 8). But Emma's disposition soon saves her from any protracted continuance of mournfulness. Experiencing herself as architect of what might otherwise have been felt to be a kind of oedipal reverse protects her from too lasting or severe a pain.

> "And you have forgotten one matter of joy to me", said Emma, "and a very considerable one—that I made the match myself. I made the match, you know, four years ago; and to have it take place and be proved in the right, when so many people said Mr Weston would never marry again, may comfort me for anything".
>
> Mr Knightley shook his head at her. Her father fondly replied, "Ah! My dear, I wish you would not make these matches and foretell things, for whatever you say always comes to pass. Pray do not make any more matches." [Mr Woodhouse, "a valetudinarian all his life", is the archetypal killjoy, opposed to anything on the side of life or relationship and thus, especially, to marriage.]
>
> "I promise you to make none for myself, Papa; but I must, indeed, for other people. It is the greatest amusement in the world! And after such success, you know!"
>
> . . . . . .
>
> "I do not understand what you mean by 'success'"; said Mr Knightley. "Success supposes endeavour . . . where is your merit? What are you proud of?—You made a lucky guess; and *that* is all that can be said". [p. 14]

This relatively light-hearted exchange is very suggestive. We immediately understand that Emma's matchmaking constitutes a defensive procedure against awareness of any desire for intimacy on her own part, as well as a way of trying out, by proxy, what intimacy might feel like. Protected by the self-imposed duty of having to stay at home to look after her child-like father, she can perpetuate the pseudo-adult role ("having been mistress of his house from a very early period") and keep at bay any risk of actually feeling dependent herself. She had been used to "doing just what she liked; highly esteeming Miss Taylor's judgement, but directed chiefly by her own" (p. 7).

Not at all consciously preoccupied with pursuing a man she might care for, Emma concerns herself, either fancifully or actually, with these issues on behalf of others, primarily on behalf of her friend Harriet Smith, through whom she can indulge her notions of matchmaking without any risk of engaging her own feelings. There is a kind of excitement and energy about Emma. She generates interest. As

Mr Knightley says: "There is an anxiety, a curiosity in what one feels for Emma. I wonder what will become of her?" The reader *is* caught up in what will occur to her next ("At this moment, an ingenious and animating suspicion was entering Emma's brain"). Much of the novel is concerned with Emma making matches, or assuming the existence of matches, only fleetingly allowing herself into any of the complex equations. One reading would be that her addiction to matchmaking is a way of protecting herself from being vulnerable to experiences of love and loss, and that her inability to relinquish her loyalty to the care of her father is based on an anxiety about exposing herself to the emotional turbulence of a different kind of intimate relationship. The central movement of the novel describes the extremely elaborate entanglement and disentanglement of projective possibilities for intimacy, an intimacy that cannot, initially, be worked on in any more direct or immediate way. A central question becomes, what is it that enables Emma, eventually, to begin to be able to take in and to appreciate the qualities and functions represented by Mr Knightley? What is it that emboldens her to risk engaging with her own sincere feelings rather than "managing" those of others?

Initially, Harriet Smith suits Emma's defensive purposes perfectly—both as a much-needed companion and as a vehicle for her projective schemes. Emma's incapacity to distinguish in whose interests her imagined attachments really are is a measure of her serious denial of the ordinary adolescent need for fantasy and experimentation, before she can recognize or develop any readiness for a lasting partner for herself. The description of her artistic talents offers a marvellous encapsulation of an adolescent's shifting tastes and enthusiasms and of Emma's narcissistic investment in admiration.

> Her many beginnings were displayed. Miniatures, half-lengths, whole-lengths, pencil, crayon, and watercolours had all been tried in turn. She had always wanted to do everything . . . she played and sang; and drew in almost every style; but steadiness had always been wanting. . . . She was not much deceived as to her own skill either as an artist or as a musician, but she was not unwilling to have others deceived, or sorry to know her reputation for accomplishment often higher than it deserved. . . . A likeness pleases everybody; and Miss Woodhouse's performances must be capital. [p. 43]

However, her portrait of Mr John Knightley does not please. "I put it away in a pet, and vowed I would never take another likeness" (p. 44).

This passage describes a more positive aspect of the projective mode, the now familiar process by which, during adolescence in particular, individuals may investigate who they are by projecting aspects of themselves into others and relating to them there, whether with acceptance or rejection. With Emma, the issue is more complicated, for instead of experimenting with possibilities herself, Harriet is proposed and promoted, with endless confusions, self-deceptions, and mistaken perceptions, and with the constant imposition of a great deal of disappointment and needless suffering. To begin with, Harriet is so malleable that Emma can more or less elicit in her what she will. Emma is an arrant projector, but she is also, as we have seen, knowingly and not unwillingly the subject of other people's projections—at times, far beyond her deserts. It is Mr Knightley who remains the touchstone of the relationship between Emma's illusory and actual ability. He retains, throughout, the capacity for judgement, duty, moral values, selflessness, and right-mindedness—a true gentleman, a true knight. "Mr Knightley, in fact, was one of the few people who could see faults in Emma Woodhouse, and the only one who ever told her them" (p. 12). He recognizes that she would never submit to anything requiring industry and patience and a subjection of fancy to understanding. He has, we are told, an exquisite manner, and good manners in Jane Austen, tend, on the whole, to be an authentic index of people's moral qualities.

When Mr Knightley questions Emma's claims to success in bringing about Miss Taylor's marriage, he is, with an honesty, straightforwardness, and, as the reader soon discovers, deep concern, trying to encourage Emma to think about the meaning and consequences of her actions. One of the problems he clearly perceives is Emma's difficulty in feeling that there is anything *to* learn: "How can Emma imagine she has anything to learn herself, while Harriet is presenting such a delightful inferiority?" (Better, he says, elsewhere, "to be without sense than to misapply it as you do".) Mr Knightley's easy access to Emma's household, outside any formal calling hours, conveys the sense that he is somehow continuously in her house/mind. Ronald Blythe (1966) describes the clever dichotomy whereby the reader "sees everything with Emma's eyes but has to judge it by Mr Knightley's standards" (p. 14). It is this very dichotomy that enables the reader to trace the evolving relationship between self and other in Emma, to follow the gradual decrease of her narcissistic projective mode in favour of a greater capacity for a realistic perception of herself and of the external world.

The relationship between Mr Knightley and Emma has much in common with that of Bion's "container/contained". As we have seen, the prototype is the relationship between mother and baby, analogous, in important ways, to that between therapist and patient. The prerequisites for thinking and learning lie in the availability of a mind capable of introjecting the baby's projective communications and evacuations, whether they be in love or in hate. Thus a person can investigate his own feelings in another personality, one that is felt to be resilient enough to contain them. In late adolescence, what becomes particularly evident is the way in which normal development is dependent on the mechanism for satisfying curiosity about the self (i.e., projective identification) being introjected in such a way as to foster an increase in thinking and in understanding. If this can happen in relation to figures in the external world, it is likely that it is also happening with figures in the internal world.

As a consequence of Mr Knightley's availability as a containing object, Emma's insistently projective mode begins to diminish to more "normal" proportions and her introjective capacities to increase. The observation of Mr Knightley's growing influence on Emma involves the reader in an experience of the process of the growth of the mind under the influence of a benign internal figure. At first Emma tends to deny any weight to Mr Knightley's admonitions. She shelters from her disquiet in the claim that they are jokes: "Mr Knightley loves to find fault with me you know—in a joke—it is all a joke. We always say what we like to one another" (p. 12). But, despite her rationalizations and self-justifications, she is troubled: "Emma made no answer, and tried to look cheerfully unconcerned, but was really feeling uncomfortable, and wanting him very much to be gone."

So absolute is Emma's emotional blindness, and so insistent her misrepresentations, that it is only much later that she can, with horror, recognize the extent of her self-deception. Yet the recognition carries with it a sense that something had been working within her for a long time—something of which she was scarcely conscious and which finally, in the face of the fear that she has lost the absolute centre of her affections, threatens internal collapse. The decisive turning point is Emma's intense remorse and the desire for reparation for her cruel snub of the elderly Miss Bates during a picnic expedition to Box Hill. Mr Knightley rounds on Emma. She mentally turns to her father for comfort and has to recognize his emotional inadequacy (as an internal figure) and his dependency on her (as an external one). Her blindness, hitherto, to her father's limitations has allowed for the perpetuation of a pseudo-mature sense of herself, offering artificial gratification because built only on idealization and denial. The reader now observes Emma herself as beginning to recognize the shift that has slowly been occurring within, a shift of which we, the readers, have long been aware. She discovers the truth of her own feelings. There is nothing indulgent in this anguished account of self-recognition. It carries with it the acute sense of shame and the biting edge of remorse and responsibility—the poised uncertainty of the turbulence of catastrophic change.

> The rest of the day, the following night, were hardly enough for her thoughts. —She was bewildered amidst the confusion of all that had rushed on her within the last few hours. Every moment had brought a fresh surprise; and every surprise must be a matter of humiliation to her.—How to understand it all! How to understand the deceptions she had been thus practising on herself, and living under!—The blunders, the blindness of her own head and heart!—She sat still, she walked about, she tried her own room, she tried the shrubbery—in every place, every posture, she perceived that she had acted most weakly; that she had been imposed on by others in a most mortifying degree; that she had been imposing on herself in a degree yet more mortifying; that she was wretched, and should probably find this day but the beginning of wretchedness.
>
> To understand, thoroughly understand her own heart, was the first endeavour. To that point went every leisure moment which her father's claims on her allowed, and every moment of involuntary absence of mind.
> . . . . . .
> With insufferable vanity she had believed herself in the secret of everybody's feelings; with unpardonable arrogance proposed to arrange everybody's destiny. She was proved to have been universally mistaken; and she had not quite done nothing—for she had done mischief. She had brought evil on Harriet, on herself, and she too much feared, on Mr Knightley. [pp. 385–389]

Yet there is also a sense that whether or not her worst fears are realized in the loss of Mr Knightley to Harriet, Emma has the strength emotionally to survive.

> When it came to such a pitch as this [that it had all been her own work], she was not able to refrain from a start, or a heavy sigh, or even from walking about the room for a few seconds—and the only source whence anything like consolation or composure could be drawn, was in the resolution of her own better conduct, and the hope that, however inferior in spirit and gaiety might be the following and every future winter of her life to the past, it would yet find her more rational, more acquainted with herself, and leave her less to regret when it were gone. [p. 396]

The relationship that allows Emma to become "more acquainted with herself" is one in which another change has also imperceptibly been occurring. It is profoundly true that when a person is able to grow as a result of learning from the inner capacities of another, that other is also deeply affected. "Those who can trust us, educate us" (*Daniel Deronda*, p. 485). Just as the analyst learns from the patient and the parent from the child, so Mr Knightley learned from Emma, and he too developed. The change here is a subtle but important one. He observes of Emma early on that, "in her mother she lost the only person able to cope with her". Clearly Mr Knightley assumes the parental mantle. It is his jealous but, as ever, selfless conviction of Emma's affection for a feared rival, Frank Churchill, that awakens him to the realization that his love for Emma is not merely parental but is rooted in the desire that she should be his wife. He too, in other words, finds an internal capacity for marriage, one that had been lacking at the opening of the book. He stumbles upon the truth about himself; not so much the early expression of his disinterested interest in Emma's declarations that she will never marry ("I wonder what will become of her"), but in his passionate longing for her—finally and so movingly understated: "If I loved you less, I might be able to talk about it more" (p. 403).

It had been Emma's belief that she had lost Mr Knightley to another. That belief revealed to her the nature of her true feelings for him. When her jealousy was fired, she discovered that in Mr Knightley she had slowly begun to invest not merely parental qualities, albeit deeply significant ones, but also, without her knowing it, aspirational ones of hope and renewal, qualities that were now represented by the idea of marriage. "It darted through her with the speed of an arrow, that Mr Knightley must marry no one but herself!" (p. 382). It was, moreover, the internal development that had been imperceptibly occurring that enabled her, despite her conviction that the object of her love was now lost, to sustain the notion of a possible future alone. Thus the reader has a sense of how Emma's development is initiated and assisted by the internal changing quality of the one to whom she is deeply attached, before she herself has any awareness of what is happening. Emma gradually moves from wishful fantasizing to the beginning of a capacity for growth and change.

The final description of her inner state defines the significance of the character shift. The key-notes have become those of self-knowledge and of sincerity, qualities on which the internal capacity for marriage is based—on the recognition of an internal presence that combines parental capacities, standards, and aspirations with sexual longing.

On the recognition of the meaning for her of someone who bears such qualities depends the move that we have followed in Emma from a vain and self-centred, albeit charming, adolescent, to a young woman who is beginning to be able to occupy a more adult sense of identity. This adult state of mind is characterized by feelings of humility, of gratitude, and of concern for the other, feelings that make mature intimacy a possibility—if, in Emma's case, still far from realized.

> What had she to wish for? Nothing but to grow more worthy of him, whose intentions and judgement had been ever so superior to her own. Nothing, but that the lessons of her past folly might teach her humility and circumspection in future. [p. 456]

Further developmental possibilities for Emma and Mr Knightley, and for the relationship between them, remain yet to be known, and, at the end of the novel, the question of her capacity genuinely to separate hangs very much in the air. She does not, for the time being at least, leave her family home and establish one elsewhere with her husband, for a condition of the marriage is that she remain with her father, to be joined there by Mr Knightley. Much is yet to be resolved.

The absence, in the novel, of a convincing internal resolution in the main characters of this central problem, both of physical separation and of psychic separateness, is also true of *Jane Eyre*. Charlotte Brontë's novel offers a wonderful and intensely poetic rendering of a courageous thirst for a "real knowledge of Life". It is an extraordinary moral and psychological investigation of Jane Eyre's childhood, her girlhood, and her emergence from adolescence into maturity. Brontë describes the process of protracted truth-seeking at its most painful and most resolute. Mr Rochester (the other central protagonist and the man whom Jane loves) has often been compared to Mr Knightley in terms both of his combination of tenderness and strength, and of the oedipal overtones of his part in the central relationship. This oedipal aspect is especially pronounced in the much more explicitly sexual and passionate attachment between Jane and her rather Byronic "Master" and, importantly, relates to the nature of the final marriage.

Jane has been much criticized for leaving Rochester and Thornfield Hall after the devastating discovery, on the day of her proposed marriage to him, that he already has a wife—the mad woman, Bertha, locked up on the third floor. Jane's suffering and mental devastation are described with a depth and poignancy that are scarcely bearable. When she falls into fitful sleep on the night of her departure from Thornfield, she dreams of one of her earliest traumatic experiences, that of being shut in the "red room" in her then home, Gateshead. Here, as a child, her terror, her sense of abandonment and the loss of any shred of sustaining goodness in her life, had driven her to near madness. It is clear from the text that this early episode had significantly oedipal connotations. The voice she hears now, in her wakeful dreaming, as a white human form emerges mysteriously from the moon is, "My daughter, flee temptation!" "Mother, I will", she replies. What this passage, and the last part of the book, imply is that in order to achieve a genuine capacity for intimacy (in this case, with Rochester), Jane still has to resolve some inner ties. She has to relinquish the ideals of infant/adolescent romance. Both she herself and he to whom she is devoted have yet more to learn about themselves. Jane has both to experience the impact of loss through renunciation and to recognize the nature of her own attachment to subjugating herself to the needs of another (St. John Rivers) rather than being able to establish a relationship of equality and reciprocity.

Rochester's accident in the fire that burns down Thornfield and kills Bertha symbolizes his becoming a changed man, with seared vision and crippled hand. In the flames he lost the "sinister" ("left" hand) part of himself, and, as a result, he began to be able to own his needs and dependency, relinquishing his proud omnipotence. Hitherto, as Jane says, he had disdained every part but that of giver and protector. Now he acknowledges how he, "can begin to experience remorse, repentance; the wish for reconcilement to my Maker" (pp. 514–515). As a consequence of his loss, anguish, and sorrow, Rochester's thoughts become directed inwards and his mind's eye sees much more clearly than he was able to before becoming blind. He experiences humility, unworthiness, gratitude, and, now, deep joy.

Charlotte Brontë seeks to establish, in this last part of the book, the basis for the internal capacity for marriage which Jane and Rochester, through their respective suffering, might finally achieve. As with Emma, that capacity seems to be essentially rooted in the *internal* presence of the loved one, an internal presence that is able to sustain the failure, absence, or fallibility of the *external*. Yet Jane's and Rochester's is a singular kind of marriage. The setting is profoundly reclusive. Ferndeane, their home, is at first sight scarcely distinguishable from the trees, "so dank and green were its decaying walls . . . it was as still as a church on a weekday; the pattering rain on the forest leaves was the only sound audible in its vicinage, 'Can there be life here?', I asked" (p. 497). Their relationship is described as almost symbiotic:

No woman was ever nearer to her mate than I am: ever more absolutely bone of his bone and flesh of his flesh. I know no weariness
of my Edward's society: he knows none of mine, any more than
we each do of the pulsation of the heart that beats in our separate
bosoms, consequently, we are ever together. To be together is for us
to be at once as free as in solitude, as gay as in company. We talk,
I believe, all day long: to talk to each other is but a more animated
and an audible thinking. All my confidence is bestowed on him, all
his confidence is devoted to me; we are precisely suited in character—perfect concord is the result. [p. 519]

With the endings of *Jane Eyre* and *Emma*, as with many nineteenth-
century novels, notably, as we have seen, with those of George Eliot,
the reader is left with qualms. The dimensions of the internal voyage
into true adulthood seem so much more extensive than the suggested
potential of the married states through which the stories find resolution. When George Eliot, towards the end of her life, said that she
had never been happy with her endings, she was perhaps reflecting
on a crisis of genre. The novel can observe and describe a process of
becoming that formally requires an ending but cannot really have
one. Yet possibly she was also recognizing a different kind of issue:
that the achievement of a committed partnership only represents a
port of reembarkation. It simultaneously marks the distance already
travelled and the distance yet to go. And so it may be that it is the
very imperfection of these unions that could be said to represent not
so much arrival as potential for further development. The final unease,
at the end of these and other novels, poses questions of whether, and
how, individuals can go on growing up within a partnership; how
they can achieve, or attain and sustain, independence of mind; how
they can come to experience and to tolerate the chosen other as they
really are, as opposed to how they may have been wished to be. This
latter process will very likely continue to involve its own kind of
losses, whether they be conscious or unconscious ones, as well as the
unquestionable gains. But that is a different story, the nature of which
is deeply affected by the distinction under discussion: that between
the external fact of marriage or partnership, and the internal "capacity" for it—that is, by the basis on which the original relationship has
been founded.

These two novels describe development as being rooted in a deli-
cate balance between introjective and projective processes. Maturity is
slowly acquired through the experience of having the more infantile

and insistent projections received and rendered acknowledgeable, bearable, and meaningful. When this is the case, not only the content of the projections themselves but also that very capacity to process them can become part of the personality. A coming-out-of-projective-identification then becomes possible, the foundation, as we have seen, for adult identity and for intimacy.

The central emotional development that takes place in these narratives represents a process to be found in much drama and fiction, one that is epitomized, perhaps, in the great nineteenth-century novels. That development, as argued in this chapter, clarifies a particular way of relating that later became known as the introjective mode, or as introjective identification. But what, precisely, that "something" really is is often unclear, or missed, in the various theoretical expositions of the process. The point about Bion's idea of learning as being a capacity based in introjection is that he is suggesting a process that is more complex than Klein's (1959) notion of the internalization of "a good and dependable object" that supports and strengthens the ego (p. 251). Learning in Bion's sense, and in the sense realized in the fictional characters described here, is based on the capacity actually to *have* emotional experiences, ones, that is, that can be felt to be meaningful. These then become the basis for further thoughts and higher levels of abstraction. Such experiences tend to be of the moment, ones that have not been excessively interfered with by other considerations: by, for example, "having an eye to the future"; or by a "sentimental attachment to the past"; or by too immediate an "awareness of consequences"; or by too nostalgic "a bond to the familiar".

Meltzer (1978) suggests that Bion's recommendation to the clinician of a temporary suspension of "memory and desire" is related to this internal situation, to Bion's awareness of the way in which a consciousness of the past and a hope for the future may disrupt, or co-opt, the experience of the present (p. 463). Being able genuinely to engage with a present emotional experience then becomes an achievement—one that is essential to the conflict and turbulence of growth and development, and one that is, for that very reason, so often resisted. In each of the novels discussed here, the decisive developmental steps taken are the result of intense emotional experiences that force those characters who have the capacity to undergo them to "think"; to think in the fundamental sense of allowing themselves to "have" their experience. These steps take place in relation to a potential partner who is also impelled to "think", to suffer, and to learn in similar ways. It is the characters' capacity genuinely to engage with emotional experience, to learn from it, and to change as a consequence that makes these ordinarily limited and flawed people into "heroes" or "heroines". It is not because they are ideally beautiful or virtuous that they achieve heroic status, but because, unlike other characters, they are prepared to struggle to become themselves in the immediacy of the anguish of their emotional engagements.

Meltzer draws attention to how evident it is in the history of our patients,

> that they have often been broken in their development by bad, painful experiences—weaning, birth of the next sibling, the primal scene, death of a love object. But it is equally apparent from the histories of great men—Keats, for example—that they have been "made" by the acceptance and assimilation of these same events. Equally, we see patients who have been "broken" by good experiences, where [those experiences] have inflamed megalomania, or, conversely, stirred intolerable feelings of gratitude and indebtedness. Freud's "character types met within analysis" could be seen to fall into this category. [1978/1994, pp. 466–467]

Recent psychoanalytic views based on the work of Bion correspond more closely to this present developmental picture than to those of Freud or of Klein. For this picture of "character" is one in which a person can begin to learn to take responsibility for himself, and to build his personality, by eventually acquiring the capacity to learn both from good and from bad experience.

These novels describe the conditions in which such growth of character can take place, in implicit contrast to all those in whom little or no development occurs. At the heart of the process lie the central challenges of the depressive position: the realistic estimation of the actual qualities of the other, and an acceptance of what is found there; the capacity to bear the loss of the external presence but nonetheless to retain that presence internally in the face of absence, of doubt and uncertainty, of loss of trust, and even of fear of betrayal by the loved one. The defining element lies not in the fact of "good" and "bad" as such, but in the different capacities to relate to and to make sense of experience.

Emma and *Jane Eyre* encompass some of the major themes of this book generally and some of the issues that belong to late adolescence in particular. The personality can grow insofar as it is able to survive psychically the disturbing experience of change and the losses that that entails. It also has to be able to establish an identification with an internal thinking figure, a focus of love and attachment, which can

eventually function independently of its external origin and representation. Psychic change and survival depend on the fledgling self
being contained and guided, whether in the course of its own intimate
relationships in the family and in life, or by an author's internal world
being given symbolic form for the reader, or by some such process in
the therapist–patient setting. Each re-evokes, as they must ever do,
the infant's earliest experiences. The late-adolescent is struggling with
his psychically emergent self. An intimate relationship may be looked
to, or even grasped at, to assuage the anxieties about separation and
the move into adult life. Depending on the internal capacity for intimacy, such a relationship may either further bind the personality to
its unseparated self or free it to go on discovering its own potential.
How the subsequent lives of Emma and Jane will unfold is uncertain.
Their choices and commitments carry no guarantees. But these choices
and commitments were made with a kind of honesty and integrity that
leave the reader somewhat hopeful.

CHAPTER FIFTEEN

The green worlds
of adolescent development

This final chapter seeks to bring together some of the threads that have traced their way through the foregoing pages and to bring them together in a positive spirit; to suggest that, despite the many indications to the contrary, some hope can, nonetheless, be found in the "inside stories" of adolescents. It falls into three sections: "There's No Clock in the Forest"; "Two Containing Poems"; "A Late-Adolescent Dream".

In *As You Like It*, as Juliet Dusinberre (2006) puts it, "Shakespeare has placed a prophetic finger on the pulse of the future" (p. 1). For this play evokes, so comprehensively, the nature of the adolescent world, both internal and external, as one apart, necessarily apart, in which the inhabitants are trying to find a way of "working out" or "working through" a sense of self-hood. That quest takes its shape—this being comedy—in the "magical" setting of a non-hierarchical, unstructured, property-less social world of possibility and opportunity. The critic Northrop Frye (1957) refers to such a setting as the "green world", which, drawing on the symbolism of the victory of summer over winter, offers the "archetypal function of literature in visualizing the world of desire, not as an escape from 'reality', but as the genuine form of the world that human life tries to imitate" (p. 184). As in *As You Like It*, the green world more generally begins in a place represented as a "normal world", moves into the green world, and "goes into a metamorphosis there in which the comic resolution is achieved, and returns to the normal world" (p. 182).

There's no clock in the forest

The main characters in *As You Like It* find themselves strangers in a strange land, that of marginal or liminal places or spaces—in this play, the Forest of Arden. Here we are invited to address the fundamental relationship between "psychic time" and "measured time"—so huge an issue during the adolescent years. Although the play is rooted in Elizabethan culture—literary, social, political, aesthetic—nonetheless it is deeply relevant to modern times. As Dusinberre puts it:

> Amongst the myths of classical pastoral and of the biblical Garden of Eden are a group of displaced persons fleeing family disruption and political corruption. In raising profound questions about the nature of liberty, renewal and regeneration posed by the new environment of the Forest, Shakespeare has created a comedy of extraordinary flexibility and depth. [2006, p. 1]

This setting includes a cross-dressed heroine, gender games, and explorations of sexual ambiguity, among much else.

There is, in the play, a sense that to resolve some relationship between psychic and measured time is to enable at least a degree of maturity to take place, given that the process of maturation is never complete. G. Stanley Hall emphasizes this point when he notes that it is a mark of genius if "the plasticity and spontaneity of adolescence persists into maturity" (Hall, 1904, vol. 1, p. 547).

As we shall see, in the quite different private spaces of an alternative version of the development of the adolescent mind, expressed in two poems of Carol Satyamurti's, we can appreciate, in a bare few stanzas, the compression of the experience of psychological and emotional growth and the expansion of meaning, despite all the odds. The paths of the two young girls described do not take them into the green worlds of experiment and otherness, but, rather, into the solitary depths of each of their efforts to find meaning to their lives.

Lastly, I bring a clinical account of a late adolescent, Karen, who, in therapy, manages to develop the capacity to negotiate a transition that had hitherto been impossible for her. This example re-evokes Alice's situation (chapter 1) and Humpty Dumpty's remark in the context of growing up: "*One* ca'n't, perhaps . . . but *two* can" (in Beer, 2016, pp. 212–214).

Now drawing on drama and poetry, I shall return to the issue of "time *lived psychically* and of time *measured*" (Jerry Sokol, personal communication, 2015). The distinction is one that is also illuminatingly explored by Virginia Woolf, in her novel *Mrs Dalloway* (1925), based, as it is, in the intellectual context of that era, particularly of the modernist writers of the twentieth century and the role of psychoanalytic thinking in their work. Elaine Showalter (1991) points out that "for Woolf, the exterior event is significant primarily for the way it triggers and releases the inner life. While an external incident or perception may be only a brief flash of chronological time, its impact upon the individual consciousness may have a much greater duration and meaning" (p. xx).

Although not an enthusiast of psychoanalysis, Virginia Woolf was, as we see in *Mrs Dalloway*, deeply interested in exploring different and simultaneous registers of human consciousness. In this present chapter, I trace the relationship between the liminal setting at the heart of, in this case, *As You Like It*, and that of contemporary life, epitomized in the process of adolescent self-discovery. (I use the term "liminal" not only horizontally—across, as here, indeterminate time—but also vertically, in terms of levels of consciousness.) For here, time as a matter of basic measurement and also as a central metaphor for different states of consciousness, is especially important for understanding the adolescent mentality.

In *Mrs Dalloway*, for example, Virginia Woolf marvellously evokes the relationship between the different time frames in the simultaneous registers that she describes. She explores the significance and meaning of the clocks of London, in particular Big Ben, in the mental worlds of those who struggle with the simultaneity of historical, quotidian, and anticipated future pain (as well as pleasure), in their mental states during the twenty-four-hour, chapterless unity of the novel's structure.

> Shredding and slicing, dividing and subdividing, the clocks of Harley Street nibbled at the June day, counselled submission, upheld authority, and pointed out in chorus the supreme advantages of a sense of proportion, until the mound of time was so far diminished that a commercial clock, suspended above a shop in Oxford Street, announced, genially and fraternally, as if it were a pleasure to Messrs Rigby and Lowndes to give information gratis, that it was half past one. [p. 112]

Time in Shakespeare's Festive Comedies also goes by in fits and starts, as Helen Gardner (1959) describes it: "It is not so much a movement onward as a space in which to work things out" (p. 30). "Working things out" is so appropriate a description of how the adolescent years are spent: how to become oneself, or one-self, in terms of the often painfully necessary integration of different parts of the personality. For time becomes relative and wholly subjective in relation to the extraordinary mood swings of the here and now. Yet all members of the adolescent community are especially aware of how clock-time ticks on in the context of social and educational constraints, ones driven by examination requirements and the general target-setting of external culture that threatens, but also challenges, the youngsters' natural habitats. The ongoing ticking of this kind of time, often so at odds with developmental states of mind and feeling, is fundamentally essential to keeping all those who have to swim in these choppy waters some-how within reach of an anchor of some kind, in order, albeit reluctantly, to maintain something of an eye to the future.

As one Shakespeare scholar, Kiernan Ryan (2009), puts it:

> *The Comedy of Errors* [the first of the, arguably, ten such comic plays] marks the outbreak of the relentless war waged by Shakespearean comedy on conceptions of time that clamp people into the predict-able scripts of their culture. The comedies have no time for the quan-tified, calibrated, sequential type of time mocked by Touchstone[1] in *As You Like It*, when he mirrors Jacques's posture of gloom in a wicked parody, which Jacques himself recounts with relish to his fellow exiles in Arden. [pp. 4–5]

Touchstone is the traditional "wise fool". At their request, he accom-panies Rosalind and Celia, cousins and the closest of friends, away from the corrupt and tyrannical Court. For, in the play's first Act, Rosalind is banished by her usurping and power-hungry uncle; along with her goes the ever-loving and loyal Celia, feeling "liberated", and both enthusiastically making their way, disguised, into the Forest of Arden. Here we encounter, too, Touchstone, who is to accompany them. Holding his own "dial" or time-piece, Touchstone solemnly pronounces that "'Tis but an hour ago since it was nine, / And after one hour more 'twill be eleven / And so from hour to hour we ripe and ripe, / And then from hour to hour we rot and rot; / And thereby hangs a tale" (II.vii.24–27). The banal nature of measured time is self-evident, yet Touchstone is also, more subtly, drawing attention to the ineluctable quality of time; time that is forever on the move towards the inevitability of death—a different register altogether.

The melancholy and humourless moralist Jacques, among the com-panions of the exiled good Duke Senior, describes his own reaction to seeing "The motley fool thus moral on the time": it is to "laugh *sans* intermission / An hour by his dial" (II.vii.32–33). Here, not even laughter escapes "the normative regime that clock-time is contracted to enforce" (Ryan, pp. 218–219). Jacques's cynical and famous disquisition on the Seven Ages of Man, later in the same scene, is undercut by the entrance of Orlando who is fleeing for his life from his wicked older brother, carrying the ancient and faithful servant, Adam (the character originally played by Shakespeare himself), on his back. For Jacques, the "Last scene of all, / That ends this strange eventful history, /Is second childishness and mere oblivion, / *Sans* teeth, *sans* eyes, *sans* taste, *sans* everything" (II.vii.164–167). The qualities of this "venerable" old man, Adam, could not be further from Jacques's grim description of aging, nor could the courtesy and graciousness of Duke Senior's welcome to the two incomers to the Forest. Orlando and Adam's entry into Arden is marked by Amiens's beautiful ballad—one of the many wonderful musical interludes in the play, as it draws comparisons between the harsh weather and man's natural cruelty to man.

> Blow, blow, thou winter wind,
> Thou art not so unkind
> As man's ingratitude.
> Thy tooth is not so keen
> Because thou art not seen,
> Although thy breath be rude.
> Hey-ho, sing hey-ho, unto the green holly.
> Most friendship is feigning, most loving mere folly.
> Then hey-ho, the holly.
> This life is most jolly.
>
> Freeze, freeze, thou bitter sky,
> That dost not bite so nigh
> As benefits forgot.
> Though thou the waters warp
> Thy sting is not so sharp
> As friend remembered not.
> Hey-ho, sing hey-ho, unto the green holly.
> Most friendship is feigning, most loving mere folly.
> Then hey-ho, the holly!
> This life is most jolly.

[II.vii.175–194]

In this pastoral setting, time and human welfare are marked by the seasons, not by the tyranny of clock-time, drawn on as a metaphor, one that governs, however inaccurately, the quotidian workaday life. Yet, as often noted, life in the Forest does, in the end, eventuate back in the pre-banishment world of the Court—albeit now one in which there is promise of enlightenment and change, by contrast with the envious destructiveness, almost motiveless malignity, of the past regime. Like so many adolescents, the dwellers in the Forest suspend time; they feel free to "fleet the time carelessly" (I.i.112–13). It remains to be seen whether they can sustain the enlightenment of this out-of-time experience (they do!), much as it remains to be seen whether the adolescent period of putative growth and development (however unpromising it may seem "in transit") can, in each individual case, be sustained (sometimes so, sometimes not).

Mental breakdown is not infrequent when youngsters, having survived the target-driven period of what Bion called a –K type of acquisitive learning, suddenly feel stripped of their erstwhile sense of achievement and self-worth. As we saw in chapter 5, they often suffer a crisis of identity and quail at the prospect of their inner capacity falling short of external expectations. The "learning about" culture has suited them as one to do with the clever accumulation of facts and information rather than a more mindful capacity for learning through being in touch with inner experiences (K), hard though that may be.

In *Feeling and Form* (1953), Suzanne Langer suggests that the essence of comedy is that it embodies in symbolic form our sense of happiness, in feeling that we can meet and master the changes and chances of life as it confronts us. In other words, she sees comedy as an imaginative expression of life triumphing over chance. Such a view constitutes the positive outcomes that are realized in Shakespeare's "green world" and, at least hopefully, in the outcome of the adolescent process more generally.

As such, Shakespeare's great Comedies might be taken as descriptions of a happy outcome of the developmental process and of adolescence in particular (although, as we have seen, the outcome often takes a bit longer than the timespan conventionally allowed for adolescence). For the comic plots, with their improbabilities, coincidences, sudden reversals, disguises and unmaskings, cross-dressings and gender experimentation present us with what Rosalind calls the "full stream of the world". It is the full stream of a particular kind of world in which the characters, to varying degrees, engage with different aspects of themselves, of hierarchies, and of societies, as they must if the final marriages—ones that are, in essence, symbols of renewal rather than of mere convention—are to take place. The very structure of comedy is that "all's well that ends well". Such symbols change, but not the significance nor the meaning.

The green worlds do not conform to the crude "goodies and bad-dies" culture of the childhood years. For the dwellers of the Forest are subject, too, to the "icy fang / And churlish chiding of the winter's wind". Yet Duke Senior can view such wintry conditions as "counsel-lors, / That feelingly persuade me what I am" (II.i.6–11). The Duke is beautifully expressing the concept of "containment", which has threaded its way through the pages of the present book: the capacity that is rooted in the earliest, passionate intimacy between mother and baby and is so central to all ages and stages in the dynamics of life to come. Here, it is the parent who is learning.

In *As You Like It*, the cruelty and suffering of the animal kingdom, with its literal pecking order and heartless attitudes, is described in much the same terms as the noblemen's jockeying for power and the remorseless relationships that prevail outside the Forest. In other words, that primitive "kingdom" is understood as representing aspects of human nature that need, at the time, to be courageously recognized, accepted, and internally learned from. These worlds, as in Amiens's ballad, represent a different vertex on the events of everyday life and a particular and peculiar liminal time, space, and place, one in which psychic realities can be negotiated and ultimately—this being com-edy—resolved. The containing structure of the play itself provides the space wherein the melee of identifications, groupings, twinnings, splittings, and pairings can be accommodated and finally resolved.

In the comedies, status in the world of the Courts, whether of Athens, of Milan, of Naples, or, as here, of Duke Frederick near the Forest of Arden, is confused with a sense of self-worth, and the enforcement of codes prevails over true value systems or ethical principles. The final marriages are often the outcome of significant experiments with bisexual aspects of the self. One might say that the great comic heroines, Viola in *Twelfth Night*, for example, and, pre-eminently, Rosalind in *As You Like It*, are constituted as heroines through their very capacities also to be Cesario and Ganymede. It is instructive, here, to cite the Arden edition footnote on Ganymede. It reads as follows:

> Rosalind's choice of name was conventional to pastoral poetry.
> . . . Ganymede, a beautiful Trojan shepherd boy, seized by Jove
> (disguised as an eagle) and swept up to Olympus to be cup-bearer
> to the Gods, was also associated with the zodiacal sign of Aquarius.
> . . . [H]e therefore came to represent Shrovetide festivity. The name
> is richly provocative of the fears of anti-theatricalists because of its
> homoerotic associations. . . . [p. 187, fn.122]

These characters "grow up", in part, by finding in themselves characteristics that their assigned conventional, social roles had hitherto precluded. Rosalind leaves that conventional self behind in Act I and, as the play proceeds, visibly matures in terms of wit, playfulness, honesty, wisdom, and self-knowledge. (She has more lines than any other female character in Shakespeare's entire oeuvre and indeed, uniquely, has an Epilogue, all to herself.) As Touchstone puts it:

> You have said.—But whether wisely or no,
> Let the forest judge.

[III.ii.118–119]

The Festive Comedies could be described as constituting the kind of psycho-sexual moratorium that the psychoanalyst Erik Erikson (1950) explores in his work on adolescence. The implication is that this moratorium, too, is an "allowable" psychic and temporal space apart, and perhaps one of time-limited sexual experimentation (though one in which some, at least, take up permanent residence). The full stream of adolescence could well be described as being, at this point of the life cycle, the most traumatic and driven; perhaps the most painful; less often, at least in retrospect, joyous; sometimes rewarding, more often undermined by extreme self-doubt, or enactment. The escape routes from this predicament may include, as we have seen, the obvious pseudo-protection of the urge for experimentation and risk-taking, often in relation to untethered sexuality or to alcohol and substance abuse; or possibly of precocious intellectual achievement (the cult of "being clever" rather than wise, to go back to Bion's –K and K formulations), or simply of confusion, crippling confusion, about any number of things—especially sexual. As hormones kick in at puberty, the world suddenly becomes a place of astonishingly intense sexual desires, of masturbation, gropings, frustration, guilt, and of both homosexual and heterosexual longings. D. H. Lawrence—to go back to where we set out—put it so resonantly:

> And now, a new world, a new heaven and a new earth. Now new relationships are formed, the old ones retire from their prominence. Now mother and father inevitably give way before masters and mistresses, brothers and sisters yield to friends. This is the period of *Schwärmerei*, of young adoration and of real initial friendships. A child before puberty has playmates. After puberty he has friends and enemies.
> . . . . . .
>   It is the hour of the stranger. Let the stranger now enter the soul.
> [1923, p. 102]

As we have seen, these troubled years are, in terms both of place—that is, internal place—and of time, "strange". They involve seemingly impossible and by no means time-specific tasks but, nonetheless, ones that are intrinsic to the inescapable process of "growing up", on the inside as well as on the outside. Much of the "work" of adolescence is that of creating, if only temporarily or partially, and whether internally or externally, a place and a time and a way of being that can be inhabited, at least in the mind, "somewhere else", while yet, in most cultures, also being bound to ordinary social norms. The creation of a "somewhere else" is intrinsic, for example, to the Pacific-island setting of Golding's *Lord of the Flies*—a place *apart* where, post plane-crash, a group of boys are stranded and cut off from the adult world, a world without which the boys' internal structures either break down or hold fast. The merited success of the Harry Potter books could be said to be rooted in J. K. Rowling's powerful insights into the developmental years of ages 11–18. She, too, draws on the "somewhere else" as a significant dimension of the youngsters' experiences. But, as we have seen, this "somewhere else" is nothing new, it has existed across time, especially in the great classical Greek and Shakespearean comedies.

The early settings of the Festive Comedies, whether expressed or inferred, are, as here, usually concerned with establishing a sense of oppression and of hierarchy and control. The political, cultural, and familial regime has to be left, or escaped from, in order for a different, and individually distinctive, way of being to develop, one that might constitute the potential for a new, and necessarily altered, generational version of birth and renewal to be established. The focus is on the complex, and often improbable, ways in which, at least in *As You Like It* and some of the other Comedies, the characters do, in the "somewhere else" of strange forests, or isles and shores, ultimately find themselves and their future partners, offering confirmation of the continuation of the natural life cycle. This is a powerful expression of hope, but, as George Eliot so eloquently put it of her own novels, the final marriages are yet but "a bourne", signifying a boundary, the beginning of the as yet unknown life to come.

In this play, the theme of time functions as measurement and as metaphor. It is also part of the notion of threshold living: as suggested, the green world of the play and the adolescent world of human life are essentially threshold and/or marginal places and spaces. Here, for a period, measured time is a restriction, a form of oppression, pending some sort of resolution. In the Comedies, life in the green world usually takes an indeterminate amount of actual time—perhaps only that of a single Midsummer Night. But this is Shakespeare's "mythic" world. In the course of actual adolescence, it takes a number of years as the complex tasks of the age are faced, undertaken, and, possibly, resolved.

In *As You Like It*, the two versions are far more polarized in the sharply contrasting worlds of this "Time" metaphor: on the one hand, the time is that of the Forest, where "there's no clock" and where seasons rather than Sovereigns hold sway. In contrast, on the other, there is that of Touchstone's description of the time of the Court by which, as we have seen, Jacques is so taken. Here, too, there are threshold experiments in terms of gender (the movements between masculine and feminine); in terms of sexuality (in the counter-positioning of homosexual and heterosexual suggestiveness); and also, in terms of class (in the relationship of Ganymede, the shepherd boy, and Rosalind, Duke Senior's daughter—one and the same person, played, of course, by a male actor).

Pushkin (1831), interestingly, leaves the time frame open: "In time, who knows the agitation of inexperience would have passed . . ." (p. lvii). In the play or poem, the time frame is held within the parameters of the art-work. The "agitation of inexperience" locates the young inhabitants somewhere between their infantile past and the possibility of a mature adult future. Rosalind soon proceeds to "demolish the spurious objectivity of the clock and demonstrate the relative nature of time, the ways in which our perception of its passing is warped by subjectivity and circumstance" (Ryan, 2009, p. 6).

Yet many—fearful of living in uncertainty and arming themselves with the pre-adolescent mechanism of self-protection and defence—can end up in a "tunnel", as Donald Meltzer (1973b) put it, during the adolescent years. The aim, so recognizable, is to get in and out the other side as quickly and as unscathed as possible, often by imitating parental *mores* rather than rebelling or, properly, painfully and mournfully separating from them. Yet when no longer protected by the family ramparts, their "doll's-house" existence starts to crumble and it becomes evident that these young people are ill-prepared for embarking on their *own* grown-up lives. In other words, many do not have the internal wherewithal to make it across the threshold.

Where *As You Like It* is concerned, my focus has been on the way in which the characters can, and do, manage to negotiate the challenging and complex terrain of the landscape that everyone has, somehow, to navigate in life. As we have seen, this place is expressed by Shake-speare in terms of the activities of the Forest.

The first time that we encounter the would-be lovers alone in the Forest, Rosalind, disguised as Ganymede, accosts Orlando in playfully superior terms:

> *Rosalind:* Do you hear forester?
> *Orlando:* Very well; what would you?
> *Rosalind:* I pray you, what is't o'clock?
> *Orlando:* You should ask me what time o'day. There's no clock in the forest.
> *Rosalind:* Then there is no true lover in the forest, else sighing every minute and groaning every hour would detect the lazy foot of time as well as a clock.
> *Orlando:* And why not the swift foot of time? Had not that been as proper?
> *Rosalind:* By no means, sir. Time travels in divers paces with divers persons. I'll tell you who Time ambles withal, who Time trots withal, who Time gallops withal and who he stands still withal.
>
> [III.ii.288–302]

There follows a humorous exchange in the course of which Rosalind, brilliantly, gives Orlando examples of the states of mind that match the speed at which Time is experienced, measured not by the clock but by mental attitude.

In *As You Like It*, notions of the acquisition of a "true" identity are not lodged in adhesive (as in imitative) or projective (as in getting into another's personality, or into their shoes) states of mind, which often constitute what are thought to be the norms of everyday exist-ence; rather, they find expression in an imaginative and compressed unfolding of events that are symbolic of internal, rather than external, realities. It is a process in relation to which, over time, contemporary adolescents variously negotiate their own relationships with the inter-nal and external worlds in which they find themselves—or, sadly, are unable to do so. It is very striking that the fictional and imaginative worlds that they inhabit in favoured books and films are, as we have seen, so often in other time-zones or planetary spaces—literally other worlds, ones that are somehow, simultaneously, inhabited as their own (see chapter 13).

In this play, the resolution is achieved with great, and wholly unre-alistic, panache in Act V, with the changes of heart both of Orlando's envious brother, Oliver, and of the usurping and tyrannical Duke

Frederick, such that, this being a comedy, all works out alright in the end. Indeed, the play concludes with *four* marriages, under the auspices of a literal *deus ex machina* with the unexpected appearance of the goddess Hymen to preside over the final proceedings.

The discovery of truth by feigning—and of what is wisdom and what folly by debate—is the centre of *As You Like It*, as it is, too, of the adolescent process at its best. But the main unifying concept in the play itself and in the tribulations of the adolescent world, both psychically and behaviourally, is that of metaphorical and actual time. Time, however, is not limitless in either of these worlds. In the play, the characters will return to the so-called "real" world from the perhaps "more real"—that of their sylvan setting. In life, the youngsters will be facing the mixed blessing of "adult life on the outside", though now, hopefully, carrying within a truer and more steady version of themselves; with, at least some sense of identity, however far, in both cases, they may still have to go.

Two containing poems

To link this vision of Shakespearean drama to any present-day poetic expression is to emphasize, albeit in wholly disparate ways, some feeling that "'twas ever so". For in exploring the fact that poetry can express other versions of the green worlds, here compressed in a few stanzas, yet also stretching across years in content, we encounter a much more private version of the ways in which the most deprived, misunderstood, and suffering self can, nonetheless, find some internal, survivalist resource. Here we engage with a very brief sense of what the Shakespearean green worlds represents, now no longer mythic, but actual. For the implication that words, be they used in the name of knowledge or of cliché—that is, at the expense of imagination—to bind rather than to free, inhibit, even arrest development, is explicitly the subject of many of the works of literature, some already explored in relation to the novel. But here I shall concentrate on two poems by Carole Satyamurti, "Between the Lines" and "Passed On". Both in their different ways are freighted with irony. In the first, the young adolescent is imprisoned by the family's culture, the vernacular of words drained of their meaning, or substituted by other words that distort and conceal reality, consigning the developing adolescent to an underground existence, "straining for language / That would let me out". The poem's rendering of the agonies of this young girl's experience, stranded in a world of suggestion, innuendo, and denial, painfully convey the suffering of one who lacks any vestige of an obvious container of meaning, while yet the poem in itself, as a poem, constitutes that very thing. It is as if the world of "home" that this adolescent inhabits constitutes a version of the trapped and deceitful Court setting of Rosalind's life when we first encounter her.

> Words were dust-sheets, blinds.
> People dying randomly, "for want of breath"
> shadowed my bed-times.
> Babies happened;
> adults buried questions under bushes.
>
> Nouns would have been too robust
> for body-parts; they were
> curt, homeless prepositions—"inside",
> "down there", "behind", "below". No word
> for what went on in darkness, overheard.
>
> Underground, straining for language
> that would let me out, I pressed to the radio
> read forbidden books. And once
> visited Mr Cole. His seventeen
> budgerigars praised God continually.
>
> He loved all words, he said, though he used
> few to force a kiss. All that summer
> I longed to ask my mother, starved myself,
> prayed, imagined skirts were getting tight,
> hoped jumping down ten stairs would put it right.
>
> My parents fought in other rooms,
> their tight-lipped murmuring muffled
> by flock wallpaper.
> What was wrong, what they had to say
> couldn't be shared with me.
>
> He crossed the threshold in a wordless
> slam of doors. "Gone to live near work"
> my mother said, before she tracked down
> my diary, broke the lock, made me cut out
> pages that guessed what silence was about.
>
> ["Between the Lines", in Satyamurti, 1987, p. 71]

This young girl, as so many, "grows up" without hope or expectation that there could exist for her an answering voice that would make sense of her world, her breathless curiosity, and her anxiety. (She "grows up", that is, on the outside, with little source of sustenance for any sort of internal, psychic growth.) There was clearly no access to the kind of emotional "common sense" that Bion describes as giving a feeling of truth to experience—as establishing the basis for psychic reality, just as the coming together of sense-impressions gives a feeling of coherence to external reality. But, as we learn at the end, perhaps this child's saving grace has been that, despite everything, she has found, in her own internal resources, some kind of "container" for her feelings—her diary, her writing—the fruit, perhaps, of her own listening (the radio) and of her reading (the books), and of her diary entries, of herself.

Here, with great eloquence, words undercut words in the description of how meaning is destroyed by euphemism, circumlocution—and silence. Yet somehow the young girl's spirit has survived to articulate the terror of sexual and emotional abuse; the knowing ignorance of the basic facts of life; the unspoken physical realities (pregnancy, birth, death); the emotional absences (stuck in the inadequacy and hypocrisy of the adult world). These are indigestible experiences, ones that tend not so much towards thought but towards action—the slam of doors, the breaking of locks, the cutting of pages.

The description of this paring down of language, from nouns to prepositions, speaks to the thinness of the emotional life of this household, to the lack of receptivity to a youngster's ignorance and anguish, in short, to the reduction of potential meaning to meaningless detail. And yet this young girl does register the significance of the silence, of the muffled murmuring. And with that extraordinary and mysterious human capacity to engage with experience and make something of it, however bleak the emotional wilderness of "home" may seem, the child/poet draws on internal resources to frame and contain her feelings. The poem condenses and communicates the pain of unmanageable experience, even encompassing the parental intrusion and destructive violation of the daughter's (diary) privacy, in that final act of abusive indignity. The mother enacts the feelings that she herself cannot contain emotionally: the primitive belief that in physically cutting out and disposing of the diary pages she would eradicate the child's knowledge, would eliminate, as if from her own mind too, the bitterness of the failed marriage.

In this poem, the evocative use of words to describe their own paucity, or absence, directly expresses the emotional paucity or absence of life lived in shadow, drained of meaning, "under dust sheets", blind to the light. Again the peeling back of the surface simplicity of this child's account of girlhood experience reveals a highly articulated and dense understanding of the profound, yet not terminal, obstacle to development posed by the lack of a properly symbolic expression of human experience, itself rooted in the lack of containment for the emotional experience itself.

Mandelstam (1977) casts the relationship between word and meaning in different, but arresting terms:

> Every word is a bundle and the meaning sticks out of it in various directions, not striving toward any one official point. When we pronounce "sun" we are, as it were, making an immense journey . . . poetry . . . rouses us and shakes us awake in the middle of a word. Then the word turns out to be far longer than we thought, and we remember that to speak means to be forever on the road. [p. 13]

"Perhaps", suggested the friend who drew my attention to this passage, "the word turning out to be far longer than we thought might apply, mightn't it, to words spoken in an analysis?" (Martina Thomson, personal communication).

As we have seen, to the basic developmental axes of love and hate (L and H), Bion added "K", signifying what he regarded as the inherent need, or desire, for the kind of knowledge that can link feeling with thinking and bring together experience of internal and external worlds.

Carole Satyamurti's poem, "Passed On", both in content and in form, describes the process of the formation of a container of meaning, while also, in itself, as in "Between the Lines", providing one.

> Before, this box contained my mother.
> For months she'd sent me out for index cards,
> scribbled with a squirrel concentration
> while I'd nag at her, seeing strength
> drain, ink-blue, from her finger-ends
> providing for a string of hard winters
> I was trying not to understand.

> Only after, opening it, I saw
> how she'd rendered herself down from flesh
> to paper, alphabetical: there for me
> in every way she could anticipate
> –*Acupuncture: conditions suited to*
> –*Books to read by age twenty-one*
> –*Choux pastry: how to make, when to use*

The cards looked after me, I'd shuffle them
to almost hear her speak. Then, my days
were box-shaped (or was I playing safe?)
for every doubt or choice, a card that fitted
–Exams: the best revision strategy
–Flowers: cut, how to make them last
–Greece: the men, what you need to know.

But then they seemed to shrink. I'd turn them over,
find them blank; the edges furred, mute,
whole areas wrong, or missing. Had she known?
The language pointed to what wasn't said.
I'd add notes of my own, strange beside
Her urgent dogmatism, loosening grip
– infinitives never telling love
* lust single issue politics when*
don't hopeless careful trust

On the beach, I built a hollow cairn,
tipped in the cards. Then I let her go.
The smoke rose thin and clear, slowly blurred.
I've kept the box for diaries, like this.

                    ["Passed On", in Satyamurti, 1987, p. 146]

Between the bald, literal statement of that first line: "Before, this box contained my mother", and the simple, metaphorical significance of the last, "I have kept the box for diaries, like this", we trace an internal odyssey of moving and recognizable complexity. Herself frozen with the denial of anticipated loss, the poet/daughter states the urgency with which a mother, ambiguously aware of her own failing mental capacities, but clearly anticipating her premature death, seeks to "squirrel away" on index cards a future ABC for her young daughter. It is an ABC of whats and wherefores, of how to and how not to live when she, the mother, has "passed on". For now, the mother was passing on, nut-like, nuggets of advice and homily to nourish her daughter during the dark winter months of her impending bereavement, attempts to assuage her own anguish and that of her daughter with notes of dated instruction.

There is a sad obsessionality about this secret project. A touching yet dogged attention to fact and detail perhaps defends this mother from the pain of her own predicament, but it also cuts her off from making the kind of emotional contact with her daughter that might have offered a more sustaining and genuine nourishment in the lonely shadows of life to come.

With a single word, or phrase, the poet powerfully conveys the daughter's nagging, but guilty, frustration, threaded with fearful antic- ipation, neither able, nor helped, to encompass the meaning of what is happening; turning the blind eye. The poet evokes the constric- tions precisely, of a meaningless "box-shaped" life of bereavement as this daughter clings to the external, concrete representations of her mother—her sense of her own self lost, or in abeyance, wholly depend- ent, for the moment, on her mother's choice and recommendations.

Only slowly does she allow herself to recognize the truth of things— the actual blanks and confusions of her mother's mind, standing also, perhaps, for the actual blanks and confusions arising from genera- tional differences. She struggles to recover her own thoughts. The fact that she eventually can achieve this possibly bespeaks her having had a mother who might well have had rich emotional capacities earlier on.

This is a painful process of mourning and working through, dur- ing which the external figure can eventually be let go and installed, instead, as an internal presence close up. With the growing acceptance that her mother herself and the importance of the index entries have "passed on", the daughter discovers that what has also been "passed on" is a container for meaning.

The box can finally function not as the square and restricted reposi- tory of the advice of a mentally fragmenting mother. Over time, this daughter could begin to take in how desperate her mother felt about "abandoning" her child, about not being able to be alongside her when she still had so much to learn. The daughter/poet can, finally, picture a mother who allows her to become herself—to contain and express the meaning of her own life, lived in her own way.

A late-adolescent dream

The final dream of an 18-year-old model, Karen, who was facing a premature interruption of therapy because of her therapist's illness, rather tentatively indicated that a similar, though perhaps less robust, introjective process was occurring. Karen had sought help for her depression. She was desperate to break a pattern of relating to men through clinging dependency, masochistically unable to separate until, like a climbing plant, she had some alternative supporting structure to which she could attach herself.

She had developed enormously in the course of her therapy, and her pain and rage of relinquishment in the final sessions was acute. Being the fourth of six siblings, her life had, from the first, constituted a kind of group experience—family attitudes were stereotyped around notions defined either by acceptability, or by opposition, to the dominant culture of the group at the time. She had had little experience of her own private feelings being registered or thought about before embarking on therapy. Having to leave so important a relationship was yet another in a long series of premature weanings, evoking intense feelings of desolation, abandonment, and anger, her early losses all too emotionally immediate. In this dream:

> I found myself in the ante-chamber of a large and beautiful house. There were doors which opened into the interior, dark passages leading off, which I felt I had access to, and was on the point of entering, but I felt uncertain and apprehensive. This small room was itself lovely, panelled like my childhood home, with many recesses and alcoves in which there were exquisite precious objects—china ornaments, glass, wood carvings. The room was pervaded by a smell of spices—they seemed like myrrh and frankincense. My eyes were drawn to one object in particular, a blue glass bowl of special fragility and beauty. I gazed at it, half believing that it belonged to me and that I had the right to take it with me, yet feeling, too, that that might be to steal. A tall, dark woman entered, apparently the owner. As we looked at each other, I "knew" that the object was indeed my own.

As the (tall, dark) therapist and patient explored this dream together, its meaning began to take shape. The dream vividly conveys Karen's life. It is as if she has Keats's Chamber of Maiden Thought (letter to J. H. Reynolds, 3 May 1818, in Gittings, 1970) in her bones. She is aware of the dark passages leading off this ante-chamber, but is frightened to move forward into them at this time, when she feels so alone. The atmosphere is sensuous, redolent of past experiences, and evocative (the frankincense and myrrh) of both birth and loss—the birth of her fledgling self and the loss, externally, of so important a relationship. Despite that loss, an internal relationship with her own parents seems to have been secured, for the house evokes features of her parents' home, something that she could now savour and appreciate, when before she had only been able to envy and resent—the shadowy recollections, as Wordsworth put it in the *Immortality Ode*,

> Which, be they what they may,
> Are yet the fountain light of all our day,
> Are yet a master light of all our seeing;
>
> [ll. 153–156]

Those memories "in feeling" were now available to be drawn on to sustain Karen, rather than being bitterly "recalled" for their absence and inadequacy.

Despite being so angry and distressed about this premature ending, and fearful too that she had somehow brought it about, Karen was also aware that the house-owner/therapist is nearby (had a place, that is, in her internal world). The felt capacity, on the one's part to make available, and on the other's to make her own, an emblem of a container of meaning—the blue glass bowl—stands as confirmation of the therapeutic work achieved and of the internalization not just of the therapist, as perceived, but also of her function in having held mental states until they could find a shape or a form, as in the dream. The dream feels something of a gift—the expression of a willingness to repair the feared damage brought about by Karen's grief-stricken rage and by her despair over being left too soon. It offers a metaphor for the internal establishing of a container of feeling. But perhaps the very fragility of the bowl was some indication of the impact of prematurity, of Karen's uncertainty. It could also be that she feared that she had internalized less the strong, functional qualities of the therapist than some kind of non-functional fragility and preciousness. She feared that she would soon be overcome with anxiety about not being sufficiently equipped to enter the dark passages of life—Keats's Mansion of Many Apartments (letter to J. H. Reynolds, 3 May 1818, in Gittings, 1970, p. 95). Keats, barely out of adolescence himself, was writing of human life and the immense burden and confusion of making one's way down what he calls "the dark passages" that lie ahead for those who have the strength to go on thinking "into the human heart" (pp. 95–96). He was using these words to describe Wordsworth, but they are so true of Keats himself. They were written when, in the aftermath of his parents' early deaths, he was having to come to terms with the imminent death of his brother and, as he clearly knew, with his own. Living among these shadows, he wrote some of his very finest poetry.

* * *

In all the lives that I have touched on in this book, both fictional and actual, I have been involved in the many-faceted process of engaging with the nature of growth and development, and the external and internal forces that promote or that impede such a process. In terms of contemporary adolescents' lives, it could certainly be argued that the negative impact of external forces is especially powerful, but this is not the note on which I wish to conclude. For in terms of "inside stories" there are grounds for hope, ones attested to by so many writers and thinkers going back to the Homeric tradition, through Plato, Aristotle, and the great writers of fiction and poetry, especially during the nineteenth and twentieth centuries.

G. Stanley Hall's wish that literature on adolescence "should be recognized as a class by itself and have a place of its own in the history of culture and of criticism" has, in the contemporary output of Young Adult fiction, been richly realized. There is, in other words, a proper recognition, now, of what Hall called "this period of transformation so all-determining for future life to which it alone can often give the key" (Hall, 1904, vol. 1, p. 589). As I mentioned in chapter 3, Aristotle's *Rhetoric,* quoted by Hall, now reads as extraordinarily contemporary. Throughout, he refers to youth in which "all things must be matters of hope" (p. 522).

In her last interview for *The Guardian*, Hanna Segal, at the age of 90, stated that:

> The important thing [adopting the vivid symbol that she first found in Cormac McCarthy's 2006 post-apocalyptic fable *The Road*] is to keep a little fire burning; however small, however hidden. I find this extraordinarily helpful: we live in a mad world, but for those of us who believe in some human values, it is terribly important that we just keep this little fire burning. It is about trusting your judgement, and the power of love. A little trust, and a little care. [in Henley, 2008]

I understand "the little fire burning" as a symbol of hope; an expression of that light within that, despite all, can keep something alight and warm—that which is needed to sustain life through catastrophically dark days.

However dark some of the days during my fifty years or so of working with adolescents, it has, despite all, been possible, throughout, to hold onto those many symbols of hope that have so enriched my working life.

Note

1. It may be helpful to bear in mind the standard meaning of a "touchstone" as "that which serves to test the true genuineness or value of anything—a test criterion" and also, as it happens, of bawdy relevance in the play, a more idiomatic term for testicles.

APPENDIX

I have tried, in these pages, to keep specialist terminology to a minimum. When drawing on specific psychoanalytic insights, however, some technical terms have been necessary and require elucidation.

At times, "object" and "object-relationships" have been referred to. These can be described as the internal representation of figures and relationships that are emotionally significant, whether positively or negatively. For example, the baby has an internal experience of goodness and well-being as a consequence of being fed, not only physically but with love and attention. As such experiences are repeated, the baby will feel that he has a source of goodness within, that he feels to be some kind of concrete presence, one that is part of him and not only something that is offered from without. He has a good relationship to a good "object".

Another term is phantasy, with a "ph" instead of the usual "f". This is drawn on in psychoanalytic writing to describe the content of the continuous inner, unconscious mental life of a person. Fantasy with an "f" denotes the term for everyday, conscious imaginative life.

There are also certain complex ideas that are fundamental to the story of development generally. They are somewhat opaque, even to those who are already familiar with them, and quite mystifying to those less well-versed in psychoanalytic theory. They are, in particular, the mechanisms of projective and introjective identification and the concept of the Oedipus complex. These notions continue to be much discussed and still do not readily lend themselves to tight definition. In the course of the book, as different versions of them appear and reappear, they gradually acquire further shape and meaning. But they need, first, to be described in their most simple form.

The psychological mechanisms of projection and introjection have their analogy in the physical processes of expelling and taking in. They are basic modes of establishing and conducting relationships, as basic as elimination and nourishment. Projection and introjection are the channels for the traffic of conscious and unconscious feeling between self and other. In the development of the personality, much depends on the force, the quality, the intensity, and the fluidity of these mechanisms or, by contrast, the intransigence.

The baby initially relates to the world and takes it in through his experience of his mother. Because she is his whole world, he is exquisitely sensitive to her moods. Her laugh will make him smile, her sadness will make him frown. When a baby is angry, he tends to be *totally* angry. With his whole being he feels his mother to be the source of his pain and anger. In wanting to get rid of this feeling, he thrusts it back into its supposed source, namely, his mother. In his eyes, his mother herself has become bad. So, he takes in the sense of having a bad mother within himself. When she comforts and feeds him and he has a good feeling, his mother again becomes good. He "projects" his bad feeling and identifies her with it. He "introjects" his experience of her as calm, satisfying, good, and he himself acquires a good feeling within. He feels himself to *be* "good".

If, on the other hand, he continually experiences a mother who rejects his communications, who seems to be impervious to his feelings, repeatedly meeting them with an emotional "blank wall", then the baby introjects something that is unresponsive to the communication of feeling and he himself may also become so. That is, he feels himself to be a version of the qualities and characteristics that he experiences first as belonging to his mother and then as belonging to him himself.

The texture of a person's experience is made up by a constant interplay between these projective and introjective mechanisms. Each term is confusing because psychoanalytic theory draws on each of them to understand so many different ideas and functions. Together, in effect, "projection" and "introjection" characterize the nature and meaning of one person's communication with another. The terms comprehend a range of motives on the part of the self (coming from different degrees of need, anxiety. or security), and a range of responses on the part of the other. When Klein (1946) first formulated the mechanism of projective identification, she described it has having different emphases and intensities. She pointed to the projection of good feelings as being the basis of empathy. She also suggested that the infant needed to get rid of, or to disown, or to evacuate, his bad feelings because they were too much for him to bear. Later, other psychoanalysts hypothesized further motives: that the baby might be seeking to feel indissolubly linked to his mother, for example, or to be the same as her, or in control of her, or indeed, simply in communication with her. In relation to this last, Bion drew attention to the fact that such projective processes, even those that seemed to be mainly for the purpose of the evacuation of bad feelings, also contained, almost always, a germ of communication. As the infant begins to realize that his crying elicits a particular response, more and more does that crying become an attempt to communicate— to communicate to his mother the fact that he is in pain or in distress.

As far as the response on the part of the mother is concerned, the term "projective identification" describes the phantasy on the baby's part that his mother herself actually feels whatever it is that he is directing towards her or is seeking to "put into" her. He feels that his mother has become the embodiment of those feelings. The mother then becomes the hated and hating self. But the term can also describe the reality of her *actually* being affected, if the original emotion or impulse is a particularly strong one and the force behind it is powerful and relentless. For a terrified baby can instil fear in his mother. She may begin to feel his feelings of fear in *reality*. She may even *act* on these feelings. Here "projective identification" involves something being put into, or pushed into, somebody else. Psychoanalytic theory concerns itself with why it is so put, or pushed, and what then happens to it.

Where an infant's cry or smile goes without any answering echo in the caretaker or mother, there will be no opportunity for the baby to take back in or to "introject" an experience of having painful feelings understood and held by a mind, or by an emotional presence, that is felt to have the care and capacity to make things tolerable for him. The bad "something" that is felt will be taken back in. It will be a "something" that is experienced as not fitting, or as a "foreign body", or as a persecutory feeling inside. In order for the baby to achieve or maintain any kind of peace of mind, this "something" will have to be got rid of again, to be re-projected. In this book, because the main focus is on development rather than on pathology, the chief concern with the introjective process is a positive one. I have not dwelt very much on sequences such as this last where there is an immediate projection-introjection-and-re-projection. Nor have I dwelt very much on those longer-term processes, where there is introjection in the course of which the baby builds up a sense of himself as somehow the same as, or engulfed by, a non-responding, cold, or distracted mother and comes *himself* to be such a person. I have not dwelt on those sequences although they do make their appearance in some of the case histories reported.

Returning to the simpler case of introjection, the experience of a sensitive, responsive mother increasingly allows the baby to feel himself also to be sensitive and responsive. He takes in an experience (the pleasure of being fed or of being understood) which he stores within—a picture of loving eyes, or an impression of being physically and emotionally contained. This is felt as if it is an *actual* taking-in of the mother's capacities (of the holding and of the loving capacities) as if these capacities were concrete objects. Through this process being repeated, the infant begins to feel the containing, loving mother as a definite presence within himself, as part of himself—as a "good object". Thus he himself gradually develops the capacity also to be containing and loving.

Introjective identification of this more positive kind leads to the strengthening of the personality insofar as the baby has been able slowly to absorb good experiences, ones that have modified infantile fears and anxieties. There is less and less necessity for the insistent or forceful projection-introjection-re-projection of the rather desperate kind that characterizes early persecutory states. Simple introjection encourages the capacity to be, and with separateness goes the increasing capacity to think for oneself and to be oneself. Projection and introjection can be described in this sort of way by reference to their simplest presentations. An observer, cognisant of ideas about them, can thus make sense of all sorts of human interrelations. By further observation and hypothesis, we learn more about them. They cannot lend themselves to outright definitions, as Martha Harris (1978) said:

> Introjection remains a mysterious process: how do involvement and reliance upon objects in the external world which are apprehended by the senses (and, as Wilfred Bion has pointed out, described in language which has been evolved to deal with external reality), become assimilated and transformed in the mind into what he calls

"psychoanalytic objects" which can contribute to the growth of the personality? This is a process about which we have almost everything to learn. [p. 168]

Projection and introjection, like so many other processes, are inherently problematic notions. They are constantly relied upon and further elaborated in the course of the book. This Appendix is intended to enable the reader to start where my account of these things begins.

Since the term Oedipus complex is so common in daily parlance, it may be helpful to draw on the mythic origins that underlie psychoanalytic thinking as it has developed over the preceding century. It is a term for a constellation that, implicitly or explicitly, is so significant in relation to the functioning of adolescent development. Freud describes a wish-fulfilling dream, or myth, of taking the place of one parent and marrying the other. The most basic version of this longing is expressed in the child's wish to keep the parent of the opposite sex for himself and to banish the parent of the same sex. Freud was struck by the way in which these, usually unconscious, wishes and desires were described in the myth of Oedipus, as retold by Sophocles in the drama *Oedipus Rex.* Here, the hero unwittingly kills his father and marries his mother. Reflecting on the impact of the play on the audience, in 1897 Freud wrote: "Each member was once, in germ and in phantasy, just such an Oedipus". The audience would see "the dream fulfilment he had transplanted into reality" (1950 [1892–1899], p. 265).

Although Freud himself drew exclusively on the drama that Sophocles based upon the myth, the brief account of the myth itself in *The Oxford Classical Dictionary* (1937) offers many sources of interest and resonance, ones that may be kept in mind as bearing on the immensely important influences, in developmental terms, of family legacies, both conscious and unconscious, from one generation to the next.

> Oedipus (OIDIPOUS), in Greek mythology, the son of Laius, the King of Thebes. When Amphion and Zethus gained possession of Thebes, Laius had taken refuge with Pelops, but had ill-requited his kindness by kidnapping his son Chrysippus, thereby bringing a curse on his own family. Laius recovered his kingdom after the death of Amphion and Zethus and married Jocasta but was warned by Apollo that his son would kill him. Accordingly, when Oedipus was born, a spike was driven through his feet and he was exposed on Mount Cithaeron. There a shepherd found him and he was taken to Polybus, King of Corinth, and Merope, his queen, who brought him up as her own son. Later, being taunted with being no true

son of Polybus, Oedipus enquired of the Delphic Oracle concerning his parentage, but was only told that he would slay his father and wed his mother. Thinking this referred to Polybus and Merope, he determined never to see Corinth again. At a place where three roads met, he encountered Laius (whom he did not know) and was ordered to make way. A quarrel followed in which Oedipus slew Laius. He went on to Thebes, which was at that time plagued by a Sphinx, a monster which asked people riddles and killed those who could not answer them. Creon, brother of Jocasta, the Regent of Thebes, offered the kingdom of Thebes to whoever should rid the country of this pest. Oedipus solved the riddle of the Sphinx, which thereupon killed itself. [Oedipus] became King of Thebes and married Jocasta. They had two sons, Eteocles and Polynices, and two daughters, Ismene and Antigone. At last, in a time of death and pestilence, the Oracle announced that these disasters would be averted if the slayer of Laius was expelled from the city. Oedipus thereupon set about discovering who had killed Laius. The result was to establish that he himself was Laius's son and his murderer. On this discovery Jocasta hanged herself and Oedipus blinded himself. Oedipus was deposed and banished. He wandered, attended by Antigone, to Colonus, in Attica where he was protected by Theseus and died. [p. 292]

REFERENCES

Abrams, M. (1954). *The Mirror and the Lamp: Romantic Theory and the Critical Tradition.* Oxford: Oxford University Press.

Ainsworth, M. D., & Bell, S. M. (1970). Attachment, exploration, and separation: Illustrated by the behavior of one-year-olds in a strange situation. *Child Development, 41*: 49–67.

Anderson, R. (2008). A psychoanalytical approach to suicide in adolescents. In: S. Briggs, A. Lemma, & W. Crouch (Eds.), *Relating to Self-Harm and Suicide: Psychoanalytic Perspectives on Practice, Theory and Prevention.* London: Routledge.

Anderson, R. (2013). Assessing the risk of self-harm in adolescence. In: M. Brownscombe Heller & S. Pollet (Eds.), *The Work of Psychoanalysts in the Public Health Sector.* London: Routledge.

Anderson, R., & Dartington, A. (Eds.) (1998). *Facing It Out: Clinical Perspectives on Adolescent Disturbance.* London: Duckworth; reprinted London: Karnac, 2002.

APA (1980). *Diagnostic and Statistical Manual of Mental Disorders* (3rd edition). Washington, DC: American Psychiatric Association.

Ariès, P. (1960). *Centuries of Childhood.* London: Pimlico, 1996.

Armstrong, D. (2005). *Organization in the Mind: Psychoanalysis, Group Relations, and Organizational Consultancy.* London: Karnac.

Atwood, M. (1989). *Cat's Eye.* London: Virago.

Austen, J. (1816). *Emma*, ed. F. Stafford. Harmondsworth: Penguin, 2015.

Baldwin, J. (1955). *Notes of a Native Son*. Boston, MA: Beacon Press.

Bateman, A. W., & Fonagy, P. (2003). The development of an attachment-based treatment program for borderline personality disorder. *Bulletin of the Menninger Clinic, 67* (2): 187–211.

Beer, G. (1996). *Virginia Woolf: The Common Ground*. Edinburgh: Edinburgh University Press.

Beer, G. (2016). *Alice in Space: The Sideways Victorian World of Lewis Carroll*. Chicago, IL: University of Chicago Press.

Bernfeld, S. (1938). Types of adolescence. *Psychoanalytic Quarterly, 7*: 243–253.

Bick, E. (1968). The experience of the skin in early object relations. *International Journal of Psychoanalysis, 49*: 484–486. Reprinted in: M. Harris & E. Bick, *Collected Papers of Martha Harris and Esther Bick*. Strath Tay: Clunie Press, 1987.

Bion, W. R. (1961). *Experiences in Groups*. London: Tavistock Publications; reprinted London: Routledge, 1989.

Bion, W. R. (1962a). *Learning from Experience*. London: Heinemann.

Bion, W. R. (1962b). A theory of thinking. *International Journal of Psychoanalysis, 43*: 306–310. Reprinted in: *Second Thoughts*. London: Heinemann, 1967.

Bion, W. R. (1963). *Elements of Psycho-Analysis*. London: Heinemann.

Bion, W. R. (1967). Commentary. In: *Second Thoughts*. London: Heinemann.

Bion, W. R. (1970). *Attention and Interpretation*. London: Tavistock.

Bion, W. R. (1982). *The Long Week-End 1897–1919*. Abingdon: Fleetwood Press.

Bion, W. R. (1991). *A Memoir of the Future: Books 1–3*. London: Karnac.

Bion, W. R. (2005). *The Tavistock Seminars*. London: Karnac.

Blythe, R. (1966). Introduction. In: J. Austen, *Emma*, ed. R. Blythe. Harmondsworth: Penguin.

Brawer, N. (2017). Thought for the day. BBC Radio 4, 24 October.

Brenman Pick, I. (1988). Adolescence: Its impact on patient and analyst. In: *Authenticity in the Psychoanalytic Encounter: The Work of Irma Brenman Pick* (pp. 135–146). London: Routledge, 2018.

Britton, R. (2003). *Sex, Death, and the Superego*. London: Karnac.

Brontë, C. (1847). *Jane Eyre*. London: Penguin, 2006.

Byatt, A. S. (1985). *Still Life*. New York: Macmillan.

Camus, A. (1946). *The Outsider*. London: Hamish Hamilton, 1946.

Collins, S. (2008–2010). *The Hunger Games Trilogy*. New York: Scholastic.

Copley, B. (1993). *The World of Adolescence: Literature, Society and Psychoanalytic Psychotherapy*. London: Free Association Books.

Craig, E. (1948). *Enquire Within*. London: Collins.

Dartington, A. (1998). The intensity of adolescence in small families. In: R. Anderson & A. Dartington (Eds.), *Facing It Out: Clinical Perspectives on Adolescent Disturbance*. London: Duckworth; reprinted London: Karnac, 2002.

Deutsch, H. (1942). Some forms of emotional disturbance and their relationship to schizophrenia. *Psychoanalytic Quarterly, 11*: 301–321.

Dickinson, E. (1862). We grow accustomed to the dark. In: *The Complete Poems,* ed. T. H. Johnson. London: Faber & Faber, 1970.

Dicks, H. (1970). *Fifty Years of the Tavistock Clinic*. London: Routledge & Kegan Paul.

Dusinberre, J. (2006). Introduction. In: W. Shakespeare, *As You Like It*, ed. J. Dusinberre. London: Arden Shakespeare.

Eliot, G. (1872). *Middlemarch*. Harmondsworth: Penguin, 1985.

Eliot, G. (1876). *Daniel Deronda*. Harmondsworth: Penguin, 1986.

Eliot, T. S. (1963). *Four Quartets*. London: Faber & Faber.

Erikson, E. H. (1950). *Childhood and Society*. New York: Norton.

Fisher, M. (2016). *The Weird and the Eerie*. London: Repeater.

Freeman, H. (2015). *When I Was Me*. London: Hot Key Books.

Freud, A. (1958). Adolescence. *Psychoanalytic Study of the Child, 13*: 255–278.

Freud, S. (1900a). *The Interpretation of Dreams. Standard Edition, 4/5*.

Freud, S. (1905d). *Three Essays on the Theory of Sexuality. Standard Edition, 7*.

Freud, S. (1910a). Five lectures on psycho-analysis. *Standard Edition, 11*: 1–56.

Freud, S. (1911b). Formulations on the two principles of mental functioning. *Standard Edition, 12*: 213–226.

Freud, S. (1917e). Mourning and melancholia. *Standard Edition, 14*: 237–258.

Freud, S. (1919h). The "uncanny". *Standard Edition, 17*: 217–256.

Freud, S. (1924c). The economic problem of masochism. *Standard Edition, 19*: 155–172.

Freud, S. (1925d). *An Autobiographical Study. Standard Edition, 20*.

Freud, S. (1933a). *New Introductory Lectures on Psycho-Analysis. Standard Edition, 22*: 3–182.

Freud, S. (1950 [1892–1899]. Extracts from the Fliess Papers. *Standard Edition, 1*: 173–280.

Frye, N. (1957). *Anatomy of Criticism*. London: Penguin.

Gardner, H. (1959). *The Business of Criticism*. Oxford: Clarendon Press.

Gathorne-Hardy, J. (1977). *The Public School Phenomenon*. London: Faber & Faber.

Gittings, R. (Ed.) (1970). *Letters of John Keats: A Selection*. Oxford: Oxford University Press.

Golding, W. (1954). *Lord of the Flies*. London: Penguin.

Graham-Harrison, E. (2017). Attackers united by youth and driven by a search for meaning. *The Guardian*, 16 September. Available at: www.theguardian.com/uk-news/2017/sep/16/terror-attackers-united-by-youth-and-search-for-meaning

Greenhalgh, T. (2017). *How to Implement Medical Health Care*. Oxford: Wiley Blackwell.

Hall, G. S. (1904). *Adolescence: Its Psychology and Its Relation to Physiology, Anthropology, Sociology, Sex, Crime, Religion and Education (Vols. 1 & 2)*. New York: D. Appleton & Co.

Hardinge, F. (2015). *The Lie Tree*. London: Macmillan.

Harris, M. (1976). Infantile elements and adult strivings in adult sexuality. *Journal of Child Psychotherapy, 10*: 121–140. Reprinted in: *The Collected Papers of Martha Harris and Esther Bick*. Strath Tay: Clunie Press, 1987.

Harris, M. (1978). Towards learning from experience in infancy and childhood. In: *Collected Papers of Martha Harris and Esther Bick*, ed. M. Harris Williams. Strath Tay: Clunie Press, 1987.

Harris, M. (1982). Growing points in psychoanalysis inspired by the work of Melanie Klein. *Journal of Child Psychotherapy, 8* (2): 165–184. Reprinted in: M. Harris & E. Bick, *The Tavistock Model: Papers on Child Development and Psychoanalytic Training* (pp. 65–92), ed. M. Harris Williams. London: Karnac, 2011.

Henley, J. (2008). Queen of darkness [Interview with Hanna Segal]. *The Guardian*, 8 September. Available at: https://www.theguardian.com/science/2008/sep/08/psychology.healthandwellbeing

Holmes, R. (1974). *Shelley: The Pursuit*. London: Quartet Books, 1976.

Isaacs, S. (1948). *Childhood and After*. London: Routledge & Kegan Paul.

Jones, E. (1922). Some problems of adolescence. *British Journal of Psychology, 13*: 31–47.

Joseph, B. (1982). Addiction to near-death. *International Journal of Psychoanalysis, 63*: 449–456.

Judt, T. (2011). *Ill Fares the Land*. London: Penguin.

Klein, M. (1921). The development of the child. In: *Love, Guilt and Reparation and Other Works 1921–1945*. London: Hogarth Press, 1975.

Klein, M. (1923). The role of the school in the libidinal development of the child. In: *Love, Guilt and Reparation and Other Works 1921–1945*. London: Hogarth Press, 1975.

Klein, M. (1928). Early stages of the Oedipus complex. In: *Love, Guilt and Reparation and Other Works 1921–1945*. London: Hogarth Press, 1975.

Klein, M. (1931). A contribution to the theory of intellectual inhibition. In:

Love, Guilt and Reparation and Other Works 1921–1945. London: Hogarth Press, 1975.

Klein, M. (1932). *The Psychoanalysis of Children*. London: Hogarth Press.

Klein, M. (1935). A contribution to the psychogenesis of manic-depressive states. In: *Love, Guilt and Reparation and Other Works 1921–1945*. London: Hogarth Press, 1975.

Klein, M. (1940). Mourning and its relation to manic-depressive states. In: *Love, Guilt and Reparation and Other Works 1921–1945*. London: Hogarth Press, 1975.

Klein, M. (1945). The Oedipus complex in the light of early anxieties. In: *Love, Guilt and Reparation and Other Works 1921–1945*. London: Hogarth Press, 1975.

Klein, M. (1946). Notes on some schizoid mechanisms. In: *Envy, Gratitude and Other Works, 1946–1963*. London: Hogarth Press, 1975.

Klein, M. (1959). Our adult world and its roots in infancy. In: *Envy, Gratitude and Other Works, 1946–1963*. London: Hogarth Press, 1975.

Klein, N. (2017). *No Is Not Enough: Defeating the New Shock Politics*. London: Allen Lane.

Knight, R. H. (1953). Borderline states. *Bulletin of the Menninger Clinic, 17* (1): 1–12.

Kohon, G. (2005). Love in a time of madness. In: A. Green & G. Kohon (Eds.), *Love and Its Vicissitudes*. London: Routledge.

Langer, S. (1953). *Feeling and Form: A Theory of Art Developed from Philosophy in a New Key*. London: Routledge & Kegan Paul.

Laufer, M. (Ed.) (1995). *The Suicidal Adolescent*. London: Karnac.

Lawrence, D. H. (1923). *Fantasia of the Unconscious/Psychoanalysis and the Unconscious*. London: Heinemann.

Lessing, D. (1962). *The Golden Notebook*. London: Michael Joseph.

Lichtenstein, H. (1964). The role of narcissism in the emergence and maintenance of a primary identity. *International Journal of Psychoanalysis, 45*: 49–56.

Maiello, S. (1995). The sound-object: A hypothesis about parental auditory experience and memory. *Journal of Child Psychotherapy, 21* (1): 23–41.

Mandelstam, O. (1977). *Selected Essays*, trans. S. Monas. Austin, TX: University of Texas Press.

Mantel, H. (2017). The Princess Myth: Hilary Mantel on Diana. *The Guardian*, 26 August. Available at: https://www.theguardian.com/books/2017/aug/26/the-princess-myth-hilary-mantel-on-diana

McCarthy, C. (2006). *The Road*. London: Picador, 2009.

McGinley, E., & Varchevker, A. (2010). *Enduring Loss: Mourning, Depression and Narcissism Throughout the Life Cycle*. London: Karnac.

Meltzer, D. (1973a). Identification and socialisation in adolescence. In: *Sexual States of Mind* (pp. 51–57). Strath Tay: Clunie Press; reprinted London: Karnac, 2008.

Meltzer, D. (1973b). *Sexual States of Mind.* Strath Tay: Clunie Press; reprinted London: Karnac, 2008.

Meltzer, D. (1973c). Terror, persecution and dread. In: *Sexual States of Mind* (pp. 99–106). Strath Tay: Clunie Press; reprinted London: Karnac, 2008.

Meltzer, D. (1978). A note on introjective processes. In: *Sincerity and Other Works: Collected Papers of Donald Meltzer*, ed. A. Hahn . London: Karnac, 1994.

Meltzer, D. (1992). *The Claustrum: An Investigation of Claustrophobic Phenomenon.* Strath Tay: Clunie Press.

Meltzer, D., & Harris Williams, M. (1988). *The Apprehension of Beauty: The Role of Aesthetic Conflict in Development, Art, Violence.* London: Karnac, 2011.

Milner, M. (1950). *On Not Being Able to Paint.* London: Heinemann; reprinted Hove: Routledge, 2010.

Ness, P. (2008). *The Knife of Never Letting Go.* London: Walker Books.

Ness, P. (2008–2010). *Chaos Walking, Books 1–3.* London: Walker Books.

Ness, P. (2015). *The Rest of Us Just Live Here.* London: Walker Books.

O'Shaughnessy, E. (1979). A clinical study of a defensive organization. *International Journal of Psychoanalysis, 62*: 359–369.

O'Shaughnessy, E. (1994). What is a clinical fact? *International Journal of Psychoanalysis, 75*: 939–947. Reprinted in: *Inquiries in Psychoanalysis: Collected Papers of Edna O'Shaughnessy.* London: Routledge, 2015.

O'Shaughnessy, E. (1999). Relating to the super-ego. *International Journal of Psychoanalysis, 80* (5): 861–870.

The Oxford Classical Dictionary (1937). Oxford: Clarendon Press.

Plath, S. (1962). Lady Lazarus. *Collected Poems.* London: Faber & Faber, 1988.

Pushkin, A. S. (1831). *Eugene Onegin,* trans. C. Johnston. Harmondsworth: Penguin, 1979.

Rey, J. H. (1979). Schizoid phenomena in the borderline. In E. B. Spillius (Ed.), *Melanie Klein Today* (pp. 203–229). London: Routledge, 1988.

Rhode, M. (2004). Different responses to trauma in two children with autistic spectrum disorder: The mouth as crossroads for the sense of self. *Journal of Child Psychotherapy, 30*: 3–20.

Riviere, J. (1952). The unconscious phantasy of an inner world reflected in examples from English literature. *International Journal of Psychoanalysis, 33*: 160–172. Reprinted in: M. Klein, P. Heimann, & R. Money-Kyrle

(Eds.), *New Directions in Psycho-Analysis*. London: Tavistock Publications, 1955.

Rosenfeld, H. (1971). A clinical approach to the psychoanalytic theory of the life and death instincts: An investigation into the aggressive aspects of narcissism, *International Journal of Psychoanalysis, 52*: 169–178.

Rosoff, M. (2004). *How I Live Now.* London: Penguin.

Rousseau, J.-J. (1762). *Emile, or On Education.* New York: Basic Books, 1979.

Rustin, M., & Trowell, J. (1991). Developing the internal observer in professionals in training. *Infant Mental Health Journal, 12* (3): 233–245.

Ryan, K. (2009). *Shakespeare's Comedies.* London: Palgrave Macmillan.

Salinger, J. D. (1951). *The Catcher in the Rye.* Boston, MA: Little, Brown & Company.

Satyamurti, C. (1987). *Switching the Dark: New and Selected Poems.* Tarset: Bloodaxe, 2005.

Savage, J. (2007). *Teenage: The Creation of Youth: 1875–1945.* London: Pimlico.

Schmideberg, M. (1947). Learning to talk. *Psychoanalytic Review, 34* (3): 296–335.

Schor, J. B. (2005). *Born to Buy: The Commercialized Child and the New Consumer Culture.* New York: Scribner; reprinted Simon & Schuster, 2014.

Segal, H. (1964). *Introduction to the Work of Melanie Klein.* London: Hogarth Press, 1973.

Shan, D. (2000). *Cirque du Freak.* London: HarperCollins.

Sherwin-White, S. (2017). *Melanie Klein Revisited: Pioneer and Revolutionary in the Psychoanalysis of Young Children.* London: Karnac.

Showalter, E. (1992). Introduction. In: V. Woolf, *Mrs Dalloway*, ed. E. Showalter. London: Penguin.

Sohn, L. (1985). Narcissistic organization, projective identification, and the formation of the identificate. *International Journal of Psychoanalysis, 66*: 201–213.

Spillius, E. (Ed.) (1988). *Melanie Klein Today: Developments in Theory and Practice. Volume 1: Mainly Theory* . London: Routledge.

Steiner, J. (1987). The interplay between pathological organizations and the paranoid-schizoid and depressive positions. In: E. B. Spillius (Ed.), *Melanie Klein Today* (pp. 324–342). London: Routledge, 1988.

Steiner, J. (1996). *Psychic Retreats: Pathological Organizations in Psychotic, Neurotic and Borderline Patients.* London: Routledge.

Steiner, J. (2006). *Seeing and Being Seen: Emerging from a Psychic Retreat.* London: Routledge.

Stern, A. (1938). Psychoanalytic investigation of and therapy in the border line group of neuroses. *Psychoanalytic Quarterly, 7*: 467–489.

Stevenson, A. (2000). *Granny Scarecrow*. Newcastle-on-Tyne: Bloodaxe Books.

Tabbia, C. (2017). The isolated adolescent. In: M. Cohen & A. Hahn (Eds.), *Doing Things Differently: The Influence of Donald Meltzer on Psychoanalytic Theory and Practice*. London: Karnac.

Tanner, T. (1971). *City of Words: American Fiction, 1950–70*. New York: Harper & Row.

Tanner, T. (1986). *Jane Austen*. London: Macmillan.

Tartt, D. (2002). *The Little Friend*. London: Bloomsbury.

Thomson, M. (1989). *On Art and Therapy: An Exploration*. London: Virago; reprinted London: Free Association Books, 1997.

Vaspe, A. (2017). *Psychoanalysis, the NHS, and Mental Health Work Today*. London: Karnac.

Waddell, M. (1998). *Inside Lives: Psychoanalysis and the Growth of the Personality*. London: Duckworth; extended edition, London: Karnac, 2002.

Waddell, M., & Williams, G. (1991). Reflections on perverse states of mind. *Free Associations, 2* (2): 203–213.

Williams, G. (1997). On gang dynamics. In: *Internal Landscapes and Foreign Bodies: Eating Disorders and Other Pathologies* (pp. 51–62). London: Duckworth.

Winnicott. D. (1971). *Playing and Reality*. London: Tavistock Publications.

Woolf, V. (1925). *Mrs Dalloway*, ed. E. Showalter. London: Penguin, 1992.

Woolf, V. (1929). *A Room of One's Own*. London: Hogarth Press.

Wordsworth, W. (1805). *William Wordsworth*, ed. S. Gill. Oxford: Oxford University Press, 1984.

Yeats, W. B. (1933). *Collected Poems*. London: Macmillan.

INDEX

abandonment:
 anxiety about, 59
 defences against, 150
Abraham, K., 6, 7
Abrams, M., 12
Abtan, B., 33
acting out, stealing as, 58
Adam Smith Society, 144
addiction, 32, 43, 91
 internet, 172
ADHD: *see* Attention Deficit
  Hyperactivity Disorder
adhesive identification, 62, 74
 adolescent dreams (case example:
  John), 63–67
adhesive room, 153
admiration, narcissistic investment
  in, 222
adolescence:
 as "Age of Experimentation", 33
 analytic work with, history of, 3–14
 as crucial developmental phase in
  human life cycle, 5, 155
 developmental transitions in, 46–60
 difficulty of diagnosis in, 172–184
 disturbed states in, 178

early, as time of transition, 46–60
 group life in, 78–92
 historical context, 3–14
 inhibition in, 6
 narcissism in, 155–171
 overview of, 31–45
 "particularly extreme case of", 177
 plasticity and spontaneity of, 234
 as process of becoming, 45
 regression to infantile states in, 38,
  41, 52, 78, 165, 179
 tasks of, 160
 as time of flux, 35
 understanding of, 8, 10, 23
adolescent(s):
 assessment of, for possible
  treatment, 115–132
 sense of disillusionment of, 210
adolescent boy, manslaughter of
  (historical vignette: Nick), 84
Adolescent Department, Tavistock
  Clinic, London, xv, xvi, 116,
  132, 172
 see also Tavistock Clinic/
  Tavistock and Portman NHS
  Foundation Trust